RESEARCHING WOMEN AND SPORT

Researching Women and Sport

Edited by

Gill Clarke

and

Barbara Humberstone

Foreword by
Jennifer Hargreaves
Consultant Editor: Jo Campling

First published 1997 by
MACMILLAN PRESS LTD
Houndmills, Basingstoke, Hampshire RG21 6XS
and London
Companies and representatives
throughout the world

ISBN 0–333–64230–9 hardcover
ISBN 0–333–64231–7 paperback

A catalogue record for this book is available
from the British Library.

This book is printed on paper suitable for recycling and
made from fully managed and sustained forest sources.

10   9   8   7   6   5   4   3   2   1
06   05   04   03   02   01   00   99   98   97

Printed in Great Britain by
The Ipswich Book Company Ltd
Ipswich, Suffolk

Contents

Acknowledgements

We would like to thank our contributors and all the past and present executive members of the Women's Sports Foundation for supporting us throughout the genesis and growing pains of this book. The Women's Sports Foundation is the only national organisation in the United Kingdom (UK) that is solely working to improve and promote opportunities for women and sport, and has its mission to pursue and promote equity for women in and through sport. The Women's Sports Foundation was one of 280 delegates from 82 countries representing governmental and non-governmental organisations, national Olympic Committees, international and national sport federations and educational and research institutions that attended the first international conference on women and sport, organised by the Sports Council, which took place in Brighton, UK from 5–8 May 1994. The conference drew up and endorsed what has become known as 'The Brighton Declaration on Women and Sport', the overriding aim of which is to develop a sporting culture that enables and values the full involvement of women in every aspect of sport. It is hoped that this international strategic approach will accelerate change and lead to a more equitable sporting culture world-wide.

Finally we are indebted to Sarah Gilroy for her insightful comments throughout the editing of this book and to Jo Campling for her constant support and helpful advice.

Gill Clarke and Barbara Humberstone

Foreword

Feminist accounts of the social world of sport – and, in particular, of women's sport – have increased in number and improved in quality in recent years. Even so, they remain small in quantity by comparison with those which marginalise or compartmentalise gender issues. Gill Clarke and Barbara Humberstone have edited a text which makes a particularly useful contribution to the field, not only because it expands the scope of investigation to include physical activities and physical education and brings together articles by women who have been actively engaged in different capacities in sport and associated activities, but also because it emphasizes the process of research. It is the first English-language book to focus in this way on feminist research in the areas of sport, physical activities and physical education. As well as attracting readers from Sports Studies, this text is relevant to those doing feminist research in other areas.

Collectively, the authors of the book highlight the complex and controversial nature of feminist research procedures and methodologies. By letting their subjects 'speak for themselves', and treating them as participants with the potential to affect the outcome of the research, orthodox relations of power in research are implicitly questioned and the gendered nature of enquiry is revealed.

The work of Gill Clarke and Barbara Humberstone in the Women's Sports Foundation (UK) (WSF) provided the impetus for their decision to seek collaborators for this collection. In fact most of the contributors have been involved in one way or another with the WSF. Because the Foundation is concerned with gender equity in and through sport, and has a committee dealing with education and research issues, it provides an important symbolic partner for the publication.

Researching Women and Sport embraces a variety of topics, representing women involved in a range of activities and from several countries. Different chapters include research about active athletes, as well as those who are involved in teaching and organisation; participants are from different social groups – for example, lesbian physical education teachers, young Muslim women, and disabled athletes; and personal and sensitive issues are included – such as problems of body image and sexual harassment and sexual abuse. The connection between empirical data and theoretical analysis is explored in several chapters, and the importance of relating personal experience to wider social implications is made clear. All the contributions are reflective in nature and connected with the personal experiences of doing feminist social research. They illustrate the clear connection between the personal and the political, signalling the relationship between the process of research and configurations of power.

The variety of subject matter and interpretation in *Researching Women and Sport* makes it a useful guide for students doing research in these areas and represents a welcome intervention in the field.

Jennifer Hargreaves
Professor of Sociology and Politics of Sport
Roehampton Institute, London

Notes on Contributors

Celia Brackenridge trained as a PE teacher and after some years teaching she became a lecturer in PE at what is now Sheffield Hallam University. During this time she played lacrosse at international level, helped to form the Women's Sports Foundation and carried out research on the social psychology of sport and on women as sports coaches. Following over twenty years as a teacher, researcher and manager, Celia is now Professor and Head of Research and Postgraduate Development in the Department of Leisure Management at Cheltenham and Gloucester College of Higher Education. Her current research is concerned with sexual abuse in sports' coaching.

Gill Clarke lectures at the University of Southampton. Prior to this she was Field Leader for PE at the Chichester Institute of Higher Education, after having taught PE in secondary schools in Hampshire. Her current research explores the lives of lesbian PE teachers. She has published articles on discourse analysis, sexuality and research methods in PE. In her spare time, she is an international hockey umpire, having officiated at the 1992 Olympic Games, the World Cup in Dublin, 1994 and umpired at the Olympic Games final in Atlanta in 1996.

Alison Dewar is a lesbian feminist physical educator. She taught in the School of Human Kinetics at the University of British Columbia. She is currently studying law at the University of Ottawa in Canada.

Anne Flintoff taught PE in secondary schools before moving to her current post as principal lecturer in sociology of education, PE and sport at Leeds Metropolitan University. Her PhD research focused on gender relations in initial teacher education in PE, and much of her teaching reflects a commitment to raising awareness of, and challenging, gender inequalities in PE and sport. Her ongoing research interests include assessing the impact of the recent moves to school based training for equality work, and exploring the nature of young women's active lifestyles in aerobics and conditioning activities.

Sarah Gilroy lectures in the sociology of sport and leisure at Chichester Institute of Higher Education. Her main research interests concern the sociology of the body, the construction of gender power relations and negotiations within households over work and leisure. Her involvement in international hockey coaching informs another area of interest concerning coaching and sport developments.

Brenda Grace completed a Masters degree in Sports Studies at the University of Alberta, Canada. This return to higher education after many years absence provided an opportunity to develop a research interest in sport advocacy work generated by ten years working in community recreation, and many more as a sportswoman. She is currently facing quite different challenges having taken a Chief Executive post with a sports centre that offers specialised facilities for people with disabilities. Her commitment to leading an active life has survived the pressures of both study and career and she continues to play her chosen sport, water polo.

Jan Graydon is Head of the School of Sports Studies at Chichester Institute of Higher Education. She is the author of many articles on various aspects of sport psychology, and consults with athletes in a number of sports. She is also a squash coach and keen player. She keeps fit for the sport by circuit training, jogging and weight training.

Tanni Grey graduated from Loughborough University of Technology with a politics degree and is currently studying for an MPhil in Sports Studies at Cardiff Institute of Higher Education. She has represented Great Britain since 1987 in wheelchair track and road racing and is a quadruple gold medallist from both the 1992 Barcelona Paralympics and the 1994 World Championship and a gold medallist at the 1996 Atlanta paralympics. She has an MBE for her services to sport and is the current world recorder holder in 100 m, 200 m, 400 m and 800 m track events.

Barbara Humberstone is Senior Lecturer in Sport and Leisure studies at Buckinghamshire College, Brunel University where she is responsible for postgraduate research students. Prior to this she taught sociology at Portsmouth University, undertakes equal opportunities consultancies and was assistant director of PE at the University of Southampton. She has taught in a number of secondary schools. Currently she is undertaking research into women in leisure/sport management and exploring the political and social context of outdoor education. She is interested in exploring social change through ethnographic methodology and has published widely on gender, equity issues, physical and outdoor education. She is a member of the European group developing networks for academics researching outdoor education and is leading the women and outdoor education group.

Sheila Scraton is Professor and reader in Leisure and Feminist Studies at Leeds Metropolitan University. Her research interests include gender, sexuality and physicality. She is currently involved in a joint cross-national study of women and sport. Her recent publications include, *Gender and Physical Education* (1993) and *Leisure and Postmodernity* (1995).

Margaret Talbot is the University Head of Sport and Carnegie Professor at Leeds Metropolitan University. For the last two decades she has been researching and writing on women's leisure, sport and physical education, and has worked with the Sports Council and other agencies to develop policies and strategies towards increased equity in sport, especially for women and young people. She was a Member of the Physical Education Group which produced the framework for National Curriculum Physical Education and was Chair of the European Sports Conference Working Group on Women and Sport from 1991–1993. She is currently leading a research project for the Commonwealth Secretariat on the barriers and opportunities faced by Commonwealth women in sport, and is working on a project with the Malaysian Ministry for Youth and Sport to analyse women's sports provision in a multi-cultural society.

Jan Wright teaches in the Faculty of Education at the University of Wollongong, Australia. Her current research interests combine the application of feminist poststructuralist theory to questions about the relationship between culture, identity, physical activity and schooling.

Hasina Zaman currently teaches leisure and sport at Tower Hamlets College in East London. She trained as a PE teacher at Greenwich University and over the past ten years has worked predominantly with Bengali/Muslim women teaching sports and outdoor education activities, particularly rock-climbing.

Introduction
Gill Clarke and Barbara Humberstone

In late 1993, we wrote to a number of women from a variety of backgrounds whom we felt could make a valuable contribution to the understanding of feminist research inviting them to contribute to this book.[1] We envisioned a book which sought to address critical issues surrounding feminist research in sport, physical activity and physical education (PE) and which would also give voice to a diversity of perspectives and theoretical standpoints. We wanted the book's focus to be on women, by women, for it seemed to us that much of the literature and related research had failed to address women's experience(s) of sport, physical activity and PE. Where research had previously focused on women much of it, as Jennifer Hargreaves (1994: 288) insightfully comments, had been linked to the experience of white Western women in Christian cultures – usually middle class and heterosexual and, we would add, able-bodied. Much too had been written about women by men, and in many instances this work tended to imply that women were some homogenous group whose experiences could be universalised. We have tried to address some of these shortcomings and universalisation, but as the reader will see, in a text such as this it has proved impossible to include all voices. We acknowledge and recognise this, and would urge others to take up the challenge to let all women's voices be heard. However, whilst we believe in the necessity for women to be heard, we also believe that it is important for us as both readers and writers that we learn how to listen to others' voices and so begin to avoid privileging some voices above others. The notion of giving voice in itself is also problematic, for as Dewar (1991: 75) rightly posits: 'What does it mean to give? What kinds of relations does this imply? What kind of power and privilege is implied in the act of giving? What does this say about how voices are heard and interpreted?' Though due to the limitations of space we have been unable to include some voices, we believe it is essential that women's differences are acknowledged and celebrated and that we continue to problematise the privileges that our various backgrounds may give us, and recognise that our notion of voice is likely to be profoundly influenced by our own life experiences and chances. Dewar (1991: 71) perceptively sums up the problem, she comments that 'The problem as I see it now is not how to give voice but to learn about different voices, hear what they have to say, and work to become allies and friends in our struggles to take on oppressive forma-

tions'. Further to this we would contend that how we choose to (mis)repre-
sent these voices is also significant. Within this text we have not only
deliberately sought to hear different voices but we have also sought to
include writing by women who are at different stages of their careers.

At the same time however we wanted to challenge traditional research
orthodoxies which appeared to us to have privileged certain ways of
knowing and researching over others and to have rendered women's presence both marginal and in many cases invisible, particularly in the field of
sports studies. Hence, we wanted a text that moved away from positivistic
and 'scientific' visions of the sporting world, to one that both drew on and
challenged these conventions, and recognised that research stories can be
told in a multiplicity of ways in order to broaden our understanding of all
women's lives. Thus, following Maynard and Purvis (1994), we wished to
add to the continuing debates around 'doing feminist research' (Maynard
and Purvis 1994: 2) through our focus upon sport, physical activity and
PE.[2] To this end, we asked our contributors to draw on their research to
illustrate and illuminate the dilemmas and issues involved in the process
of feminist research, and in so doing we have tried ' ... to move beyond
boundaries, to transgress. This is education as the practice of freedom'
(hooks 1994: 207). Drawing on hooks' clarity of vision and thought we
see writing as the practice of academic freedom, in which women should
play a significant part. Our contributors testify to this.

Chapters 1 and 2 both provide insights into an organisation run by
women for women's equity in 'sport'; the Womens Sports Foundation
(WSF). But each chapter shows the authors approaching their research in
very different ways. In Chapter 1, Gill Clarke and Barbara Humberstone
draw on the experiences of the past, and present, chairs of WSF to illustrate the contribution of life-history research. In Chapter 2, Brenda Grace
explores the workings of the WSF through a case-study approach in which
she interviewed a number of the executive members.

The life-history approach to research adopted in Chapter 1 provided the
WSF chairs with the opportunity to talk in detail about their experiences in
sport and their involvement in the organisation. What emerges are rich
descriptive biographies which highlight each chairs' commitment to sport
and to their promotion of women within sport whilst also illuminating the
strategies they adopted in dealing with tensions within the organisation. It
further exemplifies the ways in which women are both influenced by and
can challenge societal and organisational values and structures. Brenda
Grace begins her chapter (Chapter 2) by discussing various feminist theoretical standpoints before emphasising the importance of reflexivity in the
research process and demonstrating this within her own account. Her

research captures some of the tensions within an all-women organisation, drawing particular attention to the dilemmas around homophobia and heterosexism and image presentation for the WSF.

Continuing the life-history approach, Gill Clarke starts Chapter 3 by discussing some of the methodological issues that must be addressed when conducting sensitive research. She illustrates this sensitivity in her work as she highlights the complexities of the lives of lesbian PE teachers in secondary schools in England. Drawing on in-depth interviews, she illustrates some of the strategies that they may employ in order to conceal their lesbian identity as well as documenting the homophobic abuse that they may have been subjected to by colleagues and pupils alike. Rarely have young Muslim women had the opportunity to express their views about their experiences of PE and sport in a non-Islamic culture. Hasina Zaman, herself a Muslim, provides this much needed perspective in Chapter 4 where she dispels the myth that Muslim young women are passive and in some way uninterested in physical activity. She raises awareness and directs our attention to Islamic ideology whilst exploring the dilemmas affecting young Muslim women and their involvement in physical activity and how these might be addressed in a secular society.

Jan Graydon argues in Chapter 5 that sport psychology has much to offer in the understanding of sex differences when an emancipatory approach is adopted which does not reinforce stereotypes of sex difference. She draws attention to psychological research which examines girls' and boys' self-confidence and self-esteem in physical education and sport. This highlights the importance of using a combination of quantitative and qualitative research methods to gain greater insight into the meanings which participants give to their sports experience.[3] Jan Wright and Alison Dewar, in Chapter 6, highlight the ways in which women interpret and give meaning to their experiences in physical activity. They use an interpretive case study to examine how eight mature women in Canada and Australia talk about their experiences of physical education, sport and physical activity. The potential for women to be empowered through their involvement in physical activity is discussed in Chapter 7 by Sarah Gilroy. In addition to exploring some of the theoretical concerns about the body and power, she draws upon interviews with women about their involvement in physical activity to illustrate the complexities of this area of study. Élite women athletes and their experiences are frequently missing from research. Tanni Grey, in Chapter 8, seeks to redress this omission. She draws on her experiences whilst on a Winston Churchill Fellowship in Australia studying the coaching and training structures for élite wheelchair athletes. Herself an élite wheelchair athlete, she reflects on her experiences both as a woman athlete and as a wheelchair researcher.

An unspoken issue, until very recently, in women's sports coaching and training is raised in Chapter 9. Here Celia Brackenridge provides evidence that some girls and women are the recipients of unwanted sexual attention in sport and physical activity. She describes the care needed by herself and collaborative researchers in attempting to examine sensitively the experiences of those who have been sexually harassed and abused in sport. Margaret Talbot explores, in Chapter 10, how women manage their lives and their sport in the family context through the use of time profiles. Time profiles, which were one aspect of a larger research project in which 40 women were also interviewed, are shown as a useful method in feminist research. This research shows the significance that other family members play in women's lives and the ways in which women negotiate their 'own' time free from family responsibility for sport.

In Chapter 11, Anne Flintoff raises a number of pertinent issues arising out of her ethnographic research into the relationship between gender and initial teacher education in PE. She assesses, in the context of her research, aspects of contemporary debates surrounding feminist research and describes the processes by which dilemmas raised in the research come to be resolved. The practical and theoretical problems encountered in a cross-national research project concerning women and sport are explored in Chapter 12. Here, Sheila Scraton discusses the research in which she is collaborating with women researchers from a number of European countries to examine how women in these countries experience and integrate sport into their lives. In the final chapter, Barbara Humberstone uses autobiography to raise issues around power in the research process, illuminating the dialectic between ideology, structure and personal struggles. She highlights the contribution that 'grounded' theory can make to feminist research and explores a specific personal challenge to positivistic ideology in the legitimisation of ethnographic research.

The chapters that follow in this book address specific issues around feminist research in sport, physical activity and physical education, whilst illuminating a diversity of experiences and dilemmas encountered through the process of feminist research.

Notes

1 The impetus for this book came from a Women's Sports Foundation (WSF) executive meeting in which it was suggested that the 'Guidance Notes for Students' on 'Researching & Writing on Women & Sport/Leisure/PE' produced by the WSF in 1989 and edited by Celia Brackenridge should be updated. However, we decided that there was a need for an original book concerned with feminist research in sport.

2 See Maynard and Purvis (1994), which examines and analyses feminist research in some detail. Their book develops issues around power, politics and responsibility in the feminist research process through the concerns of their contributors.

3 Maynard (1994) provides an excellent discussion around the traditional opposition to quantitative methods of enquiry in favour of qualitative methods of enquiry in feminist research, arguing for each to be used in a complementary rather than competitive way.

References

Dewar, A. (1991) 'Feminist Pedagogy in Physical Education: Promises, Possibilities and Pitfalls', *Journal of Physical Education, Recreation and Dance*, 62, 6, pp. 68–71 and 75–77.

Hargreaves, J. (1994) *Sporting Females: Critical Issues in the History and Sociology of Women's Sport*, London: Routledge.

hooks, b. (1994) *Teaching to Transgress: Education as the Practice of Freedom*, London: Routledge.

Maynard, M. and Purvis, J. (Eds) (1994) *Researching Women's Lives from a Feminist Perspective*, London: Taylor & Francis.

Maynard, M. (1994) 'Methods, Practice and Epistemology: The Debate about Feminism and Research' in Maynard, M. and Purvis, J. (Eds) *Researching Women's Lives from a Feminist Perspective*, London: Taylor & Francis.

1 Managing a Women's Sport Organisation: Interpreting Biographies

Gill Clarke and Barbara Humberstone

Women in strategic positions in organisations are few and far between (Cheung-Judge and Morrison 1992; EOC 1995; Marshall 1995). Many, if not most, organisations are dominated by male values (Hearn et al. 1989; Marshall 1984). In sport this is particularly so (Humberstone 1995; White and Brackenridge 1984). Nevertheless, or perhaps as a consequence of women's under-representation, invisibility and discrimination in sport, a number of women in the UK got together in the early eighties (as have women in many other countries, see Hall 1994) and initiated the Womens Sport Foundation (UK) (WSF). Its original aims were ' ... to promote the interests of all women and girls in and through sport and demand equality of opportunity'. These aims still underpin the work of the WSF.[1] This advocacy body not only sought, ' ... to provide a voice to challenge the discrimination faced by women and girls in sport and recreation in all levels ...', but it also gave opportunities for women to become strategic managers in and through this all-woman organisation.[2]

The biographies of four key women members, all past and present chairs of the Foundation, are explored here. Through these life histories, not only are their commitments and tensions as managers illuminated, but also their sporting, educational and career experiences are illustrated. Some of the issues associated with 'doing' life-history research are also revealed.

THE RESEARCH

Members of the WSF are not a homogenous group, though they do all share an interest in and love of sport. They differ in terms of class, race, sexual identity, age, disability, body size and cultural, religious and linguistic heritage (Dewar 1993: 212). This is to some extent reflected in the diverse life stories presented here of the chairs of the organisation. The stories that follow emanate from the interviews conducted with the chairs during 1994 and 1995. Though the chairs were interviewed by the authors (Celia Brackenridge and Anita White by Gill Clarke, and Monica Vaughan and Tina Slade by Barbara Humberstone), each interview followed a broadly similar format covering similar questions. The interviews took place in the chairs' homes, except for Celia who was interviewed at her place of work. The interviews lasted for approximately ninety minutes and focused on the following issues: educational and career experiences, interest and participation in sport, and involvement with the WSF. All the interviews were tape recorded and transcribed. They were returned to the chairs for their reactions, comment, verification, and alteration.

The stories that follow highlight aspects of these women's lives and reveal the lived reality of their feminist politics. Our aims as story tellers and analysts are to provide opportunities for the reader (and writers) to identify with them as women and to learn something about each and thereby gain an insight into and understanding of their lives. What we have tried to do as authors of their stories is to let them speak from their own perspective and in their own words as much as possible, whilst attempting to analyse and interpret their stories. Nevertheless, we acknowledge that it is ultimately we who have selected the content to be included and by implication what not to include and the manner in which it has been presented. However, it would be wrong to infer from this that this was a static process, and that there was not only negotiation or compromise over the text and shape that these stories finally took. Indeed, when the stories were returned from the women some aspects of their stories were deleted on request as it was felt that they were 'too personal' and left one feeling 'personally exposed and uncomfortable'.

We believe such a process should also involve some indication of our positionality vis-à-vis this research. We are both members of the WSF (UK) Executive and serve as co-convenors of the Education and Research Group. Each of us is actively involved in sport in our spare time. Gill Clarke umpires hockey internationally and plays tennis to keep fit, and Barbara Humberstone windsurfs, rock-climbs and walks regularly. In terms of our writing, Gill Clarke identifies as a lesbian feminist and Barbara Humberstone as a heterosexual feminist. Each chair whom we interviewed is well known to us, indeed this led us to recognise the potential for harm that the telling of such stories could cause, for we were recording information that could have been deleterious to them, thus at times we felt constrained as to what information we could subsequently report. Thus, like Goodson (1992: 211) we felt '... an obligation to protect people from being managed and manipulated in the interests of research' and so returned our 'selected stories' for the chairs to approve.

FOUR LIFE HISTORIES

Celia's Story

Celia was a founder member of the WSF and its first chair from 1984 until her resignation due to ill health in 1988. She continues to be a member and was involved regionally with the WSF until moving in 1994 to take up the post of Head of Research and Postgraduate Development in the Department of Leisure Management at Cheltenham and Gloucester College of Higher Education. Outside her academic career Celia was a successful sportswoman, and played lacrosse for England for many years.

Celia was educated at a mixed primary and junior school, before moving to a private day school for girls at the age of nine. After passing her eleven-plus examination, she won a scholarship to the senior part of the school. She remembered that at home ' ... right from the beginning there was a lot of educational pressure, but not a lot of educational background. I don't remember lots of books or newspapers in the house ...'. She felt that she was '... not academic but practical'. She recalled enjoying sport from an early age and being relatively successful at it. She was selected for the school lacrosse team at fourteen, which was seen as being very young, and she was also in the tennis and swimming teams. She felt that she followed '... a fairly conventional tomboyish line at school doing all the sporty things ...'. Celia's sporting talents were further developed when at fourteen she joined a top local lacrosse club and played alongside International players. It was at this time that she '... became besotted with it and wanted to play for England...'. This was something that she later went on to do with considerable success, indeed she was made Captain of the British team and then the England team at the age of twenty seven. She also coached the English side from 1982 until 1986.

In 1968, after taking her 'A' Levels, Celia decided to go to Bedford College of Higher Education in order to become a Physical Education (PE) teacher. She spent the fourth year of her course at Cambridge University and became the first student in the UK to gain a First Class Honours Degree in PE. At Cambridge not only did she continue to excel at academic work but her sporting skills were rewarded with the gaining of 'Blues' in lacrosse and cricket. She then gained a scholarship to do a Masters degree at Leeds University. Following this she took up a teaching appointment at Bournemouth School for Girls, but after only one year's teaching and at the age of twenty four she took up her first lecturing post at Lady Mabel College. Celia described how she '... was taken on one side very sternly by a sort of matriarchal woman who was a Principal

Lecturer there and given a talking to on how I was very young and I wasn't to be led astray by these students'. After a year she was promoted to Senior Lecturer to develop the Recreation Studies Degree. In 1977 Lady Mabel College became Sheffield City Polytechnic (now Sheffield Hallam University) and in 1986 Celia was promoted to a Principal Lecturer. By then she was teaching Sports Studies, but diversification in courses followed. Celia became a '... Senior Academic Postholder ... , a Head of Department grade at Sheffield, and was promoted into the Management Team as Head of Academic Quality'. In 1994 she left to take up a Readership at Cheltenham and Gloucester College of Higher Education.[3]

Returning to the WSF, at the time of her initial involvement Celia did not see herself as being '... very politically conscious but just beginning to be ...'. She commented on how she '... suddenly realised you can't just be a feminist in sport, you have to be a feminist across the board'. Celia described it as '... a package deal, and I think that was like the scales falling from my eyes'. Celia recalled how during WSF's first year there was '... a lot of anguished conversation, what the name should be, and of course who is going to run it, where is it going to be. I got very impatient about talking and not doing anything, so I just said that I would do it and I'll do it in Sheffield if you want'. She described how the WSF was '... very typically voluntary sector, no money, lots of ambition, lots of interest but nobody really knowing how to start...'. Celia also recalled how there were '... rows like shall we have men, shall we not have men, shall we have a sliding scale of subscriptions... shall we throw our lot in with the Sports Council or stay independent. What are we going to do about lesbians, or are we going to do nothing about lesbians? And there were ferocious arguments...'. She recalled how WSF initially '... didn't have a conscious ideology, we did some quite good things and we also appeared to be a lot bigger than we were, as we were writing to Fleet Street about this and that, trying to link with other organisations... We did as much as we could on a shoestring in a rather naive way'. Celia described how she had to become '... very politically correct very quickly, because I had never done anything like this. I had never been to a women's meeting before, didn't know any lesbians, or at least I didn't think I did ...'.

The WSF later moved to an office in central London. Celia vividly remembered how, on 3 September 1988, she collapsed with back trouble before an Executive meeting and had to be lifted off the floor and taken back to Sheffield. She commented that '... it was quite clear that I wasn't going to be able to continue, and I can't remember exactly how it came about but Anita took over'. Celia noted how '... people were always reluctant to become chair because they had seen me do it and then Anita do it, and it was a bit daunting the idea of taking it over'. Celia felt however that it was '... very important that each person who does, does it their own way...'. Celia felt that it was 'A good thing that I gave up the chair because a new perspective was brought in. Anita was much more outward looking in terms of PR... I was more worried about negative issues and fighting against discrimination and writing long letters to official bodies. She got out and talked to people, she was the acceptable face for the WSF... All sorts of doors opened as soon as she took that job which could never have happened with me because I did it a different way... I was totally burned out by the time I handed over...'. She also revealed that this was a particularly stressful time for her ' ... as during this period in the late eighties I was changing sexuality, and the period of great change in my professional life also coincided with that in my personal life'. Celia's hopes for WSF in the future are that it will '... be strong enough to survive as an intermediary between sports specific organisations and an international pressure group for women. I wouldn't like there to be what I think there still is – complete political isolation between sports specific bodies and women's generic bodies'.

Anita's Story

Anita was a founder member of the WSF, and chair from 1988 to 1990. Currently she is Acting Director of National Services at the Sports Council. As a successful sportswoman Anita was an international hockey player and captained the English side that won the World Championships in 1975. Following this she was involved in coaching at club and international level.

Anita was educated at a Methodist girls' grammar school where she remembered that there were lots of opportunities for sport and that she did everything that was going because she loved it, and reached county level as a netballer, athlete and tennis player. She recalled that the school motto was '... Beyond the best, there is a better' and that she grew up with a very strong achievement orientation reinforced by parental expectations. Anita decided she'd '... become a PE teacher because ... the only role model I had of a woman who was doing the kinds of things that I liked was my PE teacher, so I just thought I'd be one, too'. Anita commented that at that time that was the only career avenue open for women to follow who were interested in sport. Anita went to Nonington PE College, an all-women's college with a strong tradition in movement and dance. She described it as '... very sheltered and very restricted... in some ways, it was an environment run by women for women'. Whilst there she was active in sport, and captained the hockey team. After leaving Anita taught for four years at a mixed Independent school in Slough. It was '… at that time that … I had to make a decision about what sport to go for …', she opted for hockey and played for Buckinghamshire and the South of England. Anita's next post was a one-year temporary PE lectureship at Berkshire College of Higher Education, and whilst there she was selected for the England hockey team. It was also at this time that she got married and recalled the support that she got from her husband throughout her hockey career. In 1971, at the age of twenty four, Anita moved to lecture at West Sussex Institute of Higher Education (WSIHE, now Chichester Institute of Higher Education (CIHE)). Anita continued to play international hockey and in 1974 she was made team captain. She believed she ' … was captain more for the leadership qualities than for my playing abilities…'. Having reached the top in her sport Anita decided to extend herself academically and in 1978 she studied full time for a Masters degree at Sussex University, and in 1980 she went to the United States, to undertake a Doctorate in the Sociology of Sport. On her return to the Institute, she was promoted to Head of the Sports Studies programme.

Anita was involved with the formation of the WSF in 1984. She described how she met Celia on her return from the USA and recognised that they shared a lot in common. 'We were both of a mind about things that needed to change in Higher Education and Physical Education, and in women's sport.' Anita remembered how she '… began to appreciate all the issues that affect women in their everyday lives, and … became … more sensitised to women's issues…'. She recalled how Celia '… really seized on, … really got into the analysis of women's issues and … brought those things to the WSF…'.

In 1988 Anita became the second chair of WSF after Celia resigned. She recalled how she was persuaded by a couple of the members to consider taking on the role, although her initial reaction was to doubt her ability to do so, for she felt that '… you couldn't possibly follow Celia, she'd been so brilliant'. Anita described some of the difficulties that she faced in undertaking the role, for her '… it was the first time that I'd tried to lead a voluntary organisation…', and she also found managing volunteers quite different to her professional management role in higher education or captaining a hockey team, and '… it was an enormous time commitment…' on top of her full time job.

Anita recounted how she became '… uneasy about some of the directions WSF was going in, in particular the issue of working with men'. Anita recalled that in the early days a lot of people were lost to the organisation because of the line that was taken of excluding men from membership. Further to this she commented that her preference would be '... to identify male allies, because I do believe that works, but, I equally respect women who think it needs to be done differently ... Celia and I differed on this point and probably would still not agree, except I think we would agree that there should be room for feminists to do things in the way they are best placed and most able'.

Anita also recalled how she had talked to the CIHE students about WSF and how she subsequently encouraged Tina (current chair of WSF) to take a more active role within the organisation. Whilst chair, Anita described how she '... tried to get the organisation accepted as a legitimate part of the sporting scene, ... I tried to establish better relationships with the CCPR and with the Sports Council ... I suppose it was a softening ... a more liberal view of trying to work with an establishment that was predominantly male ...'. She remembered also '... how the leaders in the women's sports movement at that time tended to be women in their thirties who were challenging both the male and female sports system, so we weren't much liked by anyone'. Anita expressed the belief that the '... public perception of the WSF was that it was a lesbian organisation, working out how to deal with the issue as an organisation and overcoming the homophobia we found to exist within the organisation and among ourselves was interesting... it was important for the organisation to decide whether it wanted to combat this perception actively or subtly'. She also remembered '... in the early days, there was a lot of tension between radical and liberal feminists ... I'm more of a liberal feminist and I ... believed the way to change the system was to work within it for change...'. Indeed, Anita believes that these '... are continuing debates', she commented that she would like to think that she listened to all the different viewpoints and that her concern as chair was to help the organisation to be more acceptable to the sporting world because she didn't really believe that it could be changed unless WSF worked from the inside. Anita advocated the building of bridges and forming alliances with mainstream organisations. Her role as chair was only for two years because of her appointment to the Sports Council, where it was incompatible for her to continue to hold the role of chair of an organisation seeking Sports Council funding.

As to the future of WSF, Anita considers that the organisation is '... still facing many of the dilemmas it has done over the last ten years, in particular to what extent it should remain outside and challenge the system and to what extent it should integrate with the system and try to change from within'. Anita believes that WSF '... needs to decide to what extent it should stand outside and throw bricks at the establishment and say "You guys have got it wrong"' and 'to what extent it should seek to consolidate its influence within the sporting establishment'.

Monica's Story

Monica was chair from 1989 to 1992. Prior to this she had been treasurer, when Anita was in the chair. Her first involvement with WSF was as the representative on the executive from the British Sports Association for the Disabled (BSAD). As a contestant in the swimming events in the 1976 and 1980 Paralympiad she gained five and four gold medals respectively for Britain. Monica is now a podiatrist working for the local National Health Service Trust.

Growing up on a council estate where she attended a Catholic primary school, Monica 'loved sport, any kind of sport; netball, rounders ... the football and cricket was after school', with the local lads. She then went to the Catholic co-educational comprehensive in the city, being new it had 'very good sports facilities ... including a swimming pool'. Despite the loss of her left leg above the knee at the age of four, Monica played and enjoyed all sports. She was often not picked for team games, 'until someone twigged that I might not be able to run but I could hit the ball a long way and could catch very well and had other skills'. However, after support from a teacher who taught Monica to swim front crawl, she trained with a prestigious swimming club, competing in and winning able-bodied swimming competitions. 'I'd always competed against able-bodied people, I didn't know anything about sport for people with disabilities.'

On leaving school, Monica worked for the Cheshire Homes Foundation and then trained as a State Registered Nurse. After qualifying, Salisbury District Health Authority gave Monica a three-month sabbatical from nursing to train for the 1976 Paralympics for the physically disabled. In her time Monica was an outstanding swimmer, comfortably winning nine gold Paralympic medals overall.

Taking part in and being a medal winner in the 1976 Olympics had profound effects on Monica. Despite her considerable success, she felt her swimming achievements were overlooked and her disability took centre stage. 'I came back from Canada and I was "one-legged girl sweeps board" ... the focus was on my disability whereas I had gone out to the games as a swimmer ... I was confronted with my disability which had never been a problem or issue before.'

After competing in the 1980 games, Monica decided to give up swimming competitively and she moved from her job as ward sister in a rehabilitation centre in Oxford to take up the post of southern region development officer for BSAD. Here she worked for five years developing and promoting sport for people with disabilities and became BSAD's representative on the WSF executive in 1984 while Celia was chair.

Monica was drawn to the ideals propounded by the WSF, 'here's an organisation that wants to do something' about recognition of womens' sporting abilities. 'WSF ... was very enthusiastic to welcome women with disabilities ... not in a patronising ... way but totally as women who were involved in sport ... and who had voices to be listened to'.

For Monica, through her involvement in sport, a number of personal dimensions crystallised into public issues. 'I've felt about me as a woman with a disability – or the disability and as a woman, they are actually quite similar. It's like ... being gay and having a disability are, in many ways, very similar, except that having a disability is socially acceptable and being gay is not. You are stigmatised for both. Within sport, women are also stigmatised because they are women ... Why should other people be deciding what sports we can or can't play?'

In 1987, Monica left BSAD to embark on a new career, taking a diploma in podiatric medicine and in 1989 became the chair of WSF. During her time as chair, Monica successfully led the Foundation through a number of constitutional challenges and achieved considerable sponsorship from Tambrands[4] for young womens' sports awards. Despite her achievements as a sports woman and her professional experiences. Monica felt that some people in authority in sport, 'didn't have a great deal of confidence in me as someone ... to discuss things with'. She also felt she did not have the professional background and backup that former chairs had enjoyed. The latter, who were lecturers in sport and physical education, not only had 'students who were keen' to be involved with the work of WSF, but also, 'were known nationally and internationally ... (through their) writing papers'.

Monica resigned from the chair in 1992 for a number of reasons. Her career in podiatry was developing and she wanted to focus all her energies on it. Not only was the amount of voluntary work for WSF considerable but also she was deeply concerned about the ways in which homophobia was creating tensions within WSF and between it and outside bodies. She felt that had she remained chair she would have had to overtly challenge homophobic prejudices, which were emanating largely from outside the organisation. 'I think you have to confront the issue of lesbianism because other people would actually bring it up rather than us as an organisation ... For us to deny it, which I think was happening with [our sponsors] and the Sports Council, ... is wrong and there comes a time when the organisation has to stand up and be counted ... If I had remained as chair ... that's what would have happened. That would have probably split WSF and have meant that we would have become a WSF for heterosexual women and a WSF for lesbian women ... which would have been wrong for WSF.'[5]

There is a major critique of WSF which Monica feels needs to be addressed. That is, that 'it is very much seen as a white middle class organisation. It's something Celia always tried to address ... where are the Black women, where are the Asian women? ... it goes back to the kind of image we are projecting'.[6]

Having chosen to direct her enthusiasm and energies to issues around disabilities, Monica is planning to undertake a part-time degree in disability studies and continues to practise podiatric medicine.

Tina's Story

Tina is, at the time of writing, the present chair of WSF, having been elected in 1993. After completing a BA Sports Studies degree at West Sussex Institute of Higher Education (WSIHE), Tina took an M.Sc. in Leisure Management at Loughborough University. After completion of this, and at the age of twenty three, her first post was as manager of a small rural county council leisure centre. She then moved to a city council leisure department, taking up a post as a recreation officer. Tina is now the leisure services development officer and a member of the leisure services management team.

Tina attended a girls' grammar school where lacrosse was played instead of hockey but, 'we had a rebel hockey club during lunch time'. Although never really specialising in any sport, Tina has always been eager to take part in a variety of activities. At school and college, she was a member of a number of teams such as netball, squash, hockey and basketball. She now runs with the city Running Sisters' Club. At WSIHE, Tina became interested in issues around women and sport. Gender issues were part of the course on which Anita lectured. Interested by this issue, she wrote her final dissertation on women in sports centre management, illuminating women's under-representation in leisure management. Also, through Anita's encouragement, in 1985 Tina attended her first Annual General Meeting of the WSF. There then followed a number of years in which Tina co-ordinated WSF activities in the Southern region. She was then nominated as vice-chair to support Monica and, after Monica's resignation, Tina was voted in as chair.

Tina's commitment as chair of WSF is significant and, despite the substantial demands on her time, she derives considerable pleasure from her involvement.

For Tina, on taking over the chair, 'there was such a lot to do and it was so challenging ... You can never do as much as you would want to do because there would be enough to keep a chair busy working full-time on it... So, whatever you do, it doesn't come up to your expectations because you feel you could do much more'. Tina, together with the WSF executive members and staff, successfully obtained funding from the Sports Council for a three-year national development programme. This involved the appointment of a full-time officer, Carolyn Carr. Management of this post has been very important for Tina. 'I thoroughly enjoyed being involved in the process of appointing Carolyn and also feel an obligation to ensure that she has the support and encouragement she needs and ... continuity in terms of her direct supervisor ... WSF has significant responsibility to her as an employee.'

Tina sees this appointment as valuable as it has facilitated the initiation of a number of projects which additionally require further voluntary commitment. The Sports Council's funding, Tina felt, 'is a bit like pump priming, their money will be more than matched with the valuable voluntary work by members and the executive of WSF'. She is concerned that after the three years, when the national development project ends, unless further funding is available WSF may not be able to support the types of initiative that have been possible over the last three years. Tina maintains that, 'We've done a tremendous amount but we've really only touched the surface, I believe that there's a lot more that can be done to raise the profile of the issue ... so that it becomes a part of everyday life that women should have equality of opportunity in sport at all levels and in all capacities'.

Tina is also very aware of the amount of work and effort put in by other members of the executive committee and the stresses which they experience in other aspects of their lives. 'I think you need to be realistic about what can be achieved with volunteers most of whom are also in full-time work and with family commitments. Nevertheless by encouraging an active involvement we've achieved a tremendous amount.' She is also conscious of the substantial responsibility she has as chair and frequently talks through some of the issues with Jonathan, her partner.

For Tina her professional position and voluntary work for WSF are compatible in their underlying values and aims. As an officer for the city council, Tina needs to ensure that the council is providing a leisure service which reflects the needs of the local community. 'As an officer of the council, I need to ensure that we are continually improving the service to shape it more toward the community. This often involves taking positive

action initiatives to encourage use of our facilities and services by those
who have been traditionally under-represented in sport.'

Unlike some organisations, Tina sees her current local authority as a
'supportive environment to all the sorts of policies that WSF supports',
and she feels that, 'other organisations may not have the same type of
ethos and so far I probably haven't encountered the sort of barriers that
many other people have. WSF's policies complement those of my local
authority'.

In the future, Tina would like to progress her career in local authority
management. She sees WSF as going 'from strength to strength'. 'It would
be nice to think that there is no need for an organisation such as WSF but
until then I hope we can continue to support women, raise the awareness
of the issues surrounding womens' involvement in sport, bring about
change in sport and thereby increase womens' opportunities.'

MAKING SENSE OF LIFE HISTORIES: AGENDAS AND DILEMMAS

These vignettes selected by the authors from the interviews, in collaboration with the chairs, are but partial reflections and to some extent snap-
shots of their lives. They cannot do justice to all that these women have
achieved both personally and publicly in a society which is perhaps only
now beginning to recognise the capabilities of women in organisations and
in sport. Their enthusiasm and determination, evident in these brief
glimpses, working both on behalf of the WSF and also professionally, has
arguably done much to further the cause of women, sport and physical
activity. Although the impact of their contributions is difficult to measure,
sponsorship by Tambrands and funding support by the Sports Council for
WSF projects has provided opportunities for recognition of young sports
women and raised the profile of women in sport and sport management.
Their work for the WSF has perhaps also developed their own awareness
of and sensitivity to the positions of women more generally.

The chairs are unrepresentative of women in general in terms of their
achievements (both in sport and professionally) and in their ethnicity,
class and occupational status. They are however more representative of
the few women who are in leadership/management positions in sport and
leisure in that they are largely middle class and white. Therein lies one of
the challenges facing the WSF(UK); to transform itself, as well as transforming sport.

In their various ways, the chairs have not been afraid to challenge the
inequalities and inequities in sport nor to acknowledge discordances

within this organisation. Clearly, not only are there differences in identification and in feminist standpoints between the women volunteers, but also there is the ever-present concern over the image of WSF in the wider community. Such tensions weave throughout each chair's story.

Each story tells of the commitment and energies of these chairs in working for the cause of women in all aspects of sport and physical activity. The different approaches of Celia and Anita in the infancy of the organisation are evident. Celia vigorously, overtly challenging discrimination and inequality in sport, her approach reflecting a more radical feminist standpoint, whilst Anita saw the importance of working with and influencing those in power, subtly building bridges between WSF and significant sporting bodies, her approach being more representative of a liberal feminist standpoint. This is not to say that they do not support other feminist standpoints. Building upon the awareness-raising of Celia's work, Anita's approach paved the way for major sponsorship which has supported a number of successful development projects. Monica secured and guided the organisation through its first major commercial sponsorship, and Tina played a key role in directing the Sports Council funded national development project (1993/6).

In a heterosexist and homophobic society, an all-woman advocacy body, as Anita points out, may be perceived as 'a lesbian organisation'. We would argue that there is often still the tendency in a male-dominated society to ridicule all-women organisations, unless their image is non-threatening as in the Women's Institute, which is sometimes patronisingly represented as 'all jam and Jerusalem'. Monica draws attention to the divisive effect which homophobia could have had on the organisation, challenging the united strength of both lesbian and heterosexual women on the executive.[7] One of us (Clarke 1995: 9) has drawn attention to the insidious and invidious ways in which homophobia can act to 'separate(s) heterosexual women from their lesbian sisters and prevent(s) them from sharing experiences and working together to challenge prejudices and discriminatory practices'. We both acknowledge this threat to women's strength. For Monica, rather than precipitating a division, the way forward which she chose at that time was to stand down as chair. It is ironical that there would appear to be no such similar 'negative' image for all-male organisations.

CONCLUDING REMARKS

Not only does research utilising biography give the opportunity for an individual's experiences and views to be made visible, but also it may provide insights into the ways in which women are both shaped by and can challenge societal and organisational values and structures. We have found this project stimulating and yet sometimes daunting. Certainly, the process has made us more sensitive to the problems each chair faced and more aware of what each has contributed to the development of sport and physical activity for women.

It has also developed our understanding of the tensions around processing interview data. Our attempt to 'give voice' to our research collaborators has not in itself been as straightforward as it might at first appear (see Dewar 1991: 75). What is captured on tape in an informal discussion may appear to one interviewee, when presented with a selection of their words, as acceptable whilst to another it may seem trivial and superficial. The issues for an interviewee of wishing to present a particular image creates for researchers particular ethical dilemmas which are associated with 'ownership' and representation (see Gill Clarke's Chapter 3). For us this research also raises issues around the ways in which research represents/(mis)represents its participants. How often in research are interpretations made which may be at odds with the participant's understandings and whose interpretation is privileged? This dilemma also comes into play when researchers attempt to draw upon specific theories in the analysis of their data (see Barbara Humberstone's Chapter 13).

Acknowledgements

We would like to thank Carolyn Carr (WSF National Development Officer) and Sarah Gilroy, a founder member of WSF, for their helpful comments on this chapter. In particular we wish to express our thanks to past and present chairs of the WSF for their collaboration in the writing of this chapter.

We would also like to thank Noreen Henderson for transcribing some of the life stories and Marilyn Hayward for typing endless versions of this chapter.

Notes

1   The WSF was launched in 1984 and for the first ten years was a voluntary organisation, managed by an annually elected Executive Committee. At the time of writing, the WSF has become registered as a Company limited by Guarantee and is presently awaiting the outcome of its application for charitable status. Subsequently, the management structure will undergo change, though it will continue to be run by volunteers. Its office is at Crosfield House, Mint Walk, Croydon, CR9 1B – where the National Development Officer (funded by the Sports Council) is based with the part-time membership and

advisory officer. The work which is carried out includes women and sports leadership initiatives, establishing and supporting women and sports networks, providing information and producing resources.

2   The current membership leaflet lists the main aims as being to:
     Increase awareness about the issues surroundings women's involvement in sport;
     Support women to become involved in sport at all levels and in all capacities;
     Encourage organisations to improve access to sporting opportunities for women;
     Challenge instances of inequality in sport and seek to bring about change;
     Raise the visibility of British sportswomen.

3   Celia now has a Professorship.

4   During the two years of the scheme, over £100,000 was awarded directly to young sportswomen to support them in their sporting endeavours.

5   The issue of homophobia in sport and sporting organisations is only now beginning to be addressed by significant sporting bodies such as the Sports Council. A workshop concerned with homophobia was held at the Brighton International Conference on Women and Sport, May 1994.

6   The WSF recognises that, and the WSF Development Plan for 1996–2000 seeks to actively encourage membership which is representative of the whole community and to ensure that the Executive Committee members are also representative of the community.

7   Hall (1994) identifies these tensions confronting women's sport advocacy organizations globally.

References

Cheung-Judge, M. and Morrison, C. (1992) 'What Ever Happened to Equal Opportunities?' *The Journal. Women in Organisations and Management*, 3, April, pp. 11–15.

Clarke, G. (1995) 'Homophobia and Heterosexism in Physical Education. Can we Move into a New Era?' Paper presented at the *Physical Education Association Annual Conference: Moving Into A New Era,* Twickenham, England.

Dewar, A. (1991) 'Feminist Pedagogy in Physical Education: Promises, Possibilities and Pitfalls'. *Journal of Physical Education, Recreation and Dance*, 62, 6, pp. 68–71 and 75–77.

Dewar, A. (1993) 'Would All The Generic Women In Sport Please Stand Up? Challenges Facing Feminist Sport Sociology', *Quest*, 45, 2, May, pp. 211–229.

Equal Opportunities Commission (1995) *Women and Men in Britain 1995,* Equal Opportunities Commission.

Goodson, I. F. (Ed.) (1992) *Studying Teachers' Lives,* London: Routledge.

Hall, M. A. (1994) 'Women's Sport Advocacy Organizations. Comparing Feminist Activism in Sport', *Journal of Comparative PE and Sport*, 16, 2, pp. 50–59.

Hearn, J., Sheppard, D., Tancred-Sheriff, P. and Burrell, G. (Eds) (1989) *The Sexuality of Organization,* London: Sage Publications.

Humberstone, B. (1995) 'Women and Sport Management. An Investigation of Women in Key Strategic Positions in University, Local Authority and Outdoor

Education Provision'. Paper presented in absentia at *the FISU/CESU conference*, Fukuoka, Japan.

Marshall, J. (1984) *Women Managers: Travellers in a Male World*, Chichester: Wiley.

Marshall, J. (1995) *Women Managers Moving On* London: Routledge.

White, A. and Brackenridge, C. (1984) 'Who Rules Sport? Gender Divisions in the Power Structures of British Sports' Organisations'. *Paper presented at the Olympic Scientific Conference*, University of Oregon.

2 Researching a Women's Sport Organisation

Brenda Grace

As a feminist studying sport, I consider it important to explore the connections between knowledge about women and the way that such knowledge is produced, thus:

> ... the only viable analyses of gender and sport are those that provide both a critical and historical analysis of the ideological foundations of our past and ongoing research. (Hall 1988: 331)

For me, then, the critical analysis of the research process itself is an important part of any project and is central to my attempt to operate within a feminist framework. To provide a context for discussion here, a brief background is provided of feminist critiques of traditional social science research and of the way that feminist scholars have engaged with established paradigms influential in the discipline. A look is taken at the emergence of a specifically feminist approach to research and different feminist epistemologies. In focusing on my own experiences as a graduate student researching a women's sport advocacy organisation, I attempt to draw out insights gleaned and some of the contradictions I faced from working through a feminist methodology.

DEFINING APPROACHES

Feminism includes a wide diversity of positions and analyses; accordingly feminist research embraces a range of viewpoints (Cook and Fonow 1991). While recognising this diversity, I also see feminism as a movement by which we aim towards the improvement of women's lives. The common thread that links different feminist approaches is a fundamental commitment to pursuing feminist politics. Feminist scholarship and research acknowledges that social life is structured by gender relations that are oppressive to women, is committed to changing this with an emphasis on women's empowerment and autonomy, and seeks to replace sexist intellectual traditions with a feminist paradigm (I use paradigm in the sense of a shared intellectual view of the world). The focus on transforming intellectual and cultural practices that subordinate *women* distinguishes feminist scholarship from other social and political theory within the broader paradigm of critical theory.

The relationship between epistemology and methodology is at the centre of feminist critiques of much orthodox social science research. Epistemological questions draw attention to the political implications of the research process. Stanley and Wise (1983) provide an accessible explanation of epistemology:

> An 'epistemology' is a framework or theory for specifying the constitution and generation of knowledge about the social world; that is, it concerns how to understand the nature of 'reality'. A given epistemological framework specifies not only what 'knowledge' is and how to recognise it, but who are 'knowers' and by which means someone becomes one, and also the means by which competing knowledge-claims are adjudicated and some rejected in favour of another/ others. (Stanley and Wise 1983: 188)

The assumptions which underpin the whole research process are referred to as methodology; it is the 'theory and analysis of how research should be undertaken' (Harding 1986: 2). A researcher's treatment of methodological issues, for example the relationship between the researcher and research subjects, will be guided by their epistemological orientation. Method, however, is the actual practical technique employed in gathering research data (interviewing, participant observation, surveys, the acquisition of documents, and so on).

FEMINIST CRITIQUES OF ORTHODOX SOCIAL SCIENCE RESEARCH

The changing political climate in the 1960s and 1970s generated by the women's liberation movement had an impact upon the work of many women academics working in the social sciences (Millman and Kanter 1975; Smith 1974). As a result of feminist influence, women scholars began to conduct critical analyses of the gender imbalance inherent in most traditional social science research. Feminist concerns focused on the bias towards men as both subjects and producers of academic knowledge (cf. Zalk and Gordon-Kelter 1992: 10).

Criticism of the widespread omission of women as research subjects and the distortion of social theory arising from generalising men's experiences to include women focused attention on the need to study women's experiences of, and contribution to, the social world (Spender 1981). Feminist social scientists undertook research about women with the goal of generating knowledge that would contribute to improving women's social, political and economic status. As this work increased and developed, various feminist scholars began to question existing research practice as inappropriate to the situations under study (Oakley 1981; Smith 1974, 1979; Stanley and Wise 1983). The feminist critique of male bias in methodological approaches inevitably led to a critical analysis of epistemological issues. A significant outcome of feminists experiencing a misfit between the way that research produced 'facts' and the actual social experiences of women was the realisation that for the gender issue to be addressed, it was not simply a question of adding women, but of examining the production of knowledge as a gendered process. Smith (1974, 1979, 1987) worked through a sociology of knowledge perspective to conduct a feminist analysis of the ideological foundations of social science research. In making connections between what is valued as knowledge and relations of ruling, Smith demonstrates how patriarchy is supported by mainstream intellectual practices.

The feminist challenge to 'malestream' social science traditions has largely been based on a critique of positivist epistemology. However, feminist attempts at reformulating androcentric traditions occupy a wide variety of positions; the critiques range from correcting the male bias to make the results more 'objective', to an outright rejection of the paradigm. Although positivism has historically held a central position, there have always been competing paradigms (cf. Sparkes 1992). In developing their critique of positivist epistemology and methodology, feminists drew from other anti-positivist traditions, in particular the interpretive and Marxist traditions (Acker, Barry and Esseveld 1983).

Sparkes (1992: 19) notes that as academic disciplines studying the social world became established they were greatly influenced by the legitimacy attached to 'scientific' inquiry; concepts and methods used to study the natural sciences were applied to the social sciences. Positivist assumptions are associated with Cartesian systems of thought. In this tradition, the social world is considered to exist outside an individual's perception of it and can be observed by researchers from a detached and objective stance. Positivist notions that social reality can be understood through binary categories is based upon Cartesian thought. In this mode of thought, social phenomena are divided into separate and opposite groups; subject/object, male/female, rational/emotional, public/private. In critiquing positivist epistemologies feminists drew attention to the effect of binary thinking on negating similarities and continuums and pointed out that the implicit gender structure of such categories privileges male over female.

Positivist methodologies place great emphasis on the use of prescribed methods that purport to control researcher bias and other external variables that might 'distort' the results. Quantitative methods are privileged over qualitative methods as techniques that produce objective, mathematical data. Feminist researchers argued that quantitative methods stripped away the context of the subjects being researched and that this had directly contributed to women's experiences being made invisible. Women who felt a sense of dislocation between their research experience and positivist methodologies also argued against creating an artificial separation between researcher and research subjects, pointing out that much valuable information was lost as a result (Millman and Kanter 1975). Concern was increasingly expressed about the power dynamics created by positivist research and how this was antithetical to feminist principles (Mies 1983; Roberts 1981).

The interpretive paradigm emerged in the last century as a critical reaction to positivism. This paradigm embraces a wide variety of research traditions that hold in common the rejection of a natural science approach to studying human social life. Theory is seen as grounded in the study of social experience rather than created externally and then tested for validity. Reality is not viewed as an objective 'truth' that exists separate from human experience, but rather as the subjective experience of individuals and a network of intersubjectively shared meanings between individuals (Sparkes 1992). Interpretive epistemology posits that knowledge is constructed out of human experience and is therefore imbedded with values and biases according to changing contexts and individuals. Interactional methodologies such as ethnography and phenomenology study people's social experience through an exploration of the meanings and interpretations that they themselves use to understand their lives. Interpretive methodology, and the qualitative methods associated with this approach, have been adopted by many feminist researchers who reject the rigid separation of researcher and researched. Interpretive research strategies are also valued by feminists because they are based on the epistemological assumption that the only way to know a socially constructed world is to know it from within (Hall 1985).

Neo-marxist and other critical traditions have also developed an extensive critique of positivism. Central to this is the argument that the concept of 'objectivity' and the researcher's value neutrality disguises ideological influences on knowledge production. Critical epistemologies stand in direct opposition to the liberal ideology associated with positivism.

Knowledge is seen as socially constructed and the product of humans interacting with each other and their material world. It is argued that forms of knowledge holding the most authority generally reflect the interests of the ruling group in society. Protecting these interests requires the ruling group to control the process of knowledge production and present their own view of the social world as 'objective reality'. Although feminists have critiqued these traditions for being gender-blind, they have reworked many of the ideas to expose how hierarchies of knowledge contribute to women's subordinate social position (Acker et al. 1983). The commitment of Marxist and critical theories to engaging with theory and research in order to contribute towards social change made these epistemological positions attractive to feminists challenging orthodox traditions. A key Marxist concept utilised in the development of feminist epistemology is the idea that knowledge constructed from the standpoint of those lower down the social structures provides a more complete picture of reality than that constructed only by those in the ruling group. This is considered in more detail in the following discussion which examines the emergence of feminist epistemology.

FROM CRITIQUE TO REFORMULATION: FEMINIST EPISTEMOLOGIES AND METHODOLOGIES

An extensive literature has emerged dealing with the epistemological foundations of feminist research. Within this, three main positions are acknowledged by many authors; feminist empiricism, feminist standpoint theory and feminist postmodernism (Allen and Barber 1992; Harding 1986; Hawkesworth 1989). Other feminist writers on the subject have argued that there is a broader spectrum of feminist epistemological positions that includes these models (with positions incorporating elements from one or more of them). The tensions within and between the different perspectives on the feminist research process are an indication of the expanding scope of this scholarship and its transitional stage of development (Harding 1986, 1990). They also reflect the increasing willingness of feminists to critically engage with their own theory and practice. The outline that follows is intended to highlight the central themes of these three feminist epistemologies.

Feminist empiricism maintains a positivist base, accepting notions of a social realism that can be revealed through systematic methods of observing, recording, and analysing the subject under study. However this position does reject the idea that the researcher can hold a neutral, value-free position, and maintains that the women's movement has enabled better scientific standards by drawing attention to the poor scientific standards inherent in sexism and male bias in the social sciences. Feminist empiricism has challenged the traditional approaches to social science research as not reaching its own scientific standards, but it has not addressed the foundations of the scientific standards themselves (Allen and Barber 1992; Scraton and Flintoff 1992). Sandra Harding (1990) suggests that the conservative nature of feminist empiricism enables it to have some influence within mainstream social sciences in terms of getting feminist issues on the agenda, and that this position has made a contribution to feminist scholarship. At the same time, however, she notes that an inability to transform the norms of science limits its potential for achieving social change for women.

Feminist standpoint theory is rooted in the Marxist analysis of the significance of social location in shaping an individual's understanding of reality. Where Marx theorized class and class consciousness, feminist standpoint theorists examine the implications for a feminist epistemology of women having a particular understanding of the world from their position as a less powerful social group than men. The key to this epistemological position is described by Joyce Nielsen:

> ... it is to women's advantage to know how men view the world and to be able to read, predict, and understand the interests, motivations, expectations, and attitudes of men. At the same time, however, because of the division of labour by sex found in all societies and sex-specific socialization practices, sex segregation, and other social processes that guarantee sex differences in life experience, women will know the world differently from men. It is almost as though there is a separate women's culture which is certainly not the dominant one. (Nielsen 1990: 10)

Standpoint epistemology operates from the assumption that material conditions shape and limit an individual's understanding of life. Although many aspects of women's worlds are made invisible, or silenced, because they are not valued by the men who hold positions of social, economic and political power, their everyday, lived experiences shape how women understand reality. Feminist standpoint theories posit that women have the potential for a 'double vision' which enables them to have a more complex, and less partial understanding of the social world than men (Smith 1979; Weskott 1979). Central to standpoint theory is the notion that members of an oppressed group achieve their double vision through engagement with the material reality of their oppression and as a consequence of intellectual and political struggle against inequality. This process has been termed by Marxists, and subsequently by feminists, as consciousness raising. In this sense, a standpoint is more than just a particular *view* of reality, it is rooted in the political analysis of lived experience, and is an important part of the process by which oppressed groups actively resist the dominant culture. Feminist standpoint theory has been employed by feminists committed to undertaking research *for* women rather than about women. With an emphasis on exploring the social processes that oppress women and locating the analysis in their material reality, many feminists find standpoint theory fits well with the political goals of feminist research.

A third significant dimension of developing feminist epistemology arises from the contemporary school of thought known as postmodern theory. Scholars working from this theoretical position have challenged many of the assumptions of the early feminist work on the research process. Stanley and Wise (1990) note the recent contribution of deconstructionist and postmodern ideas in providing a conceptual language for their own much earlier criticisms about monolithic feminist concepts and silenced epistemological standpoints. Postmodern theories are sceptical about all universalising claims and attempt to destabilise conceptual categories and taken-for-granted ways of knowing. Each dimension of the way our world is conceived and structured is called into question and analyzed as a construction within a particular historical and social context. From this intellectual position, feminist standpoint theory has been criticised for generalizing women's experience of oppression without sensitivity to the particular oppression experienced by marginalised women, such as women of colour, lesbians and disabled women (Allen and Barber 1992). The 'deconstructionist' critique of feminist theory and research during the past has been developed at a time when black and lesbian feminists have been increasingly challenging the failure of feminist scholarship to take account of the different experiences of oppression among women. Conflicts around the politics of difference within both the wider women's movement and academic feminism during the 1980s have drawn attention to the need to deconstruct many of the unexamined categories employed in feminist social science; 'woman', 'gender', and even 'feminism' itself.

As with the writing on feminist epistemological theory, there is a diverse literature that explores the possibilities of a feminist methodological approach. Stanley and Wise (1990: 37) point out that there is also resistance to the idea of specifically feminist methodologies based on criticisms of separatism and concerns about such claims ensuring that feminist research is relegated to the academic margins. Their criticism of feminist epistemological debates noted that there was generally little effort made to translate theory into practical research sets of research principles. Cook and Fonow (1986, 1991) studied issues relating to feminist methodology over a nine-year period and observed that despite tensions between different approaches, four common threads were apparent in feminist orientated research. These themes include: reflexivity of the research process (including consciousness raising); an action orientation; attention to the affective components of the research (insights arising from emotionality within the process); and the use of the situation at hand.

The following discussion draws upon ideas about feminist research outlined above. In seeking to operate from a feminist perspective, I attempted to engage with the historical roots of 'feminist' research as well as some of the wide ranging debates about its constitution. In the process of doing this, I found myself further than I had anticipated from arriving at clear philosophical answers, but at the same time developing my ability to question assumptions previously taken for granted. Fuelled by my readings about how to incorporate feminist principles into the research process, I approached my task with great eagerness. The demands of attempting to translate theory into practice made significant inroads into that energy; the research experience was not without contradictions, some of which became sources of insight while others remain unresolved.

FEMINIST RESEARCH ON THE WOMEN'S SPORTS FOUNDATION UK

My research, undertaken for a Master's thesis, involved a case study of the Women's Sports Foundation UK (WSF), a women's sport advocacy organisation. My rejection of positivism led me to adopt an approach based on the ideas that have emerged from feminist standpoint epistemologies. The commitment to generating knowledge from the perspectives of women went beyond merely adding women into the picture. I believe that research which begins from the experiences of women in sport, with a resolve to improve that experience, has the potential to uncover the social processes that construct sport as male territory. The implications of this for social transformation are greater than merely improving sport for women. They rest with the analysis of sport 'as a set of selected and selective social practices that embody dominant meanings, values and practices which are implicated in the creation and maintenance of hegemonic social relationships' (Dewar 1991). The feminist cultural studies perspective that informed my analysis of the WSF draws connections between sport as a cultural institution and gender inequality in all areas of social life.[1]

I conducted tape-recorded interviews with eleven women from the WSF in September 1993. Eight months later, after an initial analysis of data had been undertaken, I conducted follow-up interviews with four of these women. In identifying appropriate interviewees, I concentrated on women who had been involved in the active running of the organisation, in one or more of the following capacities; committee member, regional or specialist sub-group member, and employee of the organisation. I was able to interview all of the four women who had served as WSF chairs during the course of the organisation's history. From discussions with my interviewees about the diversity of women who had been involved with WSF, I judged my 'sample' to be fairly representative of the cross-section of women who have served on WSF committees and sub-groups. The women I talked to were heterosexual and lesbian, from different class backgrounds, working in public, private and voluntary sectors, women with international sporting experience, and women who enjoyed physical activity on a non-competitive basis. All of the women that I interviewed were in full-time work; it is significant that at the time they joined the WSF, they all had professional connections with sport. The interviewees ranged from academic women with a research interest in sport, to women working in sports management and sports development, to a woman who had played a pioneering role as a female professional sports photographer.

THE CHOICE OF TOPIC AND METHOD

Feminism emphasises the importance of linking the personal and the political, and of drawing connections between theory and practice. I endeavoured to make these connections in my choice of topic and also the way that I proceeded during the research process. The starting point for my thesis was wanting to make a contribution to understanding gender issues in sport that would proceed from studying women's experiences. Behind my decision to step into the world of graduate studies was a need to make theoretical sense of the complexity of the issues I was increasingly facing in my practical relationship with sport. My interest in researching the WSF arose largely from my experiences as a volunteer on the executive committee between 1988 and 1992.

A case study of the WSF was a good way of being able to focus specifically on the organisation and the women involved, while at the same time incorporating an historical and contextual perspective. The

choice of semi-structured interviews as the primary data collection technique reflected my commitment to trying to understand the WSF from
the position of those within the organisation. I saw my own previous
involvement with the WSF as part of this and therefore a help rather
than a hindrance. I was prepared to deal with conceptual baggage
(Kirby and McKenna 1989: 51) as part of the research process in an
attempt to keep my inside knowledge as a positive contribution to the
study. The interviews were semi-structured by my interest in three
themes that are outlined below, but I also wanted to get at the organisational issues as seen by the interviewees themselves. This was sometimes difficult. On the one hand I wanted to let the interviewee guide
the discussion, while on the other I wanted to explore aspects of the
organisational dynamics that related to the key themes. The degree to
which interviewees wanted, or were able, to talk about the themes
varied, depending on their particular experience and their level of
comfort with both the issues and myself.

My analytic strategy involved subjecting the interview and documentary
data to a content or textual analysis. My analysis therefore aimed at grasp-
ing the meaning of what was being described or recorded, and at exploring
the underlying subtleties of the text, as well as building up a comprehensive picture of what was being done by the organisation and its members.
This reflected my concern with contributing to understanding about how
and why particular issues have evolved rather than just providing a
detailed history of organisational events. The research process is neither
value-free nor objective, because there are always assumptions shaping
the research design – whether these are made visible or not.

EXPLORING KEY THEMES

In preparing this research, I drew upon my experience as a committee
member of WSF as this had given me a number of ideas about organisational issues that I felt were important and worthy of study. I identified
three key themes from these issues. The first of these centres on what
appeared to me to be the rather ambivalent relationship of the WSF to
feminism. It had seemed to me that women who were serving the organisation with a great deal of energy and commitment to the aim of improving women's lives were reluctant to adopt either the identity, or the
discourse, of feminism. A number of executive committee members
expressed concerns about the damaging effect on the WSF image of being
associated with feminism. The organisational anxiety surrounding fem-

inism is an interesting contradiction in view of the WSF description of itself and its aims:

> The Women's Sports Foundation (WSF) was founded in 1984 by a group of women working in sport who were concerned about the discrimination that women faced in sport and recreation ... WSF aims to promote the interests of all women in and through sport and to gain equal opportunities and options for all women. (Women's Sports Foundation 1992: 1)

Not all WSF committee members were reluctant to identify as feminists. At the time I was active in the organisation, the women I worked alongside appeared to include liberal and radical feminists. The tensions between these different positions seemed to further complicate the organisation's relationship with feminism. I felt that a closer examination of this relationship was important in understanding the organisational dynamics and also the gap that exists between feminism and sport.

The second theme, the politics of sexuality, is closely connected to the preceding one. I felt that it warranted exploration in its own right, precisely because it is an issue that is generally obscured in other debates, if indeed it is addressed at all. This theme centered on exploring the implications of the gender structure (women-only) of the WSF and organisational anxiety about lesbian visibility. As a WSF member I had been aware that many members were not totally supportive of the fact that the WSF was a women-only organisation. I perceived that perhaps this attitude and also the anxiety around the 'feminist' label was actually a fear of being labelled lesbian. The strength of this fear was sufficient to prevent the issues from being addressed by most of the WSF members, as far as I was aware. This was despite the fact that a number of the women in our midst were known to be lesbians, were welcomed and respected members of the organisation, and were not in themselves construed as dangerous people to be avoided at all costs. Within our committee this apparent fear did not seem to be discussed or analysed. While I was a member, it seemed that we did not try to understand why it was so powerful, and what its implications were for the WSF's aim of reaching out to women from all walks of life. Although it was a sensitive subject, I hoped to be able to gain an understanding of this issue from different member's perspectives.

The third theme that I felt was significant in the organisation relates to issues of difference. This was characterised by the difficulty the WSF encountered in attempting to work towards a common goal for women in sport, while at the same time attempting to maintain a commitment to differences among women. During my volunteer years, I was aware that the various executive committees over the years had largely comprised white, professional women and that this was a matter of concern to the WSF. Although the work of the organisation reflected its commitment to promoting and valuing the sporting involvement of women of colour, women with disabilities, and women of all ages, we were far from being representative in our organisational structures. This issue was often clouded by conceptual difficulties; should we assume a similarity about women's inequality in sport so that we may proceed in a united way with our cause? Or should we look at how we are different and what needs to be done about this, at the risk of losing our unified efforts to improve sport for women? We found it difficult to address issues of power among women and the processes at work that privileged some women's needs, while making others invisible. This conflict is not a new one for women joining together to fight against sexism; it has been a particular characteristic of debates in the women's movement during the 1980s (Lovenduski and Randall 1993). I wanted to try and understand what lay behind the tensions and confusion that surrounded dealing with differences among women.

INSIDER STATUS

One of the particular things about this study was that I was known to most of the women I interviewed, albeit not particularly well, as I discovered when doing the interviews. To those who had been involved in the WSF before my time I was a stranger, but one with a great deal of inside knowledge. I generally felt that my insider status was a bonus, the fact that I had been involved in the WSF helped me to be trusted and to be seen as Brenda-who-is-now-a-student, rather than some distant academic who had come to slice up the organisation without having a clue about what it was like trying to struggle along in difficult circumstances. Reinharz (1992: 26) notes the controversy that exists in mainstream and feminist research about the comparative benefit of being known to one's interviewees. Although I felt my insider status was beneficial to my project, as an element of the research process it was undoubtedly the source of more anxiety and greater reflexivity than any other. In this section I want to discuss the relationship between myself as researcher and the women I interviewed, with particular attention to the dynamics of power.

I was committed to the feminist principle of sensitivity to issues of power in the research relationship and tried to find ways of reducing, or at least acknowledging, where I held relative power. I felt the key to this was reciprocity and self-disclosure; I gave continual recognition during the interview that I too had been part of the WSF and was therefore involved in the issues we were discussing. Sometimes I was worried that parts of the interview were more like a conversation than an interview. While transcribing, I felt reassured that these moments often contributed greatly to building rapport in the interview and encouraged my interviewee to talk more comfortably about what were sometimes very personal and difficult issues. Some women shared feelings and thoughts that were obviously painful, and even told me things that had not been spoken about with anyone else. Although I was attempting to acknowledge the issue of relative power within our relationship by developing an atmosphere of mutual trust, I became aware that this actually made the research subjects more vulnerable.

The control over converting the information I was collecting into research findings gave me a particular form of power as the researcher. Even though all my interviewees were quite aware that they could withdraw from the project at any time and were able to chose what they told me, giving me an interview meant that they had to trust me to treat whatever they said appropriately. The authority dimension of power was actually quite variable. I made a point of locating myself in the same critical plane as my interviewees; after all I was *only* a student doing a research project and had recently been one of the group. I tried to make it clear I didn't see myself as having superior knowledge which authorised me to study the WSF.

A number of the women with whom I spoke I saw as having greater authority than myself, in terms of their life experience, political knowledge and personal achievements. An example of the shifting power dynamics in my researcher/interviewee relationship was my experience of interviewing women who were well established in their academic careers. Here the tables of power seemed turned completely. I was more than conscious that their co-operative involvement in talking to me was accompanied by a professional scrutiny of what I was doing; *I* was the vulnerable partner in the relationship now. One of the academic women whom I interviewed began the conversation with a casual question, 'What is your hypothesis for investigating the WSF?' I was temporarily thrown, having assumed that an established *feminist* academic would, like myself, have rejected positivist research strategies. I nervously gulped out my reasons for approaching the research in the way that I was, wondering how far my loss of credibility was going to detract from the interview, only to be met with a chuckle and 'Thank God for that'. I presume I passed the test.

My methodological stance which underpinned my project seemed fairly clear in my mind as I set off enthusiastically to conduct my interviews. By the time I was bogged down with analysing the data, I began to have some sharp moments of self-doubt about what I thought I was trying to do. Much of this revolved around how to use my interview material in a way that let the women's voices speak for themselves, while also respecting my promise of confidentiality. Most graduate students have a well founded suspicion that no-one will ever read the product of their academic toil except their research committee. I had every intention of providing the WSF and all the women who were kind enough to be involved in the project with a copy of the final work, in keeping with my feminist principle of reciprocity. In this sense, it was potentially going to be a very public document, and those who looked at it would very likely, at the very least, skim the thing to see if they were obviously visible and if so, how they were portrayed. My beneficial insider status brought with it the particular pressure of facing the judgement of my work by my peers. I was continually aware of this while writing up the project in terms of dealing with different realities.

THE MANAGEMENT OF DIFFERENT REALITIES AND UNDERSTANDINGS OF THE RESEARCHER

Feminist epistemologies reject the positivist view of the researcher as value-neutral, pointing out that the researcher's particular social and historical location affects what they can know, and how they can know it (Nielsen 1990; Roberts 1981; Stanley and Wise 1983). Part of my responsibility in representing other people's reality in writing up the research involves acknowledging my particular social experience as white, middle-class, able-bodied and heterosexual. In choosing to address issues of difference and the politics of sexuality in my research, my analysis attempts to deal with the experiences of women of colour, lesbians and women who are differently abled. This created a problematic dimension to the research. The issues discussed in the study focus on the dynamics of power both in gender relations and also among women who experience differing social and economic status. My own position as a women of relative privilege not only shapes my ability to understand the issues, but inevitably affects the political credibility of the analysis. I was constantly aware of this contradiction while writing about the WSF's struggles over lesbian visibility throughout its history, and while arguing that the WSF had a key role to play in challenging homophobia in sport. I feel that my attempt at exploring issues of power as one who has not experienced the oppression does not invalidate the inquiry, but it does undoubtedly raise questions about the ownership of the problems and potential solutions.

In addition to these issues, I knew that some of the women that I interviewed held very different political positions from me. I had to find a way to represent the experiences of other women in my work, whilst making it clear I speak not on their behalf, but from the point of view of someone with a dissimilar background. My 'intellectual autobiography' (Stanley and Wise 1990), that is the process by which my understandings and conclusions have been reached, is considered in my discussion of reflexivity of the research (cf. Grace 1995). I endeavoured to make it clear that the 'results' of this research are not a representation of the organisation as such, but a construction of the reality of WSF that has been shaped by the researcher.

REFLEXIVITY OF THE RESEARCH PROCESS

Cook and Fonow (1991: 2) describe reflexivity as 'the tendency of feminists to reflect upon, examine critically, and explore analytically the nature of the research process'. The importance of reflexivity arises from the feminist assertion that all aspects of the research process are of interest and importance, because they all affect the way that the knowledge produced by the research is constructed. (Bowles and Klein 1983; Scraton and Flintoff 1992). I see reflexivity as a source of insight as well as a means of opening up the research process.

Stanley and Wise (1983) suggest that emotionality is an important aspect of reflexivity for the researcher. My experience suggests that this process begins with the initial contact with the research subjects and, rather like an echo, has a delayed reaction that carries its effects on beyond the completion of the project. Even while writing up this thesis, I found myself looking again and again at my reaction to some of the material and events, continually trying to make sense of it all. The interviews were highly personal interchanges and contained moments of great hilarity, but also some bitterness and a measure of sadness. The sheer energy given by women, slogging away to keep the WSF growing over the years, was clearly discernible in the interviews, together with evidence of the toll in burn-out that such commitment often takes. I had witnessed this in my own involvement, but was powerfully reminded of the problems by the interview conversations. It was moving to hear the personal histories of women struggling to make changes to improve their own and other women's lives.

I believe that it is impossible not to have an emotional involvement in interactive research. For me it created a sense of enormous responsibility towards both my research participants and the WSF, and became the source of growing anxiety as I approached the end of the thesis project. This sense of responsibility goes beyond my rationalised ethical stance of keeping the research subjects informed of what was going on, giving assurances of confidentiality and making it clear that they were able to participate on their own terms. The comment of one WSF member struck a particular chord, 'You won't write anything in your thesis that might hurt the organisation will you?' At the time it was easy to respond reassuringly. I saw myself engaged in an undertaking that was intended to be helpful to the WSF. That comment has come back to haunt me on a number of occasions. What did the question (and my reassurance) imply? That I should not make any references to conflict? That I should not create a negative overall impression of the WSF? (I had assumed uncritically that my previous connection and my research interest indicated that I valued the organisation.) That I must not write about lesbianism, or feminism, in a way that might damage the WSF?

As I thought through these problems, I became very aware that what *I* think is useful in the analysis of the organisation, others may find uncomfortable. My intention is not to offend and I hope that I have treated the opinions of all the women who helped me to conduct the research with the respect that they deserve. That is not to say that I share the same perspective or political interpretation of events as each woman with whom I spoke. I have endeavoured to address how this has shaped the research. In trying to understand why this caused me so much concern I find myself considering the problematic issue of organising around the monolithic category 'woman' which takes no account of the power dynamics at play between us.

For me, one of the most difficult things to reconcile emotionally is what I perceive as the great sense of disappointment felt by women drawn together for a common cause only to find that their differences divide them more than their commonalties unite them. By this I do not mean that disagreements, or personality clashes, threaten the organisation, although of course every organisation has such ups and downs. I am referring more to differences and commonalties in the sense of women's social and political location. The emotion runs deep when conflict centres on individual's very sense of themselves and their world; their way of relating to others around them. Such conflict may not always be dramatic, nor even visible, but the tensions are experienced just as strongly when competing needs or politics are tidied away in the interests of organisational harmony.

The emotions that surrounded my research experience related to these problems. I was moved by the women's intense commitment to working collectively towards the goals of WSF, saddened by the experiences recounted that suggested this had not always worked, and desperately wondering how I was going to deliver a thesis that addressed the politics of this without alienating anybody within the organisation. One thing is for certain; my relationship with the women I interviewed, and the organisation, has shifted to new ground and cannot return to its previous location. Some of the women in the organisation will be less than comfortable with my political analysis, others will feel disappointed that I did not go far enough.

The final comment concerning my analysis of the 'feminist' research process concerns consciousness raising. Ongoing reflexivity throughout my project has made me realise how the project has affected my own understanding of the WSF, the women who work for it and the issues at stake. Because I approached the research as a feminist project, perhaps it is not particularly surprising that my consciousness has evolved as a consequence.

Cook and Fonow (1991: 3) discuss the process of consciousness raising that can occur through reflexivity of the research:

> ... consciousness of oppression can lead to a creative insight that is generated by experiencing contradictions ... transformation occurs, during which something hidden is revealed about the formerly taken-for-granted aspects of sexual asymmetry. Thus, in this model, previously hidden phenomena which are apprehended as a contradiction can lead to one or more of the following: an emotional catharsis; an academic insight and resulting intellectual product; and increased politicisation and corresponding activism. (Cook and Fonow 1991: 3)

For me, likewise, the process of analysing the issues that I chose to explore and of engaging with a wide range of feminist literature has given me a new position from which to analyse and articulate those issues. It is perhaps significant that this perspective is considerably more radical than the one from which I started.

Notes

1   My study of the WSF drew from feminist cultural analyses of sport which theorise sport as a cultural institution playing a fundamental role in the social production and reproduction of unequal gender relations. The theories

demonstrate how ideologies of natural difference present socially-constructed meanings of masculinity and femininity as rooted in biology, and therefore immutable. Because sport is located in bodily practices, those who control it hold a great deal of cultural power over what it means to be male and what it means to be female. It is not just a coincidence that the interests of those who rule sport (and society) are served by the maintenance of ideologies of natural difference. Exploring the implications of social relations being shaped by the cultural institution of sport also raises questions about relative privileges held by different women, and how these are reproduced through sporting practices.

References

Acker, J., Barry, K. and Esseveld, J. (1983) 'Objectivity and Truth: Problems in Doing Feminist Research', *Women's Studies International Forum*, 6, 4, pp. 423–435.

Allen, K. R. and Barber, K. M. (1992) 'Ethical and Epistemological Tensions in Applying a Postmodern Perspective to Feminist Research', *Psychology of Woman Quarterly*, 16, pp. 1–15.

Bowles, G. and Klein, D. R. (1983) *Theories of Women's Studies*, London: Routledge and Kegan Paul.

Cook, J. and Fonow, M. M. (1986) 'Knowledge and Women's Interests: Issues of Epistemology and Methodology in Feminist Social Science Research', *Sociological Inquiry*, 56, pp. 2–29.

Cook, J. and Fonow, M. M. (1991) (Eds) *Beyond Methodology: Feminist Scholarship As Lived Research*, Bloomington, IL: Indiana University Press.

Dewar, A. M. (1991) 'Incorporation or Resistance?: Towards Analysis of Women's Responses to Sexual Oppression in Sport', *International Review for the Sociology of Sport*, 26, pp. 15–22.

Grace, B. M. (1995) 'Women, Sport and the Challenge of Politics: A Case Study of the Women's Sports Foundation (UK)'. Unpublished Master's thesis University of Alberta, Canada.

Hall, M. A. (1985) 'Knowledge and Epistemological Questions in the Social Analysis of Sport', *Sociology of Sport Journal*, 2, 1, pp. 25–42.

Hall, M. A. (1988) 'This Discourse of Gender and Sport: from Femininity to Feminism', *Sociology of Sport Journal*, 5, 3 pp. 330–340.

Hall, M. A. (1990) 'How Should We Theorise Gender and Sport?' in Messner, M. and Sabo, D. (Eds) *Sport, Men and the Gender Order*, Champaign, IL: Human Kinetics.

Harding, S. (1986) *The Science Question in Feminism*, Milton Keynes: Open University Press.

Harding, S. (1987) 'Introduction: Is There a Feminist Methodology?' in Harding, S. (Ed.) *Feminism and Methodology*, Milton Keynes: Open University Press.

Harding, S. (1990) 'Feminism, Science and the Enlightenment Critiques' in Nicholson, L. J. (Ed.) *Feminism and Postmodernism*, New York and London: Routledge.

Hawkesworth, M. E. (1989) 'Knowers, Knowing, Known: Feminist Theory and Claims of Truth', *Signs*, 14, pp. 533–557.

Kirby, S. and McKenna, K. (1989) *Experience, Research, Social Change: Methods from the Margins*, Toronto: Garamond Press.

Lovenduski, J. and Randall, V. (1993) *Contemporary Feminism: Women in Politics in Britain*, Oxford and New York: University Press.

Mies, M. (1983) 'Towards a Methodology for Feminist Research' in Bowles, G. and Klein, D. R. (Eds) *Theories of Women's Studies*, London: Routledge and Kegan Paul.

Millman, M. and Kanter, R. M. (1975) 'Editorial Introduction' in Millman, M. and Kanter, R. M. (Eds) *Another Voice*, Garden City: Anchor Books.

Nielsen, J. (1990) *Feminist Research Methods*, Boulder, CO: Westview.

Oakley, A. (1981) 'Interviewing Women: A Contradiction in Terms' in Roberts, H. (Ed.) *Doing Feminist Research*, London: Routledge and Kegan Paul.

Reinharz, S. (1992) *Feminist Methods in Social Research*, Oxford: Oxford University Press.

Roberts, H. (Ed.) (1981) *Doing Feminist Research*, London: Routledge and Kegan Paul.

Scraton, S. and Flintoff, A. (1992) 'Feminist Research and Physical Education' in Sparkes, A. (Ed.) *Research in Physical Education and Sport*, London: Falmer Press.

Smith, D. (1974) 'Women's Perspective as a Radical Critique of Sociology', *Sociological Inquiry*, 44, pp. 7–13.

Smith, D. (1979) 'A Sociology for Women' in Sherman, J. and Beck, E. (Eds) *The Prism of Sex: Essays in the Sociology of Knowledge*, Madison: University of Wisconsin Press.

Smith, D. (1987) *The Everyday World as Problematic: A Feminist Sociology*, Boston: Northeastern Press and Milton Keynes: Open University Press.

Sparkes, A. (Ed.) (1992) *Research in Physical Education and Sport*, London: Falmer Press.

Spender, D. (1981) *Men's Studies Modified*, Oxford: Pergamon.

Stanley, E. and Wise, S. (Eds) (1983) *Breaking out: Feminist Consciousness and Feminist Research*, London: Routledge and Kegan Paul.

Stanley, E. and Wise, S. (1990) 'Method, Methodology and Epistemology in Feminist Research Processes' in Stanley, E. (Ed.) *Feminist Praxis: Research, Theory and Epistemology in Feminist Sociology*, London: Routledge.

Weskott, M. (1979) 'Feminist Criticism of the Social Sciences', *Harvard Educational Review*, 49, pp. 422–430.

Women's Sports Foundation (1992) *Networking for Women's Sport*, London: WSF.

Zalk, S. R. and Gordon-Kelter, J. (1992) 'Feminism, Revolution and Knowledge' in Zalk, S. R. and Gordon-Kelter, J. (Eds) *Revolutions in Knowledge: Feminism in the Social Sciences*, Boulder, CO: Westview Press.

3 Playing a Part: The Lives of Lesbian Physical Education Teachers

Gill Clarke

The diversity and complexity of the lives of lesbian physical education teachers in secondary schools in England are the focus of this research, which begins from the standpoint of women. Like Smith (1987) I seek to make women the subject and not the object of analysis. The intention is to reveal something of their lived experiences and to challenge the oppressive structures that 'force' them to conceal their lesbian identity within the schooling context, and through this process give voice to their silenced voices (see Dewar 1991). At the same time it is acknowledged that we are all differently positioned and privileged and that this impacts on how we view and interpret our own lives as well as those we seek to understand. Thus, whilst I am arguing for the need to begin from the standpoint of the lives of these lesbian teachers, and to make their lived experiences central such a stance should not be viewed as a panacea and unproblematic. It is imperative that the differences between women are not obscured, nor any commonality falsely universalised. Such an approach for me involves a commitment to lesbian feminism, since as Jeffreys (1993: xii) aptly comments '... [it] transforms feminism by calling the naturalness of heterosexuality into doubt, by pointing out that it is a political institution and seeking to bring that institution to an end in the interests of women's freedom and sexual self-determination. Most importantly lesbian feminism sees the creation of a world fit for lesbians as a world in which all women will be free'. Like Dewar though (1993: 211), I believe that we have been guilty of developing theories in which white, middle-class women's experiences are falsely universalised as representative of all women's experiences. Further to this, I make no claim that this group of lesbian physical education teachers is representative, indeed I believe there is no generic lesbian woman. As Harding (1991: 266) notes, even the term '... "lesbian lives" is a cultural abstraction; race, class, sexuality, culture, and history construct different patterns of daily activity for lesbians as they do for the lives of other'. This research lies within the critical interpretative paradigm (see Sparkes 1992) and is grounded in the voices and experiences of

36

the lesbian women interviewed. It accepts that no research is ever final and that it is only the present frozen in time, therefore the experiences relayed here need to be located within their social, cultural and herstorical contexts.

The research is openly ideological for, like Lather (1986) and Sears (1992), I believe that all research is value-based, hence this research is committed to the challenging of the status quo, rejection of compulsory heterosexuality, and to the building of a more just and equitable society.

THE CONTEXT OF THE CONCEALMENT OF LESBIAN IDENTITY

If we are to begin to understand the lives of lesbian teachers then they must be understood within a social and political context that often renders their presence both invisible and marginal. Invisibility often becomes a measure of survival and avoidance of harassment and discrimination within the classroom, rarely is sexual orientation placed on the educational agenda unless it is where a teacher's employment is about to be curtailed. For example, teacher Austin Allen was sacked after admitting, when asked in a classroom, that he was gay. His job was saved only after his Union threatened an all-out strike (see Vallee et al. 1992). Another example of the hostile climate for homosexual teachers was demonstrated by Hackney Council, who sought to suspend lesbian headteacher Jane Brown after she refused to allow her pupils to attend a ballet performance of *Romeo and Juliet*. This controversy began in January 1994 when one of her reasons for not allowing this visit was singled out and ridiculed by the national press, namely, her wish not to reinforce the notion that passion is the exclusive property of heterosexuals. 'IN FACT a lot of other good reasons were put forward when the original offer for the seats was made. Many Kingsmead parents could not afford the £7 they would still have to contribute towards the trip. The hire fee for the coach would have cost the equivalent of a full term's swimming lessons...' (Kingsmead Support Group Newsletter 1994: 1). Despite these other reasons the press continued to harass Jane Brown and to besiege her home. Such was the harassment that she was forced to go into hiding to escape media attention and death threats, meanwhile she continued to go into work. In March of the same year 'the school suffered a graffiti attack of homophobic abuse levelled at Jane' (Kingsmead Support Group Newsletter No. 3 March 1994). In March 1995 the school received a glowing report from the Office for Standards in Education (OFSTED) which singled out the 'strong and supportive' and 'committed' leadership provided by headteacher Jane Brown.

June 1995 saw the Governor's inquiry find Jane Brown innocent of blame over the ballet trip (*The Times*, June 10 1995). Lesbian, gay and bisexual teachers' professional existence are threatened by such examples of homophobia and heterosexism, it is no wonder that most 'choose' to keep their identity hidden and that many now feel even more threatened and vulnerable by what has happened to Jane Brown. The introduction of Section 28 of the Local Government Act (1988) serves to legitimate dominant discourses of compulsory heterosexuality through making unlawful the promotion and acceptability in school of homosexuality as a 'pretended family relationship' and continues to function to keep many teachers afraid of revealing their real identity. Colvin and Hawksley (1989) describe the legislation as an oppressive and retrograde piece of legislation which threatens to undo hard-won advances in equal opportunities awareness and anti-discrimination practice. They comment further: 'Section 28 is also a bad law. Imprecisely drafted and dangerously open to misinterpretation, its implications are potentially far reaching. Already operating to encourage damaging self-censorship, Section 28 strikes at the civil liberties of us all' (Back cover). This then is in part the backdrop in front of which these lesbian voices must be heard and read.

RESEARCHING LESBIAN LIVES: ISSUES OF ACCESS AND CONFIDENTIALITY

The data for this chapter are drawn from in-depth interviews conducted with fourteen white lesbian physical education teachers during 1993/4. Access was difficult due to the prevailing climate of fear of exposure and loss of employment that surrounds lesbian and gay teachers and forces many of them to remain an invisible and silent presence within our schools. Making contact was problematic, however this was made initially through lesbians known to me, who made contact with other lesbians, to see if they were willing to talk in confidence about their lives. This created a 'snowballing' effect where one woman put me in contact with another and so on. Contact was also made in this manner because such are the silences that it is not always possible to identify with any degree of certainty those women who are lesbian (see Squirrell 1989b). The interviews generally took place in the women's homes. Each was sent a letter prior to the interview outlining the research aims, plus a copy of the interview schedule and information about the procedures that would be adopted to protect their identity. All the women were given a pseudonym, the first woman interviewed chose a name beginning with the letter 'A', the second a name beginning with 'B' and so on. (I refer to the interviews as the 'alphabet interviews', after Sue Grafton's on-going alphabet series of detective stories featuring the female private eye Kinsey Millhone.) The interview focused on four main areas for discussion: lesbian identity, activities of teaching, relationships with pupils and relationships with colleagues. These discussion areas arose from my reading of other researchers' work on lesbian teachers, (see Griffin 1991 and Khayatt 1992) together with my own experience of teaching physical education in secondary schools. Permission to tape record the interviews was also sought. All were happy for this to occur, except for one woman who preferred not to have the interview recorded as she felt uncomfortable with the tape recorder on, and another woman who chose to write about her own life. The interviews generally lasted for approximately ninety minutes. When I first started the interviews in September 1993 they tended to last for a much shorter period, but as I became more confident in talking and listening so they became progressively longer (see Clarke 1994). The interviews were then transcribed and returned for comments, corrections, deletions and so on. Following this, the transcripts were analysed according to the main topics of the interview as outlined in the interview schedule.

LOCATING THE WOMEN

The women interviewees were white, able-bodied and aged between twenty three and forty seven. Some were single, some had been married, some were currently in long-standing lesbian relationships, none had children, they came from a variety of working and middle class backgrounds. The length of time that they had taught for varied between just over a year to twenty five years. At the time of the research they were teaching in a variety of establishments: mixed comprehensive schools, girls' schools, church schools and independent schools, these being located in inner cities, urban and / or rural areas.

At all stages it has been my desire to keep the women involved in the research but also in the subsequent dissemination of it. Throughout this process they have had the power of veto over their voices and how they were and are to be used and represented. Thus, where I have written about their lives I have sent them copies for their comment. However, it would be simplistic and naive to assume that these small collaborative actions have solved the problems of exploitation and (mis)representation.

MANAGING A LESBIAN IDENTITY IN THE CONTEXT OF
SECONDARY SCHOOLS

There has been virtually no research in England that has focused
specifically on the lives of lesbian physical education teachers. Sparkes
(1994) has written the life history of a lesbian physical education teacher.
His research records the daily experiences of oppression that she faces and
highlights the range of identity management strategies that she employs to
protect against threats to her substantial sense of self. Squirrell (1989a, b)
has written more generally on issues of teachers and sexual orientation
and Epstein (1994) has edited a collection of articles under the title
Challenging Lesbian and Gay Inequalities in Education. Griffin (1991),
writing in the United States, records that fewer than ten studies have
focused, at least in part, on the experiences of gay and lesbian educators.
Her pioneering research (1992) has illustrated how teachers manage their
gay or lesbian identities in school, and she outlines four categories that her
research participants described that they employed: passing, covering,
being implicitly out and being explicitly out. These were seen as being
part of a continuum, from passing being the safest strategy to explicitly
out which involved the most risk. Woods (1992) (who was a Doctoral
student of Griffin), in describing the experiences of lesbian physical educators in the United States, shows how the majority of her participants
conceal their sexual orientation. From her data two identity management
techniques emerged: strategies to conceal one's lesbian identity and risk-
taking behaviours that could disclose one's lesbian identity. She sub-
divided the strategies that they used to conceal their lesbian identity into
three categories: (i) passing as heterosexual, (ii) personal censoring / self
distancing from students, teachers and administrators; and (iii) personal
censoring / self distancing from any association with homosexuality. The
following sections illustrate how a lesbian identity is concealed from
teaching colleagues and pupils alike within secondary schools in England.

CONSTRUCTING BARRIERS TO CONCEAL A LESBIAN IDENTITY

All the women built barriers around themselves in order to conceal their
lesbian identity from both colleagues and pupils. Elaborate boundaries and
mechanisms for deceiving were thus established and entry into their 'real'
world was not allowed for fear of exposure and / or disclosure and in their
views the possible loss of their jobs. Whilst building these self protective
barriers the women wanted to be valued for their teaching effectiveness, yet

they were worried that if their lesbian identity was revealed then they would be perceived, particularly by their colleagues, in a different and non-positive light. The following comment by Caroline illustrates how she fears losing her job and how she believes that if her sexuality were public knowledge she would be viewed differently by her colleagues. She feared this would lead to her becoming isolated in the staffroom, and she expressed it as:

> Fear, of ultimately losing my job, ... I pride myself that I could pro-bably have a conversation with anyone at the moment in the staffroom and I would be scared that people would not actually talk to me ... You become more of a victim in school than you do of your home life.

In connection with this, another of the teachers, Deb, reported that if her head found out, she thought that she could make someone's life hell if they were gay, particularly if they were a woman. Thus, we can see how in order to be seen to be at least pseudo-heterosexual different scripts have to be adopted within school, as opposed to those that might be adopted in the private home world, as we shall see later in this chapter. The school script requires the lesbian physical education teacher to be above reproach and to live a double life, as Ethel revealed:

> I am two people ... it's not easy to remember to say the right things in one place and the right things not to worry in another ... you slip into two modes depending on where you are and what you are doing.

Barbara also talked about the difficulty of remembering what she'd said to people in the staffroom and how she'd got herself 'legged up so many times'. ('Legged up' is slang for getting confused or muddled.)

Conversations in staffrooms with colleagues become the site for the possible revealing of lesbian identity. Hence conversations about home life are often avoided, or where they focus on partners and children they are steered by the participants to less threatening frames of reference. As Ethel commented,

> I don't tend to join in conversations when they talk about other halves or if they ask me a question related to that or related to their children I'll usually turn it around by saying 'my brother's like that' if they're talking about their husbands and if they're talking about children then I say 'my god children'.

Barbara also talked of worrying about what they (colleagues) might ask. She safeguarded her identity by not saying too much about home. But she also felt that it was hard that she couldn't mention her partner, but they could mention their husbands and children. It is clear then how the self is thus further censored and denied. Despite these concerns Barbara felt that her lesbian identity was relatively safe:

> ... because I'm young, I don't think that they have thought about it, if I was older and still wasn't married and still didn't have a boyfriend then may be, but at the moment I can get away with it because I'm younger.

Compulsory heterosexuality remains the order of the day and these lesbian physical education teachers were forced to comply with it, thereby maintaining the status quo of dominant hegemonic femininity if their sexuality was not to be revealed. Many of the women talked about how their teaching colleagues were always trying to find them a boyfriend, for instance Caroline remarked:

> I'm getting older ... a lot of them are desperately trying to find me a fella. Even going as far as saying you're your own worst enemy, because if you will play netball which is a female sport you will never meet someone, 'take my husband, I met him at the Catholic Ramblers, that's what you need to do' ... sometimes I can laugh it off and sometimes I feel if only you knew. I've got a better relationship than you'll ever dream about.

Ethel also made reference to one colleague who was always trying to find her a man:

> ... she's always been worried for me as far as finding a man is concerned that I'm still single and she must be totally blinkered because she's known me a long time and knows that I've shared a house with two different women. It's not as if she doesn't know me but it just becomes a joke.

In order to protect their identity they are forced not only to listen to such comments but in a sense also to take them on board and to receive them in a positive way. Thus, in order to maintain an 'acceptable' heterosexual identity these comments are not challenged for fear of exposure. Annie's comments illustrate this claim.

> ... you don't think about it, you accept things and that's the way it goes. Most of the time there shouldn't be anything to be scared of, but you are frightened of losing friends and frightened of being exposed to people, ridiculed I suppose ...

Anti lesbian or gay remarks made in conversations also had to be endured for fear of it '... start(ing) to become painfully obvious that I was pro-that type of sexuality ...' (Ethel).

Acceptance and non challenge of these remarks become a way of survival for these teachers, for as Ethel commented, if she was to challenge these remarks then '... it might open a whole new can of worms that I don't want to'.

CONCEALING PERSONAL IDENTITY FROM PUPILS

Not only does identity have to be hidden from teaching colleagues but it also has to remain hidden from pupils in order to guard against possible harassment and verbal abuse from them. All of the women talked in some detail about how they avoided getting 'too close' to pupils so as not to place themselves in at-risk situations. These so called risk situations centred around a number of related issues to do with the body, sexuality and physicality. However, it is beyond the scope of this chapter to do little more than to allude to these issues here. Nevertheless, as the body is dominant in physical education, there is much fear amongst the teachers over both supervising pupils through showers and in changing rooms, and also in supporting children during activities such as gymnastics. Barbara when talking about making the children have showers commented:

> I'm very wary of the kids thinking we're watching them ... we're starting a policy now of all kids have got to have showers, I try and say to the kids 'no one is watching you and we're all the same and if you do think people are watching you I'm sure it's in your imagination, I'm certainly not going to stand there and watch you have a shower.' I'm very wary when they walk past and turn the other way if they've got nothing on or just underwear on ... You're also very wary if you are supporting them in gym ... where you hold them and you just think this is completely stupid ... because there is no way you think anything like that, or, but are they thinking that of you, ... you're on very dodgy ground, they could accuse you of anything...

The very physicality of the subject clearly poses an additional threat to the revelation of the teacher's lesbian identities and leaves them wary as to how they may be perceived by others when they have to support / touch pupils. For some, these fears have become a living nightmare of victimisation and abuse. Caroline recalled in graphic detail how she had been terrorised by a group 'of older youths' outside her house:

> ... they kicked the side of my door in. They would come down in a pack of fifteen or twenty, some on bikes and running and they would

bang sticks on the window or kick the side of my car in. I went one day and all the locks on my car had been polyfillered up. I came back from the cinema in Barbara's car and they had put a brick through every single one of my windows. There was cash in the car and they had not made an attempt to take anything ... the terrorising all sort of came with dyke and lezzie P.E. teacher and I thought these people actually hate me and for nothing more than my sexuality or my job ...

The 'hassle', as Caroline described it, appears to have stopped for the time being. In her anger and desperation she had tried to run the lads over, she then went over to them and said sorry and told them that she'd had loads of hassle with her car and asked them if they happened to know who the lads were. She then asked them to keep an eye on her car as her boyfriend worked away:

I really laid it on thick about having this boyfriend, being the damsel in distress because I'd been left alone, and tried to evoke sympathy...

This incident vividly illustrates how a lesbian teacher is forced into lying about her identity in order to prevent further risk to her identity and life. Reference here to a mythical (heterosexual) man seems to have been her saviour. Whilst this example may possibly be extreme, what was not rare were instances of name calling by pupils of these teachers within schools. These were often either addressed directly to them or took the form of snide comments as they walked past pupils within the school buildings. The teachers responded by ignoring the comments as much as possible, again for fear of bringing too much attention to themselves. Graffiti about two of these teachers had also appeared in their schools. Ethel described how she disliked intensely the name calling behind her back, she said:

I'd rather they did it to my face as the youngsters did when they were obviously concerned and they asked me questions ... I could cope with that. I don't like things shouted down corridors, that makes me feel uncomfortable and unhappy.

These teachers also described how they were anxious not to get too friendly with pupils for fear that they would be asked personal questions about their lives. This fear also affected the relationships that they felt able to construct during extra curricular activities – a time where traditionally teachers have felt able to develop more informal and friendly relations with their pupils.

All the teachers mentioned how, on occasions, they had been asked questions by pupils as to whether or not they had boyfriends and who they lived with. In response to these probing personal questions they either lied about having a boyfriend, some even going so far as to give names to these non existent men, or they gave ambiguous answers that would keep the pupils guessing as to their personal relationships. Deb commented:

> I don't deny anything. I am ambiguous in what I say to them, just because I don't want them knowing my lifestyle ... It's a sort of game with the kids, when someone rings me up ... after school it just sparks off 'oh Miss Henderson is on the phone to her boyfriend' and I will play up to it. 'Oh, what makes you think I'm talking to him ...?'

Not only are these situations threatening to the maintenance of a pseudo 'straight' identity but other situations where they may be required to give moral support to their pupils who may be wrestling with their own sexuality or other personal problems often cause them alarm and distress. Barbara described how she had often ended up 'shoving a kid away who probably needed her' because she was afraid of what the situation might lead to. That is, that the pupil might find out about her sexuality, and hence she was afraid that the ultimate scenario would be dismissal from her job. Two of the other women reported how pupils had come out to them but they had been afraid to counsel them further because to do so might be to run the risk of having their cover blown and also because of their fear of losing status and their job. Neither felt comfortable about this, indeed Caroline saw the steering away of one pupil from homosexuality to heterosexuality as being '... not very loyal advice, not very loyal to my sexuality'. Caroline, like the other participants, felt far too vulnerable to get involved.

THE INTERFACE BETWEEN THE PUBLIC WORLD OF THE SCHOOL AND THE PRIVATE WORLD OF THE HOME

As we have seen, the participants in this study were fearful of both colleagues and pupils discovering the reality of their carefully concealed lesbian identities. The scenarios portrayed earlier illustrate some of the strategies they have employed in order to distance themselves from not only their pupils but also their colleagues. In comparison to this the private world of the home was somehow seen as sacrosanct and entry to it either verbally or physically was rarely allowed, primarily for fear of disclosure of a lesbian identity. Hence, in schools, if these lesbian teachers had partners then they were rarely mentioned, nor were they often taken to school functions. Barbara said that she was afraid of being 'sussed' by staff and pupils if she took her partner to school events. For all of the teachers there were occasions when they would never talk about how they had spent their weekends away from school. Severely censored and acceptable vignettes devoid of any reference to homosexuality were all that might be recounted after the break from school.

Some of the women had visited lesbian and gay clubs in the past, a few continued to do so on an infrequent basis. Part of the reason for visiting these social clubs infrequently was due to fear of bumping into people that they might know, people whose very presence in the club could threaten their concealed identity. Again these were not just imagined fears, Caroline recalled how when coming out of a gay club the police intimidated them and how she was frightened of being arrested and the consequences that this might have for her job. Further to this she described two chance meetings whilst she had been at a gay club. The first involved a pupil and the second a parent. She described the first as harrowing, this was when a sixth form pupil turned up at the gay club. Caroline's main fear was '... of upsetting her (the pupil) and scared of her blowing up and blowing my cover literally'. This same pupil came to see her on the Monday after the meeting and asked her not to tell anybody about it as she said that she would die if the sixth form got to know. Caroline admitted that she was glad that the pupil had approached her first, and that she'd told the pupil to '... be very, very careful and to think long and hard before she visited places like that ...' What is apparent from these comments is the way that compulsory heterosexuality and homophobia traps many women and thereby has the potential to push them into narrowly prescribed and socially acceptable gender roles. We can see too how pupils are denied lesbian role models, and how lesbian teachers are denied the opportunity to be themselves. The second incident that caused Caroline concern was when she met the mother of one of her pupils in this club. Again, it was the fear of disclosure of her lesbian identity, that might eventually result in the loss of her job, that caused her so much worry. In fact, it turned out that though the woman had told her daughter she was lesbian, she had not told her that she went to clubs. Thus, Caroline felt that her secret identity was safe with this parent. She said '... I think I actually trust her, but the consequences could have been dire'. Caroline's fear of being discovered and sacked, was such that she could visualise

... this sort of scenario of our Headmistress, I'm convinced she's gay, ... one of the teacher Governors I know is gay and two more of the senior teachers are gay, all women ... I have this awful idea ... they would get rid of me basically so they wouldn't blow their own cover. I think that I would get a far less sympathetic response than I would from heterosexual senior teachers. I think they wouldn't want to be seen supporting something that I'd done, [and] privately they did.

CONCLUDING REMARKS

This chapter has revealed a partial picture of the lives and lifestyles of lesbian physical education teachers in England. It is not so dissimilar to the picture described by Woods (1992) of lesbian teachers' existence in the United States, in so far as this preliminary analysis has illustrated how these teachers employed strategies to pass as heterosexual, and in so doing engaged in self censorship about their 'real' lives and distanced themselves from any association with homosexuality. All concealed their identities within school to a greater or lesser extent. However, to attempt to place their experiences further within the framework used by Griffin (1992) or Woods (1992), at this stage, would I believe be in danger of being reductionist and run the risk of objectifying their experiences. That is not to say that they did not, at some stages of their teaching careers, employ some of the identity management strategies that Griffin and Woods identified in their research. A fuller picture of their lives may however be revealed on completion of the data analysis.

What is clear is that within a heterosexist and homophobic world these teachers are afraid to reveal their lesbian identities. Thus, we have seen some of the strategies that they are forced to employ in order to survive and conceal their identity. We have seen how they feel unable to join in staffroom conversations about families and partners and how they are frequently urged to find a boyfriend. Not only are their relationships with colleagues stunted by these pressures but they also feel the need to distance themselves from pupils, again to preserve and protect their lesbian identity. They are forced to lead double lives, one for school and another at home. Indeed Ethel said that she felt like Jekyll and Hyde, and that such was the pressure to be seen to be heterosexual that her actions had become almost subconscious and virtually automatic and that she was nearly unaware of doing it, as it had become such a conditioned part of her life. In addition to these double lives we have also seen how some of these women have been victimised and harassed by their pupils. What is also evident is that this group of teachers are oppressed by patriarchy and compulsory heterosexuality. That is not to deny that there are other multifarious factors that contribute to their oppression and marginality within the teaching context and the world at large. (See Pharr's (1988) analysis of homophobia, for she clearly demonstrates the common elements of oppressions, through showing how each is terrible and destructive.) Thus it is important that we see and read these lives within the context of many interconnected oppressions.

This research continues to seek to give voice to their silenced voices and in so doing to render visible their oppressions and to challenge and change this unjust social order which leaves these teachers caught in the closet of the classroom. The words of Caroline when asked how she felt about being involved in the research provide a fitting and moving conclusion to this chapter:

> ... it is something that is very important ... I know that I would like to read it because I would be fascinated to know what other people's experiences have been and what their thoughts are ... I think it is extremely important and it's probably not given the respect it deserves ... there are a lot of people living an extremely lonely inner existence and they are living a lie at school and often they are living a lie at home as well, and where do these people find out how other people are feeling, and equally there are a lot of ... staff that you live a lie to, who don't know you are living a lie. It would be nice to say if only you knew, and I think this is an opportunity to let people know, and people do need to know.

Acknowledgements

I should like to express my thanks to the women who have shared their life stories with me.

This chapter is a revised version of a paper presented at the North American Society for the Sociology of Sport Annual Meeting, November 3–6, 1993, Ottawa, Canada.

References

Clarke, G. (1994) 'The Research That Dare Not Speak its Name: Doing Controversial Research in physical education', *Conference Proceedings of the 10th Commonwealth and Scientific Congress, Access to Active Living*, 10–14 August 1994, University of Victoria, Canada.
Colvin, M. with Hawksley, J. (1989) *Section 28: A practical guide to the law and its implications*, London: National Council for Civil Liberties.
Dewar, A. (1991) 'Feminist Pedagogy in Physical Education: Promises, Possibilities, and Pitfalls', *Journal of Physical Education, Recreation and Dance*, 62, 6, pp. 68–71 and 75–77.
Dewar, A. (1993) 'Would All the Generic Women in Sport Please Stand Up? Challenges Facing Feminist Sport Sociology', *Quest* 45, 2, pp. 211–229.

Epstein, D. (Ed.) (1994) *Challenging Lesbian and Gay Inequalities in Education*, Buckingham: Open University Press.

Griffin, P. (1991) 'Identity Management Strategies Among Lesbian and Gay Educators', *Qualitative Studies in Education*, 4, 3, pp. 189–202.

Griffin, P. (1992) 'From Hiding Out to Coming Out: Empowering Lesbian and Gay Educators' in Harbeck, K. (Ed.) *Coming Out of the Classroom Closet: Gay and Lesbian Students, Teachers, and Curricula*, New York: Harrington Park Press.

Harding, S. (1991) *Whose Science? Whose Knowledge? Thinking from women's lives*, Milton Keynes: Open University Press.

Jeffreys, S. (1993) *The Lesbian Heresy. A Feminist Perspective on the Lesbian Sexual Revolution*, London: The Women's Press.

Khayatt, M.D. (1992) *Lesbian Teachers*, Albany: State University of New York Press.

Kingsmead Support Group Newsletter, 3, March 1994.

Kitzinger, C. (1987) *The Social Construction of Lesbianism*, London: SAGE publications.

Lather, P. (1986) 'Issues of Validity in Openly Ideological Research: Between a Rock and a Hard Place', *Interchange*, 17, 4, Winter, pp. 63–84.

Moses, A. E. (1978) *Identity Management in Lesbian Women*, USA: Praeger Publishers.

Pharr, S. (1988) *Homophobia: A Weapon of Sexism*, USA: Chardon Press.

Ponse, B. (1976) 'Secrecy in the Lesbian World', *Urban Life*, 5, 3, pp. 313–338.

Rich, A. (1980) 'Compulsory Heterosexuality and Lesbian Existence', *Signs: Journal of Women in Culture and Society*, 5, 4, pp. 631–660.

Sears, J. T. (1992) 'Researching the Other/Searching for Self: Qualitative Research on (Homo)Sexuality in Education', *Theory into Practice*, XXX1, 2, Spring, pp. 147–156.

Smith, D. E. (1987) *The Everyday World As Problematic World: A Feminist Sociology*, Milton Keynes: Open University Press.

Sparkes, A. C. (Ed.) (1992) *Research in Physical Education and Sport: Exploring Alternative Visions*, London: Falmer Press.

Sparkes, A. C. (1994) 'Self, Silence and Invisibility as a Beginning teacher: A Life History of Lesbian Experience', *British Journal of Sociology of Education*, 15, 1, pp. 93–118.

Squirrell, G. (1989a) 'In Passing … Teachers and Sexual Orientation' in Acker, S. (Ed.) *Teachers, Gender and Careers*, Lewes: Falmer Press.

Squirrell, G. (1989b) 'Teachers and Issues of Sexual Orientation', *Gender and Education*, 1, 1, pp. 17–34.

The Times, June 10, 1995

Troiden, R. R. (1988) *Gay and Lesbian Identity: A Sociological Analysis*, New York: General Hall, Inc.

Vallee, M., Redwood, H. and Evenden, M. (1992) *Out, Proud and Militant: The Fight for Lesbian and Gay Rights and the Fight for Socialism*, London: Militant.

Woods, S. (1992) 'Describing the Experience of Lesbian Physical Educators: A Phenomenological Study' in Sparkes, A. C. (Ed.) *Research in Physical Education and Sport: Exploring Alternative Visions*, London: Falmer Press.

4 Islam, Well-being and Physical Activity: Perceptions of Muslim Young Women

Hasina Zaman

Islam is not a mere belief system, an ideology or a religion in the usual sense in which these words are understood. Rather it is a total way of life, a complete system governing all aspects of man's existence, both individual and collective. (Hanifa 1974: 9)

Centuries of conflict between the 'Christian West' and 'Islamic East' have led to the development of misconceptions about Islam. Most of the negative stereotypes and even fabrications appear, I would suggest, largely as the result of systematic efforts by the West to 'demonise' Islam and Muslims. According to Edward Said (1978, 81, 93), this 'demonisation' was a partial step in the West's efforts to subjugate and control the Levant.[1]

One area in which these misconceptions about Islam have persisted is in the West's perceptions of the role, status and needs of Muslim women (see Abu Odeh 1993). Consequently, most well-intentioned attempts to deal with issues confronting British Muslim women have failed essentially because of the West's misunderstandings and inability to challenge past prejudice. Instead of trying to deal with the real issues around Muslim women's needs, both non-Muslims and feminists appear often as anti-Islamic crusaders. Their approach is essentially limited and its consequences may be the exacerbation rather than resolution of the problem for Muslim women.

Halstead (1991) clearly exposes the dichotomy confronting radical feminism when it engages with Islam and Muslim women. In attempting to come to terms with the ideological conflict Islam presents, most feminists appear to end up championing Western male prejudices against Muslim women. This situation has not been conducive to any kind of co-operation and leaves little space for some feminists to contemplate that they might share something in common with Muslims, such as the case for single-sex education.

50

Some leading Muslim women writers, however, have recently been requesting more understanding. Ali (1992), for instance, has argued that the issue confronting Muslim women should not be reduced to 'dress', because 'Islam provides a fascinating example of how ethnicity, community and gender can collide in strange and unexpected ways ... Islam can provide the intellectual strength and cohesion' (Ali 1992: 113). Consequently, I argue that in looking to the needs of Muslim women we must take seriously the Islamic framework which informs Muslim women's sense of self.

Moreover, the eurocentric and hard-line position taken by some feminists has had undesirable results for Muslim women who are concerned with changes in their society. This is so for Kabbani who notes that due to:

> ... increasing repression, coupled with the reactionary and colonial views of western feminism and the so called other progressive groupings in Europe, I, like a lot of other Muslim women, have been pushed into positions that I don't necessarily want to adopt ... I find it absolutely insulting and contemptuous to be told by the West how I should feel about my religion, how I should be as a Muslim ... I challenge that to the very end, and I challenge it not as a secularist, but as a Muslim. (Kabbani 1992/3: 43)

MUSLIM YOUNG WOMEN'S NEEDS AND PHYSICAL EDUCATION

Physical education, sport and physical activities do not take place in a vacuum. The creation and provision of facilities are normally the result of a wide variety of factors. These include prevailing political attitudes, available resources and, most important of all, the existing power structure and any accompanying mechanism of patronage. In Britain, physical education for 'minority' groups is frequently considered under the auspices of all-pervasive but largely ineffectual equal opportunity policies. Regardless of the political background of the commentators on the matter, the needs, issues and problems of physical education are invariably pinned on the banner of 'equality'. Three distinctive models appear to have emerged in this pursuit of equality; assimilation, integration and separation.

The assimilation model is based on the notion that minority groups need to be absorbed into the dominant culture. Evans (1990: 144) critiques this model arguing against a 'version of equal opportunities which, with its emphasis mainly on the issues of access, has little to do with egalitarian concern, with social justice, or the structure or structuring of opportunity both inside or outside schools'. One manifestation of this approach, according to Nelligan (1991: 12), would be a situation whereby netball 'was played by most boys in the same enthusiastic way as they play the other games, with few adverse comments'. Logically, this model would support the teaching of physical education in both mixed and single sex classes and would consider it natural for men to teach girls in such activities as dance, educational gymnastics and so on.

The assimilation model presents several fundamental problems in relation to Muslim pupils. Carrington and Leaman (1986: 222) observed that for Muslim pupils:

> ... mixed physical education will not be an option available to staff ... Muslim parents raise objection to it on both religious and moral grounds, arguing that mixed physical education may bring their daughters into direct contact with males in what is regarded as a shameful and potentially compromising situation ... staff should take cognisance of the value and beliefs of Muslim girls and their parents when planning both curricular and extra-curricular activities.

A major shortcoming of this approach, for Muslim girls, is its narrow concept of 'equality' which depends merely on access. Religious preferences are generally ignored and so go unacknowledged.

Caroll and Hollinshed (1993) attempted to understand how the religious beliefs of Muslim girls impinged on their experiences of physical education by focusing on four so called 'problems' or areas of apparent 'conflict' concerning religious values. Problems which emerged related to the inadequacy of clothing for physical education, truancy due to communal showers, participation in sporting activities during the fasting month of Ramadan and daughters returning home late from school after extra curricular activities at school.[2] Siraj-Blatchford (1993) criticised the study because it was 'problem' led. She claims that it is eurocentric in its understanding of the teaching of physical education. In conclusion, she points out that the 'study takes as its "foundation" the very racist and sexist structures that the research professes to understand and undermine' (Siraj-Blatchford 1993: 90).

The integration model is the outcome of multicultural notions of equality. Its aim is to encourage integration into the dominant society whilst maintaining facets of the original subculture. Essentially the model reflects a tendency toward 'multiculturalism'.

A major criticism of the model, according to Figueroa (1993: 90), has been its obsession with cultural tokenism and its inability to problematise racism. Moreover, he suggests that any attempt at anti-racist education which might address these issues has been attacked for being 'negative' and ideological. For Muslim girls, the model offers a limited understanding of their position. The suggestion that Muslim girls might be allowed to wear tracksuits instead of regulation shorts during physical education classes is merely symbolical as it fails to take account of issues around 'respect' and/or 'equal treatment of difference'. The needs of Muslim girls – based on their faith and culture – go much deeper and are more extensive than mere 'dress' instructions. For Muslim girls, as Daly (1991: 31) reminds us, 'religion means a whole way of life not just worship or beliefs. It determines how to dress, what to eat, how to behave'.

Carrington, Chivers and Williams' (1986) study revealed the dangers of succumbing to stereotypical conceptions of Muslim cultures and of gender relations in Muslim society, in particular. According to this study Muslim girls will continue to be disadvantaged in physical education unless physical education teachers and policy makers challenge these stereotypical misconceptions and confront structural racism.

The separation model is based on the principal of gender differentiation. Most of its support has come from feminist writers such as Talbot (1988), Scraton (1986) and Sfeir (1985). Scraton (1986) outlines the historical basis and assumptions underlying this model. Notions of 'separate' and 'different' physical opportunities and experiences were the basis of the traditional separate and distinct physical education for girls which until recently was a central concept in schooling. Talbot (1988: 32) argues that, for women, 'achievement or so called equality does not consist merely of being free to do whatever men have done, but first (it is necessary) to question the moral and human consequences of the structures and procedures which have been created by a patriarchal society'. She argues that women should not be seen as the 'problem', rather it is the social structures which constrain women's sporting activities which need to be problematised. In this chapter, I am arguing that these structures are not only patriarchal but also racist.

According to Sfeir (1985), Muslim women in the West can participate in a sport only within a secular context, but never as a 'Muslim'. She also blames this on the 'patriarchal' nature of Muslim societies and male chauvinism. The most profound deficiency of the separation model is that while it does attempt to understand Muslim women as women, it fails totally to appreciate that they are first and foremost Muslims. Hence the gains made in gender terms become insignificant when compared to the loss Muslim women suffer because of the denial of their Muslim identity.

It is important to recognise that Muslims in Tower Hamlets, where this research was undertaken, are, like Muslims elsewhere, becoming more aware of their Muslim identity. Part of that identity search entails considering how they should look after themselves. Thus to make sense of the perceptions of young Muslim women, physical educationalists and physical activity providers need to understand and respect the way in which these women shape and are shaped by Islam and their Muslim identities. The overemphasis upon 'constraints' acting on Muslim girls and women, rather than attempting to understand the girls' perceptions of health and well-being, has led to the creation of limited conception of these issues in both physical education and sports provision. This chapter attempts to go beyond previous research concerned with Muslim young women and physical activity by locating them within their faith which is practised within the structures of dominant Western ideologies. In so doing young Muslim women's perceptions of health and well-being are illuminated. Consideration is also given to the ways in which Islamic ideology defines well-being in the context of physical health, the connections between 'Islamic ideals' and 'Muslim realities' for Muslim young women and their particular experiences of physical education and physical activity.

ISLAM AND THE BODY

According to the Islamic world view, the human being – man or woman – is created by God in a naturally good and pure state, free from sin. The concept of *fitra* (the primordial norm), is at once the measure of truth in our actions and being, and at the same time the quality of harmony between ourselves and the cosmos. This is the Islamic framework of the purpose for oneself, and in connection to this Muslims have various responsibilities which they have to carry out in their daily lives.

Islam, Physical Activity and Physical Education

The Prophet Mohammed (may peace and blessing be upon him) (pbuh) himself prayed for God's protection against laziness and incompetence. He stressed physical activity and exercise and regularly participated in horse-riding, swimming, archery, wrestling, running and mountaineering. It is interesting to note that all the sports recommended are endurance-based, apart from archery which is classified as a fine motor skill sport.

The Prophet Mohammed (pbuh) said the following about the human body: 'In the body there lies a small piece of flesh; when it is good the rest of the body is good also, and when it is corrupt the rest of the body becomes corrupt: it is the heart' (Imam Al-hadad 1989: 15). The emphasis here is on the heart, therefore it can be argued that a fit and strong heart is central to the well-being of a Muslim.

Prayer and Physical Exercise

Islam has prescribed exercise as part of a daily routine for Muslims. This takes the form of five obligatory daily prayers. The prayers, which are performed at five different times during the day, consist of seventeen circles of body movements. The Qur'an (Ali 1989) says (verse 77 sura 22) *'bow down* and *prostrate* yourselves and worship your Lord'. According to Dayyab and Qarqaz (1982) it is 'part of God's wisdom that s/he who undertakes devotions in answer to the call of his/her Lord shall at the same time be engaged in an excellent set of exercise'. During prayers Muslims have to stand still, bow, kneel and prostrate. The movements are controlled and synchronised and exercise most of the large and small muscle groups in the body. Fleming and Khan (1994) suggest that the daily prayers for Muslims act as spiritual exercise which refreshes and they argue there is a close relationship between sport and Islam.

THE RESEARCH PROCESS

This research was undertaken as the project aspect of my physical education degree. As a consequence of my own experience as a Muslim woman concerned with physical education and Muslim women's well being, I wanted to illuminate Muslim women's experiences. Consequently, tape recorded interviews were undertaken with Muslim girls and young women from a school in the East End of London which has a 96 per cent intake of Muslim girls. Seventeen Muslim Bangladeshi and Indian girls and young women were interviewed. The interviews involved ten year-eleven girls, three year-thirteen girls and four ex-pupils, whose ages were between twenty one and twenty four. I wanted to develop trust and respect with those whom I interviewed, and the interviewees needed to feel safe and comfortable in order to share their views with me. To do this, I had to create a situation in which there was a two-way relationship. As I wanted to be able to probe more deeply into their views and go beyond surface issues, I therefore chose not to use a rigid-schedule interview scheme because many issues were complex and needed disentangling.

Not only was I an ex-physical education student teacher at the school, but also I belonged to the same community as my research participants. These connections had both advantages and disadvantages. One of the advantages was that I could empathise more closely with the young women because of our shared identity. For example, when certain words or terms were used in Arabic or Bengali, I could relate to the participants and assist them to express themselves. The potential disadvantages were that the participants might think that, being of the same background and community, I might use the information against them in some way. I was also conscious of the power relationship between me as the interviewer and the girls/young women as the informants (Oakley 1982). There were times when I felt I had to be provocative and (re)focus the discussion because I wanted to challenge the stereotypical image of Muslim girls.

The Interviews and Participants

Ten Muslim girls (Halima, Ruksana, Jamila, Ayesha, Sabiha, Aliya, Rahima, Anisa, Kaleema and Latifa)[3] from year eleven were interviewed in two groups of five during lunchtime, which lasted for thirty minutes. As these girls had experienced five years of physical education and would soon be leaving school, I felt that they would be in a position to think about how they might continue keeping fit or looking after their physical health. Initially the participants were very nervous as they did not know what to expect from the interview. The content of each interview was not always easy to tackle as some of it was fairly complex and difficult for both myself and the participants to grapple with, particularly with groups of this size.

Three year-thirteen Muslim girls (Jabin, Nafida and Nooree), who were currently studying A levels were interviewed for fifteen minutes, during youth-club time. Due to its location, the interview had many distractions and was difficult to carry out. Consequently, the participants did not appear to grasp the issues easily, not because they were incapable but because there were too many external factors affecting the discussion. I also ran out of time. We attempted to continue the discussion the next day but they felt that there was nothing more to add.

As regards the ex-pupils, Salma was in her final year studying for a degree in Social Policy. The interview took place at her house and lasted for fifty minutes. This interview was one of the most successful as Salma was able to examine the social structure in relation to her Muslim identity,

Islam and wider gender issues. Rukia was an ex-pupil and is studying for an MSc in Information Technology whilst working part-time as a lecturer at the local Further Education College. Initially Rukia did not want to be interviewed, as she felt she had nothing to say. However, she agreed and the interview took place at her house and lasted for about forty minutes. The interview was full of rich, detailed personal experiences as she explained how she had attempted to keep fit but had, along the way, faced many problems.

Farida and Mymuna were two ex-pupils who were best friends at school and still continue to be so. Farida graduated from university after undertaking a degree in biology. She now works part-time as a youth/nursery worker. Mymuna works for the local authority as a Road Safety Officer. Both participants were known to me from their childhood. The interview took place during lunch in a noisy cafe. It was difficult to concentrate and develop issues fully as there was too much noise. However, many contrasting views and experiences were aired. This chapter illuminates some of the views and experiences of these young women.

PERCEPTIONS OF PHYSICAL ACTIVITY IN THE CONTEXT OF THE MUSLIM FAITH

Halima was asked how she would feel if physical education was made available within the context of Muslim religion. She commented:

> Well, if it was part of your religion I would be more motivated, but it isn't. It is about looking after your body, it doesn't necessarily mean going out and jumping about, because it depends what type of fitness you want. So, I think I would do it anyway because it is enjoyable, but I am not so regular with doing my exercise. Maybe if it was part of my religion I would be regular.

Halima could not see the connection between her Islamic faith and the benefits of physical education, but she stated that if regular exercise was part of her faith she would be more likely to try to be more fit.

However, Salma said that as a 'Muslim or as a human being', the importance of being healthy and sustaining good health outweighed other achievements in life, such as material wealth or gaining careers-related qualifications and happiness. She remarked:

> I mean it is very important to look after your body. Cause your body is you really you. If you are not healthy then you can't live life and enjoy it, because if you are unhealthy you might have the money, you might

have everything else materially. You might have the qualifications you can never be happy, but if you are healthy you feel happy don't you. As a Muslim it's part of your religion that we should be healthy, isn't it? In order to live as a full human being you have to be healthy. So I think as Muslims it is important for us to be healthy.

Another ex-pupil, Rukia, shared similar perceptions about the importance of looking after the body:

... 'cause if you are not healthy ... well you have to be healthy to have a lot of vitality in you ... don't you ... if you are healthy, you feel good about yourself, as a Muslim. ... I am a Muslim, but I don't know how it's related to my religion, I don't know anything about that. But I assume that all human beings have to be healthy, so they have to do things for their well-being ... I don't think Islam disagrees with peoples' good health and looking after the body.

In Islam, holistic (mind, body and soul) well-being is an obligation and there are numerous exhortations, advice and guidance on how an individual should attempt to achieve well-being whilst recognising the person as an integrated whole. Islam sees no dichotomy between the spirit, the mind and the body. Attempting to achieve well-being is an Islamic responsibility for every Muslim. However, for a Muslim the human body is not perceived as a 'temple' but rather as a manifestation of respect and love for God. The obligation to be well was identified by Halima when she commented: 'It is our duty to keep ourselves fit and look after ourselves'.

A healthy body and mind, in Islam, are viewed as gifts from the Creator. In Islam there are 'duties that you owe to yourself and *rights* your body and mind have upon you' (Hamid 1989: 25–6). It is the body that has a *right* over you and not the other way round. Ayesha, a pupil, expressed similar ideas but pointed out the practical benefits of looking after the body as a gift.

... people who are really religious they might think that God gave your body as a gift, you should try your best to look after it. It is your duty to be healthy and try to have a longer life expectancy.

Salma, Rukia and Mymuna felt that Western media portrayed a fitness culture which is inherently un-Islamic because it is dominated by a 'body beautiful' image, that is, it is a particular physique or shape of the body which is paramount and in this sense the body becomes treated like a 'temple'. Arguably, the fitness industry has concentrated on improving the outer image, placing particular value on looking good. Unfortunately, this displaces the prime aim of regular physical activity for health benefits. Consequently, keeping fit is often associated with slimness for women and a muscular body shape for men. For Farida, an ex-pupil, the world of fitness is associated with vanity.

What do you mean look after the body, ... if you are talking about fitness and training, doesn't that mean it's vanity almost. I don't know what the Muslim rule is set down for exercise and looking after the body, but I do think it (fitness) is maybe vanity. But you are supposed to keep yourself clean, obviously for prayers and other things ... keep yourself clean and that's as far as I know about keeping your body well.

In reality, Muslims have not had the opportunity to develop Islamic notions of what the physical education curriculum should consist of, neither from an ideological nor a practical perspective. Therefore, for the Muslim young women interviewed, involvement in physical activity and sport was a difficult struggle. It was difficult for them since Western societal values have divorced physical fitness and health from Muslim reality.

PHYSICAL ACTIVITY AND MUSLIM YOUNG WOMEN'S DILEMMAS

The young women and girls who were interviewed took part in various types of physical activities and sports. In some cases, as we can see from the following comments, they were positively influenced by their experience of physical education.

Latifa: I really like doing PE, because it keeps your body really healthy, it relieves stress, it's really good. We usually sit around all day. But, if I do PE once a week and then after all my body aches. It's because you don't do it regular that is why your body aches. The only other exercise I have is my three minutes walk to school and that's it.

Many times the issue of regular exercise was raised, for example Salma expressed her interest in rock-climbing and remarked,

Rock-climbing that's something that I am really enthusiastic about. I only went once and I really, really enjoyed it, I just can't explain it, it's like I really felt good, it's like you forget about everything and you just concentrate on you know ... climbing that rock and it was really enjoyable, I just really enjoyed it and I suppose it is partly to do with the

environment, as well … you know the open air and everything, I would
like to do more of that and everything. I would like to do more of that, I
wish I had the money and the time.

However, most Muslim young women experienced a variety of dilemmas
in relation to their participation in physical activity. These dilemmas are a
consequence not only of living in a non-Islamic society, but also because
of the perceived conflict between their cultural traditions and Islam. These
dilemmas are illustrated below.

Salma:　Islam allows us (to participate in) sports, but Bengali culture
does not allow it I think, because it's a patriarchal culture isn't
it. It is also very influenced by colonialism. During colonialism
men had to protect the women didn't they, so the men had to
exercise and be more strict on purdah[4] and along with that
women were not allowed to participate in any sort of outdoor
activities. I mean sport is one. She was too busy doing cooking
and cleaning that happens in an agricultural society, she does
not really have the time to exercise. Also in Bangladesh,
lifestyle is different, she does not need to be all covered because
she would be in her own village and she has so much space to
roam around. There won't be any non-related males around for
her to totally hide herself. In Britain or in any industrial society
as soon as you walk out of the door you are in front of
strangers, strange men that you have to start wearing purdah,
you can't go anywhere without the men feeling that you are
unprotected. So I think that Asian people and Muslim men in
particular are very protective about the women and it can
become negative only when you come into a setting where they
have to protect you too much.

Salma here clearly identifies the impact of colonialism upon Muslim cultural traditions in general and Muslim women in the West in particular.
She also highlights the problems for Muslims and in particular for Muslim
women of having to fit their lives into a non-Islamic society. This means
that if women want to participate in sports, they tend to have to give up
their Islamic values in order to adopt a Western lifestyle. Salma also highlights some cultural and structural factors that make it difficult for Muslim
women to be involved in physical activity.

Salma:　I think it is very difficult living in a non Islamic society, because
the society is not structured so you can live as a Muslim. I mean
you can't be in purdah as a woman and take part in the social

activities of that society. You can't really 'cause it's always mixed, so that's a lot of factors that work together to stop a Muslim woman from taking part in sports. First of all, she can't go into any sports centre unless its got facilities that are accessible for her, which they don't have. The second is that Muslim women around here tend to be Asian women who have a lot of family responsibilities, 'cause the family is structured where they don't have the time ... culturally it's not encouraged either. So there are three factors that all work negatively, that stop her. I think all these factors worked in my situation.

Family responsibilities, cultural values and a lack of understanding of and respect for Muslim women's views and needs in local leisure and physical education provision are pertinent considerations which can inhibit their involvement in physical activity. This lack of understanding of Muslim women's values is highlighted by Rukia who vividly describes her distressing experience when going along to what she thought to be a women-only swimming session.

Rukia: I don't think that being a Muslim woman should prevent you from doing sports. I go to 'women-only' ... because you know that my religion says that I shouldn't expose my body to men, but you know that when I went to women's night, I assumed that it will be all women and even lifeguards or the safety people would be women and I was shocked that it was men. But I tried to get into the pool as soon as I could, that is the only thing that ruined my swimming apart from that I like swimming.

Rukia had a similar uncomfortable and off-putting experience when changing in communal changing rooms. She said,

... that's what puts a lot of girls off because you know in our school ... you were supposed to get showered in a communal thing and a lot of the girls didn't like doing that, the Muslim girls', cause they didn't like showing their body ... shall I tell you that once I went to this dance workshop, that was the first time I saw ladies all naked in front of each other (laughs) and I was so shocked. Until then I was thinking of taking up dance and we went to that workshop ... after seeing that I didn't want to go anymore.

A number of the young women interviewed also spoke of conflict between cultural traditions and Islamic views. They believed Bangladeshi culture tended to disapprove of women doing sport:

Nooree: Well – culturally it is not really encouraged, you know Bangladeshi culture doesn't really encourage women to partici-pate in physical education. It is looked upon as being 'unfeminine'.

Jabin: It's the men, who stop them. Some are just too sexist and think that sports are for men and why should women do it. They think why should girls play football, if I watch football, my brother he goes 'why are you watching it? you shouldn't be interested in these kinds of things'. They think we should just do sewing, knit-ting and housework. If I ask my brother to do any housework, he tells me to shut up (laughs).

There is clear evidence from the young women that whilst their parents may be trying to maintain their cultural values in their expressed concern over their daughters' involvement in physical activity, some young women wish to look to the teaching of Islam rather than their parents' views.

Salma The Qur'an and Sunnah have the framework, whereas culture and tradition don't. That is the main clash that is going on with parents and their children, 'cause the parents see their culture as important, 'cause they can't apply it here.

The concern of parents has partly developed because physical activity is presented in a Westernised leisure form which falls outside of religious and cultural activities. Jamila commented.

'Cause they [parents] are always worried about 'people' and what people will say, you know. They [parents] say if you go on your own and you travel or walk, what are people going to say. They are worried about people and not themselves. Especially if it's mixed.

Even when the activities are women-only, Sabiha suggests that some Muslim parents perceive it as inappropriate for their daughters,

Then they are going to say you are going to get too Westernised or something like that. They will say always something to prevent you. They will say why do you need to exercise? Why don't you stay at home and do it? Why do you need to do all that to your body? Do you want to show off to men, you are alright like that. That's what parents are likely to say. I don't think my parents will say that, but others might.

Thus even with women-only sessions, there is a belief that physical activ-ity is a Western activity and that daughters may lose their Muslim values as perceived by their parents, as we see in the following discussion:

Halima: Parents don't allow girls to do it, it's something that is not expected.

HZ: Because it is not Islam is it?

Aliya   No it's not Islam, it's the culture actually. It's the culture. People want to say it is religion, they would just say it. They [parents] get Islam confused with culture, that's what I think. That's why we tend to get the wrong end of the stick and [people] misunderstand Islam and make Islam look bad. Parents twists things around to suit themselves rather than what it [Islam] actually is saying. They might not allow girls to go out, so they just say Islam says this. They don't really know the facts, they just have their own opinions and tell us it as Islam.

It appears also that an interrelated issue, constantly on parent's minds, is one of safety. Green et al. (1987) point to women's considerable concern over safety and its influence on their leisure activities. Tower Hamlets has suffered from a long history of racial and sexual attacks and Muslim parents require reassurance that their daughters will not come to harm if they go out to a sports centre. Furthermore, they are worried about the reaction of their neighbours in the community, as it is not accepted or expected that Muslim young women take part in any sports with serious intentions in case of any potential injury. Ruksana says,

I wanted to go into sports but my parents are not very happy about that. I suggested to my mum that I take up badminton. Partly she didn't want me to, you know its a cultural thing, … women taking part in sports – it's not really encouraged. She [mum] starts telling me what are the people going to say if they know that you play sports. They are to think that it's not very feminine is it. She thinks that I might hurt myself as well (laughs).

What is apparent from this research is the awareness of the young women of differences between the teaching of Islam and their parents' cultural views shaped within a non-Islamic racist and sexist society.

REDUCING THE BARRIERS – VALUING DIFFERENCE

For Salma there is much to be done to enable Muslim women to participate comfortably in physical activities,

I think it is really good thing to get Muslim women to take up physical activity more, it's very important for them, but I really don't see how you are going to do that. Because it's really difficult, because the factors are so wide, ... you know in order to eradicate that problem you have to attack everything ... that goes along with it.

Clearly, Salma sees Muslim women's participation in sport not merely as a problem of access but also as a consequence of the racism deeply embedded in societal structures. Nevertheless, despite these factors, Anisa suggested various practical solutions which could enable greater participation by Muslim women and girls in physical activity. She suggests the following:

Cover up more and have things like separate swimming pools for males and females so it doesn't matter. You won't have men watching you or anything. You can wear leggins or tights and a T-shirt and you can't then see the shape. In Bangladesh the women do it [swim] with their clothes on.

Modest dressing and behaviour for both men and women in Islam needs to be seen in context. There is a paradox here that has been cultivated because non-Muslims perhaps either find Muslim women's dress threatening or believe Muslim women are oppressed and made subservient through it. However, Muslim women who choose to wear the *hijab* see it as carrying out the duties of the Islamic code of dressing. Muslim women and their dress have been attacked particularly by the media. But it is a logical step for the Muslim community to defend their rights: for Muslim women, modesty is an important attribute. However, Western thought often perceives such an attribute as showing deficiency and acquiescence. In a sense, in Western society, modesty is largely equated with shyness, passivity and weakness. For Muslims modesty is seen in terms of humility, a positive attribute which for Muslim women provides them with the freedom of not having to conform to Western styles and fashion and provides them with liberation from the male gaze.

CONCLUDING REMARKS

This chapter has sought to raise awareness of Islamic ideology and physical activity. It has raised the issue of the Islamic notion of 'rights of the body' in the context of physical health and well-being. 'Sport' as it is made available to Muslim women is largely perceived as both Western and masculine. The Muslim, young women interviewed revealed a variety of factors which inhibit their involvement in physical activities. These included family responsibilities, cultural values and the lack of understanding of, and respect for, Muslim women's views.

It is clear that a major problem surrounding participation is the ways in which sport, physical activity and physical education are organised and made available and not necessarily the activities themselves. If we genuinely want to increase the participation of Muslim young women, then Muslim values need to influence and inform the context in the way activities are structured and accessed.

A starting point lies for both sport providers and physical educationalists in their willingness to recognise and genuinely address their anti-Islamic views, particularly in relation to Muslim women. This may be addressed through the development of training awareness programmes for sport professionals in collaboration with members of the Muslim community, particularly women. This is a crucial process as it can bring providers and users together to debate Muslim needs and enable Muslim women to be actively involved in structural change. For example, the training of providers in consultation with Muslim women could inform and influence the design of new sports/leisure centres, such as exclusively women-only provision with total screening, creche facilities, changing and shower cubicles and access into activity areas where women are not exposed to male staff/user gaze. Furthermore, local authorities need to work in conjunction with educational establishments to develop National Governing Body coaching awards for Muslim women. This would enable Muslim women to become positive role-models as sports coaches within the Muslim community. It is not any 'passivity' on the part of Muslim young women which inhibits their participation in physical activity, rather it is the racist and sexist society in which they live. If people can overcome their deep-rooted prejudices and encourage Muslim women to take leading positions in sports development and careers within the PE field, then some headway can be made in meeting the needs of Muslim young women and girls in sport, physical activity and physical education.

Acknowledgements

I would like to thank all the Muslim young women who took part in this study.

In addition Muslim women may or may not subscribe to the particular standpoint highlighted in this chapter.

Notes

1   Levant refers to the Eastern part of Mediterranean countries.
2   Ramadan is one of the pillars of Islam. Ramadan or fasting lasts for thirty days. In order to fast a Muslim must, between sunrise and sunset, abstain

from eating, drinking, smoking, use of bad language or thought and sexual intercourse.
3   All the names are pseudonyms.
4   Hijab and purdah are modest outer covering. Women cover all parts except the hands, face and feet. Clothing has to be loose and non-transparent. Recently the term 'hijab' is used to denote the covering of hair.

References

Ali, A. (1989) *The Holy Qur'an*, (translated), Washington: Amana Corporation.

Ali, Y. (1992) 'Muslim Women and the Politics of Ethnicity and Culture in Northern England' in Sahgal, G. and Guval-Davis, N. (Eds), *Refusing Holy Orders*, London: Virago.

Abu Odeh, L. (1993) 'Post-Colonial Feminism and the Veil: Thinking the Difference', *Feminist Review*, 43, pp. 26–37.

Carrington, B. Chivers, T. & Williams, T. (1987) 'Gender, Leisure and Sport: A Case-study of Young People of South Asian Descent', *Leisure Studies*, 6, 3, pp. 265–279.

Carrington, B. and Leaman, O. (1986) 'Equal Opportunities and Physical Education' in Evans, J. (Ed.) *Physical Education, Sport and Schooling. Studies in the Sociology of Physical Education*, Lewes: Falmer Press.

Carroll, B. and Hollinshed, G. (1993) 'Ethnicity and Conflict in Physical Education', *British Educational Research Journal*, 19, 1, pp. 59–76.

Daly, D. (1991) 'Multicultural Issues in Physical Education', *The British Journal of Physical Education*, 22, 1, pp. 31–32.

Dayyab and Qarqaz. (1982) *Medicine in the Holy Qur'an* Damacus, Syria: Muassat Al-Qurran (translated from Arabic by Mohammed Lamani).

Evans, J. (1990) 'Ability, Position, and Privilege in School Pysical Education' in Kirk, D. and Tinning, R. (Eds) *Physical Education, Curriculum and Culture*, Lewes: Falmer Press.

Figueroa, P. (1993) 'Equality, Multiculturalism, Antiracism and Physical Education in the National Curriculum' in Evans, J. (Ed.) *Education, Equality and Physical Education*, Lewes: Falmer Press.

Fleming, S. and Khan, M.N. (1994) Islam and Sport. Observations on the Experiences of Pakistanis in Pakistan and Bangladeshis in Bangladesh, in Duffy, P. and Dugdale, L. (Eds) *Looking Ahead to the 21st century*, Champaign, IL: Human Kinetics.

Green, E., Hebron, S. and Woodward, D. (1987) 'Women, Leisure and Social Control' in Hammer, J. and Maynard, M. (Eds) *Women, Violence and Social Control*, London: Macmillan Press.

Hanifa, S. (1974) *What Every Muslim Should know About Islam*, Pakistan: Lahore Press.

Halstead, M. (1991) 'Radical Feminism, Islam and the Single-sex School Debate', *Gender and Education*, 3, 3, pp. 263–277.

Hamid, A. (1989) *Islam the Natural Way*, Leicester: Mels.

Kabbani, R. (1992/3) 'Gender Jihad', *Spare Rib*, p. 43.

Imam Al-Hadad. (1989) *The Book of Assistance*, London: Quilliam Press.

Nelligan, C. (1991) 'Equality of Opportunity in Physical Education' *The Bulletin of Physical Education*, 27, 1, pp. 12–13.

Oakley, A. (1982) *Subject Women*, London: Fontana.

Said, E. (1978) *Orientalism*, Peregrine Books.

Said, E. (1981) *Covering Islam*, London: Routledge & Kegan Paul.

Said, E. (1993) *Culture and Imperialism*, London: Chatto.

Scraton, S. (1986) 'Images of Femininity and the Teaching of Girl's Physical Education' in Evans, J. (Ed.) *Physical Education, Sport and Schooling*, Lewes: Falmer Press.

Sfier, L. (1985) 'The Status of Muslim Women in Sport: Conflict between Cultural Tradition and Modernisation', *International Review for Sociology of Sport*, 20, 4, pp. 301.

Siraj-Blatchford, I. (1993) 'Ethnicity and Conflict in Physical Education: A critique of Carroll and Hollinshead's Case Study', *British Educational Research Journal*, 19, 1, pp. 77–82.

Talbot, M. (1988) 'Understanding the Relationship between Women and Sport. The Contribution of British Feminist Approach in Leisure and Cultural Studies', *International Review of Sociology of Sport*, 23, 1, pp. 31–39.

Self-confidence and Self-esteem in Physical Education and Sport

Jan Graydon

Probably one of the most important factors for people, men or women, striving for excellence in sport, or trying out new activities, is the issue of self-confidence. It has been shown that self-confidence is linked with continuing sports involvement (Feltz and Petchlikoff 1983) as well as with persistence in physically demanding tasks (Weinberg, Gould and Jackson 1979).

Various terms have been used in the sports literature to cover similar phenomena, including self-confidence, self-efficacy, perceived competence and self-esteem. Self-confidence and self-esteem have usually been regarded as general beliefs about one's own capabilities, while self-efficacy has been used by Bandura (1977) to indicate a belief about one's abilities to perform a specific activity or achieve a specific outcome. Perceived competence (Harter 1985) is also specific and refers to one's ability at a particular skill or field of endeavour (for detailed definitions and a thorough review see Feltz 1988). Clearly in sport and physical activity we are concerned with specific activities in the physical domain.

To date much research has suggested that females frequently lack confidence in their ability to perform sport-oriented tasks as compared to their male counterparts (Lirgg 1991). Lirgg and Feltz (1989) have suggested that female lack of confidence only occurs under certain conditions and have outlined various strategies for enhancing female confidence in the sporting domain. There is a growing body of work which suggests that these strategies are needed and can be successful. It is therefore the intention of this chapter to examine some of the research in the related areas of self-confidence, self-esteem and their enhancement. Finally the value of this mainly quantitative research is discussed with reference to recent critiques of the value of sport psychology research to women.

SELF-CONFIDENCE AND THE EFFECTS OF GENDER

The low self-confidence experienced by many females anticipating physical activity is well documented. A recent meta-analysis (Lirgg

68

1991) showed that, compared to males, females tended to display less confidence in their physical ability, although this effect was not large and was more pronounced in those tasks normally considered to be masculine oriented. This finding provided support for Lenney's view that females would display 'situational vulnerability' in that females' lack of confidence was not general, but particular to certain situations (Lenney 1977). Unfortunately, many of these situations tend to be sporting situations as many sporting tasks are deemed to be masculine in orientation. A recent study by Clifton and Gill (1994) into perceptions of confidence when contemplating the activity of cheerleading, a generally feminine-oriented task, has shown no lack of confidence on the part of women.

Lirgg (1992) has called for a systematic study of the psychological antecedents of lack of confidence in girls and how socialisation affects these. This would seem an ambitious task, but one which should help to provide girls and women with more positive experiences and thus expectations.

What is clear is that there are gender differences appearing in self-confidence and perceived physical competence quite early in life. Work on 10–11 year old boys and girls in primary classes (Granleese et al. 1988; Fazey and Keely 1992) has shown that at this age girls report their perceived physical competence to be lower than boys. The analysis by Fazey and Keely went further and examined children's perceived physical competence with respect to the reported gender appropriateness of the activity. The children were asked to rate the gender appropriateness of several activities and then to indicate how they perceived their athletic competence with respect to male-appropriate, female-appropriate and neutral activities. Evidence from this study indicated that boys showed higher levels of perceived competence than girls, but that the gender appropriateness of the activity affected the outcome. Boys indicated higher levels of perceived competence than girls on male-appropriate and neutral activities, whereas there were no gender differences on the female-appropriate tasks. These results are instructive and further support Lenney's notions of situational vulnerability, in that girls felt selectively disadvantaged in boys' activities. However, what is arguably of more concern is that activities classified as neutral (swimming, tennis, rounders) also resulted in lower perceived competence on the girls' part. This finding is in agreement with the work of Petruzello and Corbin (1988) with undergraduate students. Despite the suggestion by Lirgg and Feltz (1989) that one strategy for enhancing females' self-confidence would be to avoid sex-typing activities, Fazey and Keely's findings would indicate that this may be of limited value.

Furthermore, for boys in the research there was no evidence of situational vulnerability, since there was no significant difference between boys' and girls' estimates of competence on the female-appropriate activities (netball, skipping, hopscotch). It is worth noting that only one of the female-appropriate activities, netball, is taught in school and likely to be carried on into adolescence and beyond. This is patently not the case for the masculine-typed activities (boys' own ratings) of cricket, and rugby. This may raise issues about the girls' continued involvement in, and enjoyment of, physical activity in later years.

In summary then it can be seen that there is a growing body of evidence to support the notion of situational vulnerability in females in sport. Male-appropriate activities tend to elicit lower levels of self-confidence from females than female-appropriate activities. However, what is probably worth emphasising is that female-appropriate sporting activities result only in female estimates of confidence equalling those of males. Female estimates of higher levels of self-confidence are conspicuous by their absence, except in physical activity settings (for example, the cheerleading study by Clifton and Gill 1994). Sport may therefore be seen to be a particularly problematic area of achievement for females.

COMPETITIVE STATE ANXIETY AND SELF-CONFIDENCE

The Competitive State Anxiety Inventory-2 (Martens et al. 1990) is a multidimensional measure which consists of three subscales, namely cognitive anxiety, somatic anxiety and self-confidence. It is frequently used to assess pre-competition levels of anxiety at various times leading up to a competitive situation, for example the study of Jones, Cale and Kerwin (1988). When used with undergraduate students, Jones and Cale (1989) found that females differed from males in the patterning of the pre-competitive anxiety and self-confidence in the period leading up to a prestigious competition. Females were found to experience a decrease in self-confidence on the day of competition. Such a decrease was not found for the males. This finding could have serious consequences for the competitive performance of the females and could bear some serious investigation into its antecedents.

Given the levels of 'situational vulnerability' of schoolgirls in sporting activities outlined above, it may be expected that one consequence of these low levels of perceived competence may be elevated levels of competitive anxiety in gender-typed activities. This could be important when attempting to introduce children to new activities.

This issue was addressed in a recent study (Graydon et al. 1995) which examined levels of pre-competitive anxiety in schoolchildren aged 13–14 years of age. The activities chosen (netball and soccer) were those taught exclusively to boys or girls within a particular school. The boys were overall less anxious and more confident than the girls irrespective of the activity. With respect to the effect of participation in the activities it was found that the boys were less confident before the netball than the football task, whereas the girls were less confident before the football task. Of significance psychologically, if not statistically, was the finding that there was little difference at all between the boys and girls anticipating the netball task, whereas for the football task this difference was large, with the girls' anxiety being much greater. These results support those of Fazey and Keely (1992) and give cause for concern.

It could be argued that these feelings reflect the proposal of Lirgg and Feltz (1989) who noted that self-confidence levels increase as skill proficiency increases. It is likely that the girls in the study would not have any grounds for feeling competent about football skills as they do not play any kicking games. On the other hand the boys do play ball-catching games, possibly even basketball, and so would therefore have grounds for feeling reasonably confident. These findings have obvious implications for planning the introduction to unfamiliar activities.

The results from the anxiety subscales largely mirrored those for self-confidence with the girls showing the greatest anxiety before the football task. A further analysis of this study looked at the children's heart rates prior to participation. Although no significant effects were found there was a noticeable trend in the data. This showed a rise in the boys' heart rates pre-netball, and a rise in the girls' heart rates pre-football.

Again support is found for the 'situational vulnerability' idea with respect to self-confidence, but to this is added the findings about anxiety and the feelings of the children when confronted by different sporting activities. We tend to avoid what makes us feel fear and anxiety. It would seem that teachers should be aware of the possible feelings of anxiety experienced by children and monitor their teaching style accordingly. One of the suggested strategies advanced by Lirgg and Feltz (1989) is also targeted at reducing the feelings of anxiety experienced by girls in some sports settings.

PHYSICAL SELF-PERCEPTION

An issue related to self-confidence is the concept of physical self-perception documented and operationalised by Fox and Corbin (1989).

These authors constructed a multidimensional scale which comprises four subscales: perceived sport competence, physical strength, physical conditioning and body attractiveness. Together these subscales combine to give an estimate of general physical self-worth or physical self-esteem described by the authors as an important contributor to global self-esteem. Given the results of the work already outlined on perceived athletic competence in schoolchildren, it is not surprising to find similar gender differences in responses to the Physical Self-perception Profile (PSPP).

Pountney and Graydon (1993) used the scale to study a group of 105 schoolchildren aged 13–14 years. On the overall general physical self-worth scale the boys gave significantly higher estimates than the girls, a result which was mirrored in all the subscales. This is clearly of great concern and is further compounded by the finding that almost 40 per cent of the girls considered themselves to be overweight. Only 6 per cent of the boys felt themselves to be overweight. A further analysis revealed that scores on the PSPP were related to attitudes towards sport and physical education for the girls but not for the boys. This showed that, for the girls, the higher the feelings of physical self-worth, the more positive the attitudes towards sport and physical education.

Clearly a correlational study of this nature cannot imply causality, but it would appear that many girls are locked in a self-destructive spiral. Low perceptions of physical self-worth are associated with negative attitudes towards sport and physical education in school, which in turn probably reinforce low estimates of perceived athletic competence and physical self-worth. The problem would seem to be how to break out of this negative spiral.

INTERVENTION STUDIES

One obvious method might be to create an environment in physical education classes which is designed to enhance perceived competence, whether this be for girls or boys. Such an environment might be found by examining the achievement-motivational climate of the class, in particular the way in which the achievement goals of the children are fostered.

Briefly, two achievement goal perspectives have been described. These are task and ego orientation. Nicholls (1984) has described a person having an ego orientation as being a person who judges their perceived ability in comparison to others, that is; success means being better than someone else. A task-oriented person is someone whose goals are self-referenced, that is, they are concerned with task mastery and improving their own performance irrespective of others. Task orientation is believed to be linked to positive achievement behaviours (Nicholls 1984) and is generally held to be favourable and to be fostered.

Linford and Fazey (1994) conducted a study with 11–12 year old boys and girls being taught in regular physical education classes. The aim of the study was to examine if teaching style (interpersonal competition oriented versus individual improvement oriented) would affect the physical self-perception of the pupils. They were able to demonstrate that those children taught in an environment which emphasised 'individual improvement, personal bests and skill development' (Linford and Fazey 1994: 199) were able to show significant increases in physical self-perception. This effect was particularly pronounced for those children who initially scored lowest on the self-perception measure. Whether this increase would be maintained after the conclusion of the intervention, and whether it would lead to increased enjoyment of, and participation in, physical activity is not known, but at least this important work has shown that it is possible to break the links creating this destructive spiral.

Teaching strategy was also addressed in some recent work by Lirgg (1993). Working with middle school and high school students of a similar age to those of Linford and Fazey (1994), Lirgg's study examined the effect of changing students who had been taught in mixed (co-ed) classes to same-sex classes over 10 units of basketball. It was found that the boys in the same-sex classes decreased significantly in their confidence in learning basketball. The girls on the other hand did not change significantly in their confidence levels, although there was a visible trend in the direction of increased self-confidence in the same-sex classes and decreasing self-confidence in those students continuing in mixed classes. Little indication is provided with respect to teaching style, although it may be assumed to be fairly task oriented as it is stated that there was '… little emphasis on competition between students' (Lirgg 1993: 327).

With much current debate and opinion about the relative merits of mixed versus single sex physical education it would be well to consider carefully the possible effects on self-perception, particularly for the girls.

It appears from these studies that for adolescents self-confidence, or perceived physical competence, is somewhat fragile and changing. However, the learning environment we provide may have important effects on how adolescents see themselves and therefore possibly on how they view physical activity.

The issue of physical self-perception has been previously addressed with respect to adolescent schoolchildren. It is well documented however (Cash et al. 1986) that many women suffer from feelings of physical inadequacy and dissatisfaction with body image. The search for slimness, or thinness, has spawned a multimillion pound industry which appears to flourish on the feelings of inadequacy that society seems to impose on many women.

The phenomenon of 'social physique anxiety' has recently been documented (Hart et al. 1989), and has been shown to influence attitudes towards exercise participation (Crawford and Eklund 1994). Not surprisingly, if women are anxious about their bodies they are not likely to wish to exhibit them in public wearing flimsy or figure-hugging clothing.

With these issues in mind a study was designed (Graydon and Farrington 1993) to investigate the effects of a women-only programme of aerobics or weight training on the parameters of the PSPP (Fox and Corbin 1989), and on subjects' views of body image as depicted by portrait analysis analysed by an art therapist.

It was found that both exercise programmes resulted in positive changes in aspects of the PSPP. These changes were unrelated to any measurable morphological changes resulting from the programmes. The self-portrait analyses provided valuable insights into the processes which had occurred for many of the women, and provided a useful addition to the quantitative data. It appeared to the art therapist that the women were becoming more aware of their bodies and that many women were 'looking at themselves for the first time' (Graydon and Farrington 1993: 124). Some, however, showed striking positive changes in their views of themselves, becoming more relaxed and confident.

Again it would appear that women's often negative perceptions of themselves can be challenged. However, for exercise promoters the problem with this work is to attract women to the programme in the first place. Work with schoolchildren may be easier in that they are captive participants!

CRITICISMS OF TRADITIONAL RESEARCH METHODS AND FUTURE STRATEGIES

The focus of this chapter has been chiefly concerned with estimates of self-confidence and self-esteem in women and girls and possible ways in which this can be influenced. The research outlined has used the concepts and methods of psychology, mainly quantitative and located frequently within the context of gender differences. These issues have come in for frequent criticism from feminists and from feminist psychologists (see, for example, Squire 1989). The criticisms of gender difference (or sex difference as it used to be known) work have been chiefly that such an approach has merely served to reinforce gender stereotypes without offering meaningful explanations for either theorists or practitioners (Fasting 1993).

The viewpoint advanced in this chapter is that an approach based on gender differences as outlined by Hollway (1991) is useful in identifying the position of women and girls within the sporting arena. Hollway has described a gender-difference approach as:

> … explanatory rather than descriptive, relational rather than comparative, emancipatory rather than normative and dynamic rather than static. (Hollway 1991: 32)

The challenge for sport psychology is to ensure that the above conditions are met and that we are not merely reinforcing stereotypes of sex differences. This task is not to be underestimated, and it is not claimed here that we have all the answers yet, nor even all the right questions! However, given the importance of feelings of self-confidence and self-esteem for women's continued participation in sport, it would seem important to examine how women feel about different sporting contexts, and how situations can indeed be made more 'dynamic'.

It has been clearly shown that feelings of competence and self-worth are not static. They can be influenced in children by teaching style (Linford and Fazey 1994), mixed or single-sex teaching (Lirgg 1993), and for adults by the provision of programmes of physical activity which, while having as an ostensible aim the modification of physical parameters, can influence feelings about physical self-image (Graydon and Farrington 1993).

The issue of self-esteem, self-worth and the enhancement of these to the benefit of women's and girls' psychological health comes close to the popular issue, within feminist writings, of empowerment. Basically this revolves around women being able to realise their own power and to use it to challenge their positions in the world. In a critique of the notion of power within psychology, Kitzinger (1991) has argued that this notion can be dangerous in that it can often result in the victim blaming herself, or himself, if disaster strikes or if things are not up to expectations:

> The notion of the free, autonomous, self-fulfilled and authentic woman possessed of a personal power innocent of coercion – an ideal which informs most feminist psychological engagement with the concept of power – is simply an individualist myth which actively obscures the operation of power. (Kitzinger 1991: 24)

The operation of power as advanced by Kitzinger is generally seen as involving the patriarchal structures and culture within which we are

obliged to operate, and which have to be challenged. Sport, with its
emphasis on masculine values, is often seen as the epitome of patriarchal
structure, thus it is not surprising that women frequently feel less than
confident in their interactions with it. If women are not to turn their backs
on the whole thing then it would appear that they have either to change it
or to use it for their own purposes and to grow from their experiences.
Very often women may use a mixture of these tactics.

Fasting (1994) has presented some examples, drawn from various cultures, of how women have made their own particular sports or activities
more 'user-friendly', and tailored to their own needs. Evidence has been
presented in this chapter which would both support the need for these
strategies and show in some measure how women and girls can grow in
confidence with appropriate sporting experiences. The autonomous
woman can grow in personal power, but on a collective level the power
structures can also be challenged. It should not be forgotten, however, that
it takes immense personal power to challenge an entrenched institution.

The issue of methodology, qualitative or quantitative, has been debated
in mainstream psychology for some time, with varying positions being
adopted. Sport psychology has usually opted for a quantitative positivistic
approach to data collection, with qualitative analysis being the exception
(Bredemeier et al. 1991). For Bredemeier et al. a qualitative approach was
adopted in order to get closer to ('inside the head of') the participants, as a
method of accessing the personal meanings of their sports experiences.
These investigators studied women who were involved in five forms of
physical activity encompassing competitive and non-competitive activities, individual and team events. Data were gathered by semi-structured
interview in order to access the participants' epistemological perspectives
on their involvement. The results are too detailed to outline here, but it is
clear that this approach provides a very different, and fresh, perspective to
the traditional quantitative style much favoured by sport psychology. One
study mentioned previously (Graydon and Farrington 1993) used a combination of quantitative and qualitative techniques, as it was felt that the two
perspectives could complement and inform each other so that a fuller
picture would emerge. Both methodologies could then be seen as complementary, not in competition, with neither being of more value or more
worthwhile than the other. A recent article by Krane (1994) has drawn
attention to the need for qualitative studies in sport psychology to provide
'rich descriptions of mental states ... unobtainable through traditional
quantitative methods' (Krane 1994: 396). The application of new paradigms could delve deeper to gain a fuller understanding of the mental
states associated with levels of self-confidence.

The area of self-confidence and self-esteem is held to be a crucial one for girls and women involved in, or contemplating, physical activity. The view that has been advanced here is that much has been learned using a gender-difference approach. This approach is able to inform researchers and practitioners interested in fostering a love of, and enjoyment in, physical activity for all. As Hollway (1991: 32) has argued, we must take care not to 'throw out the baby with the bathwater'. That is to say, knowledge is advanced by both traditional and new approaches. The challenge is now to go forward and to show how we can change the sometimes tentative, sometimes negative, feelings of girls and women into positive ones which will foster and enhance their enjoyment of the activities which have brought so much pleasure to many of us.

Acknowledgements

With many thanks to Dr. Sandy Wolfson for her helpful comments on an earlier draft of this chapter.

References

Bandura, A. (1977) 'Self-Efficacy: Toward a Unifying Theory of Behavioral Change', *Psychological Review*, 84, pp. 191–215.

Bredemeier, B. J. L., Desertrain, G. S., Fisher, L. A., Getty, D., Slocum, N. E., Stephens, D. E. and Warren, J. M. (1991) 'Epistemological Perspectives among Women Who Participate in Physical Activity', *Journal of Applied Sport Psychology*, 3, pp. 87–107.

Cash, T. F., Winstead, B. W., and Janda, L. H. (1986) 'The Great American Shape-up: Body Image Survey Report', *Psychology Today*, 20, pp. 30–37.

Clifton, R. T. and Gill, D. L. (1994) 'Gender Differences in Self-confidence on a Feminine-typed Task', *Journal of Sport and Exercise Psychology*, 16, pp. 150–162.

Crawford, S. and Eklund, R. C. (1994) 'Social Physique Anxiety, Reasons for Exercise, and Attitudes Toward Exercise Settings', *Journal of Sport and Exercise Psychology*, 16, pp. 70–82.

Fasting, K. (1993) 'The Development of Gender as a Socio-Cultural Perspective: Implications for Sport Psychology', *Proceedings of 8th World Congress in Sport Psychology*, Lisbon, pp. 81–91.

Fasting, K. (1994) 'The Male Model of Exercise and Sport – A Challenge for Girls and Women', *Proceedings of 10th Commonwealth and Scientific Congress*, University of Victoria, pp. 42–49.

Fazey, D. M. A. and Keely, P. (1992) 'Children's Perceived Athletic Competence in Sex-stereotyped Physical Activities', *Journal of Sports Science*, 10, pp. 623–624.

Feltz, D. L. (1988) 'Self-Confidence and Sports Performance' in Pandolf, K. B. (Ed.) *Exercise and Sports Science Reviews*, New York: Macmillan.

Feltz, D. L. and Petchlikoff, L. (1983) 'Perceived Competence Among Interscholastic Sports Participants and Dropouts', *Canadian Journal of Applied Sports Science*, 8, pp. 231–235.

Fox, K. R. and Corbin, C. B. (1989) 'The Physical Self-Perception Profile: Development and Preliminary Validation', *Journal of Sport and Exercise Psychology*, 11, pp. 408–430.

Granleese, J., Trew, K. and Turner, I. (1988) 'Sex Differences in Perceived Competence', *British Journal of Social Psychology*, 27, pp. 181–184.

Graydon, J. and Farrington, T. (1993) 'The Effects of Weight Training and Aerobics on Body Image in Women' in Gies-Stuber, P. and Hartman-Tews, I. (Eds) *Proceedings of Conference 'Frauen und Sport in Europa'*, Germany: Academia Verlag.

Graydon, J., Whelan, S., Keen, S. and Dowling, C. (1995) 'The Effect of Gender and Gender Appropriateness of Activities on Self-confidence and Anxiety' in Vanfraechem-Raway, R. and Vanden Auweele, Y. (Eds) *Proceedings of IX Fepsac Conference*, Brussels, pp. 339–346.

Hart, E. A., Leary, M. R. and Rejeski, W. J. (1989) 'The Measurement of Social Physique Anxiety', *Journal of Sport and Exercise Psychology*, 11, pp. 94–101.

Harter, S. (1985) 'Competence as a Dimension of Self-Evaluation: Toward a Comprehensive Model of Self-Worth' in Leahy, R. L. (Ed.) *The Development of the Self*, New York: Academic Press Inc.

Hollway, W. (1991) 'The Psychologization of Feminism or the Feminization of Psychology', *Feminism and Psychology*, 1, pp. 29–37.

Jones G., and Cale, A. (1989) 'Precompetition Temporal Patterning of Anxiety and Self-confidence in Males and Females', *Journal of Sport Behaviour*, 12, pp. 183–195.

Jones, J., Cale, A., and Kerwin, D. (1988) 'Multi-dimensional Competitive State Anxiety and Psychomotor Performance', *Australian Journal of Science and Medicine in Sport*, 20, pp. 3–7.

Kitzinger, C. (1991) 'Feminism, Psychology and the Paradox of Power', *Feminism and Psychology*, 1, pp. 11–129.

Krane, V. (1994) 'A Feminist Perspective on Contemporary Sport Psychology Research', *The Sport Psychologist*, 8, 393–410.

Lenney, E. (1977) 'Women's Self-Confidence in Achievement Settings', *Psychological Bulletin*, 84, pp. 1–13.

Linford, J. and Fazey, D. M. A. (1994) 'Goal Orientation of Physical Education Lessons and the Perceived Competence Levels of Young Adolescents', *Journal of Sports Science*, 12, pp. 199–200.

Lirgg, C. D. (1991) 'Gender Differences in Self-confidence in Physical Activity: A Meta-analysis of Recent Studies', *Journal of Sport and Exercise Psychology*, 13, pp. 294–310.

Lirgg, C. D. (1992) 'Girls and Women, Sport, and Self-confidence', *Quest*, 44, pp. 158–178.

Lirgg, C. D. (1993) 'Effects of Same-Sex Versus Coeducational Physical Education on the Self-perceptions of Middle and High School Students', *Research Quarterly for Exercise and Sport*, 64, pp. 324–334.

Lirgg, C. D. and Feltz, D. L. (1989) 'Female Self-confidence in Sport: Myths, Realities, and Enhancement Strategies', *Journal of Physical Education and Dance*, March, pp. 49–54.

Martens, R., Burton, D., Vealey, R. S., Bump, L. A. and Smith, D. E. (1990) 'The Competitive State Anxiety Inventory-2 (CSAI-2)' in Martens, R., Vealey, R. and Burton D. (Eds) *Competitive Anxiety in Sport*, Champaign, IL: Human Kinetics.

Nicholls, J. G. (1984) 'Striving to Demonstrate and Develop Ability: A Theory of Achievement Motivation' in Nicholls, J. G. (Ed.) *The Development of Achievement Motivation*, Greenwich CT: JAI Press.

Petruzello, S. J. and Corbin, C. B. (1988) 'The Effects of Performance Feedback on Female Self-confidence', *Journal of Sport and Exercise Psychology*, 10, pp. 174–183.

Pountney, J. and Graydon, J. (1993). Unpublished data.

Squire, C. (1989) *Significant Differences – Feminism in Psychology*, London: Routledge.

Weinberg, R., Gould, D., and Jackson, A. (1979) 'Expectations and Performance: An Empirical Test of Bandura's Self-efficacy Theory', *Journal of Sport Psychology*, 1, pp. 320–331

6 On Pleasure and Pain: Women Speak Out About Physical Activity

Jan Wright and Alison Dewar

The idea for this chapter began over dinner in Vancouver when a group of women, all with a background in physical education and sport, began talking about the absences in the institutional discourses explaining participation and non-participation in physical activity. The available discourses in Australia and North America seemed to come, for the most part, out of social psychology and were primarily concerned with identifying motivational factors which could be measured on various inventories (see, for instance, Eccles and Harold 1991). These inventories seemed to have been administered primarily to college and school students and investigated factors such as self-perception of ability, perceived task value (Eccles and Harold 1991), self-efficacy (McAuley 1992) and sport commitment (Scanlan and Simons 1992).

These explanations had few resonances with our own experiences of physical activity nor did they seem to take into account the movement of the body as a source of the kinaesthetic/sensual pleasures which we described to each other. For all of us physical activity has been characterised by intensely pleasurable experiences, descriptions of which were rarely taken up in the literature. Moreover some of us had friends who for most of their lives had very little to do with physical activity, who would have been regarded as non-participators in their youth but were now finding pleasure in a diverse range of activities very few of which were associated with the traditional activities taught in schools or taken up by school-aged girls in the community.

There was clearly a need to talk and write about movement in ways other than those that have hitherto been available. We believed that a fruitful beginning might well be made with the experiences of adult women who had sought out or constructed their own pleasure from physical activities. We were looking also for an engagement with movement activities which could be transformative, which had the potential for changing subjectivities and also women's social reality. Further we believed that the documentation of women's experience required a research approach which allowed for the expression of the participants' voice more directly than that allowed by the quantitative approaches which had previously been used to write about motivation.

THE BODY AND PHYSICAL ACTIVITY

There has been an increasing focus in feminist work, in philosophy and sociology, on the body as the subject/object of study. Central to this work has been an understanding of the body as constituted within complex historical and social circumstances rather than as a natural/biological phenomenon which is given. Recent work in sociology from writers such as Mike Featherstone (1991) and Chris Shilling (1993) has focused on the ways in which the body is constituted as a commodity in an affluent western consumer society which links pleasure with the display of the products of consumption. In such a context the body becomes a bearer of 'symbolic value' where what is most highly valued is the youthful, trim and sensual body. Such a body is clearly unavailable for most of the population, despite the promises of the fitness, cosmetics and other industries that their products if purchased will produce it. The body thus becomes a project to be worked at and accomplished as part of an individual's self-identity, a project which for many is endless, self-defeating and all-consuming. This is a preoccupation which, according to Shilling (1993), generates a constant sense of anxiety.

> In contemporary consumer culture this has helped promote among people the experience of both becoming their bodies, in the sense of identifying themselves either negatively or positively with the 'exterior' of the body, and of being regularly anxious about the possibility that their body will let them down or 'fall apart' if they withdraw from its constant work and scrutiny. (Shilling 1993: 35)

A discourse which links physical activity and work on the body with fitness and health (Colqhoun 1990; Tinning 1985) also contributes to the normalisation of this process. Health is taken to be evidenced by a slim, slightly muscled body for women and a well-defined muscular body for men, assumed to be achieved through frequent exercise and appropriate diet. The corollary is to assume that if your body does not measure up then you are unhealthy and in some way lacking – a strong moral imperative towards thinness. Since health is taken to be an individual responsibility, to be fat or not thin suggests moral laxity, a lack of self-control, 'she's let herself go'.

Although Michel Foucault has been criticised by Shilling and by feminist writers (Bartky 1990) as being insensitive to gender issues and overly deterministic, his work has still been taken up and used by feminists to understand western women's preoccupation with their bodies and the related prevalence of eating disorders. Susan Bordo (1989) and Susan Lee Bartky (1990), for instance, use Foucault's notion of 'docile bodies' to describe the meticulous processes of self-disciplining, the work women do on their bodies to transform them for public consumption. Throughout the literature this process is always characterised by a sense of lack, of never being good enough, of never measuring up to the ideal (Chernin 1983; Smith 1988; Bordo 1989).

While it is clear from the feminist and other writings on the body that bodily appearance is central to social identity and to what it means to be appropriately masculine and feminine in a patriarchal society, far less attention has been paid to the relationship between the moving body and social identity. Feminists writing in the area of dance have begun to explore how particular inscriptions of the body are developed or challenged in and through dance (Dempster 1988; Rothfield 1994). However, it is the more direct connection between physical activity and feminine and masculine identity taken up in the work of Iris Marion Young (1980) and Bob Connell (1983) which has particular pertinence to this project. In particular, Young uses the work of Merleau-Ponty to argue that it is 'the ordinary purposive orientation of the body as a whole towards things and its environment which initially defines the relation of a subject to its world' (Young 1980: 139). It follows then that how we move is intimately linked to relations of power both in terms of other people/subjects and our environment. This would also suggest that changing the way we move, the way the body is deployed in 'purposive' movement, can change our relation with the world.

In general most of the recent literature paints a bleak picture, particularly for women and girls where the body is couched as a deeply problematic site associated with feelings of unhappiness, frustration and lack, whereby bodies are experienced as constraining, as preventing them from becoming all they would want to become (Shilling 1993). On the other hand, Shilling also suggests that the potential inherent in the possibility of changing the body – that is, that the body need not be taken as pre-given – can also be a source of pleasure in the control that can be exerted over one's own body and the opportunities this may provide to challenge social definitions.

While this literature has acknowledged and indeed is primarily focused on the female and male bodies as constituted within differing social and cultural circumstances, and at least one writer has also taken up questions of social class (Bourdieu 1986), few have gone beyond such parameters to explore the multiplicity of diversity of bodies and experience. For instance, most of the feminist literature dealing with body shape and eating disorders has taken for granted the homogeneity of the female body and women's desires, ignoring the diversity of women's experience. While it has taken up difference in terms of fatness and thinness, it has for the most part taken the female body to be young, white, middle class and above all heterosexual – that is the female body constituted always with an eye to the male *Other*.

This chapter then intends to problematise such notions of the body in relation to women's participation in physical activity by listening to the stories of lesbian and heterosexual women who are in their late 30s or older, as they talk about their experiences, their pleasures and pains in relation to their participation in physical activity. We began this project tentatively. We shared our ideas with friends and colleagues. We 'played' with our original ideas and tried to name, develop and construct themes that would allow us to have conversations about our bodies, about pleasure and pain.

We agreed that we would start by collecting women's stories. We began with women who were interested in being part of this dialogue – women who wanted to have a dialogue about their bodies and their relationships to them. We did this by creating narratives about our experiences as a way of beginning the process of naming the ways in which our bodies are critical to how we construct and express ourselves as women, feminist, lesbian and heterosexual, white, able bodied young and old, working class and middle class, and as Australian and Canadian.

These narratives are our first attempts to explore connections as yet unnamed and unexplored in the literature. They are a beginning and are presented here as an attempt to begin to draw connections, to explore difference and to put bodies/our bodies into the conversation. The women we worked with were not chosen to 'represent' particular realities; rather they were willing to work with us to explore and learn about our bodies. Together we were concerned about starting a process that might allow the creation of rich conversations where we could explore layers of meaning, question ourselves and each other about our bodies and our relationships to and with our bodies in the context of our lives. This chapter is part of that beginning.

We interviewed six women in Australia (Carol, Jillian, Tina, Cynthia, Jenny and Val) and five in Canada (Diana, Marnie, Wendy, Michelle and Claire) who were friends and colleagues or contacted through friends. The women ranged in age from 35 to 78 and all of the women in Canada and three of the women in Australia are lesbian, the remaining three in Australia are heterosexual. All but two of the women would describe themselves as feminists and have incorporated this into the way they conduct their lives, including the way in which they take up physical activity and the time they have to pursue it. Only three have children and these are now in late adolescence or adults. This in itself makes the group rather different from those usually researched. There was however an important commonality, which emerged from the analysis of interviews, which separates the experiences of this group from those experiences described, for instance, in the literature on women's leisure. In one way or another these women have, through a combination of the circumstances of their lives and their choices in terms of relationships and politics, a great deal more freedom to take up leisure activities than many of their peers.

On the other hand, as Henderson (1989: 229) has pointed out, 'leisure involvement for women may be a means of liberation from restrictive gender roles and thus a means for empowerment'. With the women in the study this has worked both ways – for some, changes in their identity (coming out as a lesbian) have provided the catalyst for a radically different relationship with their bodies while for others the more powerful sense of embodiment arrived at through their participation in physical activity has helped them to construct a different social reality. This is not to say that for many of the women their relationship with physical activity and their body was unproblematic. Quite the opposite, more than a few of the women carried very negative baggage about themselves and physical activity, which they often attributed to the alienating experiences they had in school physical education.

PAINS AND PLEASURES: THEMES IN WOMEN'S PARTICIPATION IN PHYSICAL ACTIVITY

These women are active and have been active in a variety of ways since early childhood – certainly some more than others and some more consistently than others. Very few of the women, however, have patterns of activity that fit with those traditionally researched – that is, very few participated in organised competitive activities/sports for any length of time. For most, competitive sports were associated with school in ways which left residues of anger and disenchantment with such activities. In contrast, their sources of pleasure in physical activity, past and present, are more likely to be associated with activities which are less likely to be competitive, less routine, more connected to sensual feelings of flow and rhythm and participated in with friends or significant others. What is also apparent is the very diversity of activities the women describe, both individually and collectively. These range from the pleasure of being able to competently perform practical activities such as chopping wood to the different and diverse pleasures from activities such as belly dancing, skating and walking. One aspect of the difference in activities has to do with the very different environments of Canada as compared to Australia – for instance, the cold winters of Canada lend themselves to activities such as ice skating and skiing, whereas the Australians were more likely to talk about swimming and surfing.

STORIES ABOUT PHYSICAL EDUCATION

For most of the women physical education and school sport were either barely mentioned or were described in very negative terms, with the exception of Val for whom almost any kind of physical activity would have had the potential for pleasure. However, even for Val her memories of school physical activity seem to be primarily associated with one sport and the fun of playing with and going away with her team. For the other women the pleasures they eventually found in physical activity were rarely connected with the kinds of physical activity they experienced at school. And for some of the women their school physical education experiences left strong negative feelings, including feelings of humiliation, anger and anxiety about their physical ability. For some, such feelings left them with long term feelings of inadequacy which have influenced their ability and desire to participate in physical activities generally; for others, it has been more specifically directed to the rejection of those activities most closely associated with their school physical education experiences, namely competitive games and sport.

Part of the problem was that their physical education teachers did not seem interested in those students who were not top performers; they felt that they were invisible or marginalised in physical education classes. Some of the women also felt that there was very little sympathy (or perhaps empathy would be a more appropriate term) with those students who did not fit the appropriate body shape or, in Diana's experience, whose performance did not measure up to those expectations which her long, lean body shape might have suggested. In the following quotes a number of specific practices are described which have provided for each of the women their own specific sources of humiliation or fear. For instance, the very common phenomenon, which still seems to survive despite its obvious destructive effects, of the process of team selection whereby student captains are left to choose their teams, one by one, from their expectant and often very anxious peers. Several of the women also contrasted the negative experiences of most of their formal physical education and sport with the enjoyment experienced from more playlike activities in less structured settings both inside and outside school. The following quote from Claire takes up a number of these points.

Claire: Well I can think of when I was really young thoroughly enjoying it (physical activity) like probably four, five, six, the first couple of years of school and because it was pretty unstructured and it was great, I would do this, that and the other and sports day was the highlight of my life when I was that age, but then subsequent to that if you want brief glimpses, I'd say, one thing that recurs frequently is clearly the idea that kids would pick teams; I mean talking about somebody like myself who is tall, skinny, awkward, not very physically adept.

Alison: So you felt that when you were in...

Claire: Well just basically, if you want sort of highlights I can think of standing there and always being the last one picked for a team and I think that is the cruellest way to get kids to play organised sport, where they used to have two teams and get some young kid who is pretty good to pick her mates for the team.

Some of the women also mentioned feeling invisible or marginalised because of teacher preferences for the better performers, for those who most resembled the teachers themselves.

Carol: Yes and from high school we had a sports mistress who was **a woman to be seen**. She represented Australia or New South Wales (one or the other but I think it was Australia) in hockey and a couple of other things as well. Very keen and only interested in young women who were athletic and interested in developing and all those sorts of things. She couldn't come to grips with anybody who had any different approach to sport and consequently I think the vast majority of us (young women I am talking about because we had segregated physical education classes) turned the vast majority of us off sport. Consequently, I used to wag sport almost from I'd say halfway through first year but certainly by the end of first year, every sports day I would be gone.

There was also the sense that the activities in physical education in no way assisted students to like their bodies, to feel more connected with them. This came particularly with hindsight as some of the women, having now found activities from which such feelings of bodily connectedness are available, looked back at their school experiences and found such pleasures notably lacking. For instance, in the following quote, Carol describes the immense pleasure she experienced from her tap dancing when what they did and how they did it was motivated by the enjoyment of making up dances to radical music with her feminist friends. She compares how this changed and how she left tap dancing with the arrival of a new teacher who was concerned primarily with quality of performance.

Carol: Not long after that we were going to organise the next show and the teacher stopped; she said she couldn't come for that period, and so we thought we would use another young woman who was a tap dancer and she came along and within two lessons, a week's span, everybody had stopped going because she was just 'oh, no you can't do that, it would be embarrassing' and it was just awful and I couldn't bear to be in the same room with her after that. She got another woman to dance with her and they danced at the next one themselves and they were very good, they were excellent but nobody enjoyed it in the same way that they had enjoyed the others. The Steel City tappers we were. It was because they were perfectionists, the same ethos, you know, you do it to show people how good you are. A waste of time. We were there for the social and the political and the enjoyment type aspect and they (the women who performed to demonstrate virtuosity) completely missed the point I think.

Jan: That is an important thing. I think school is incredibly guilty of missing the point.

Carol: I think they completely missed the point in terms of trying to connect people with their bodies and their bodies with their lives. It's like 'okay now get into this, this is all physical', with no concept that the physical is also connected to a whole lot of other social stuff as well. I think sometimes that's why rap dancing and stuff like that has been really successful because it's integrated those two really well.

The fear of failing, of being incompetent, of not measuring up, is a recurrent theme in connection with physical education or sport experiences. The legacy of such experiences for some of the women is an ongoing fear of being too scared to try because of the burden of expectations of standards to meet which, if not met, leave one feeling discouraged and useless. Diana, for instance, described her experiences on a long and challenging canoe trip where account was taken of those who had very little experience of canoeing. The respect shown by the more experienced canoeists for those who were less experienced is contrasted with her experiences in physical education where she felt forced to do tasks which terrified her.

Diana: For two people who really have barely been in a canoe, I mean it was really...

Michelle: And it was done at a pace, you see I think the difference is, it was done in a very respectful way that...

Diana: And it wasn't all up to you...

Michelle: No, right, and you go at the pace of whoever is the slowest so it doesn't feel then like, you know, like some people are just madly paddling and within ten minutes they're off in the horizon and you say 'just forget it, I can't do it'.

Diana: Yeah, I would have been really discouraged.

Michelle: It's too bad in a way that phys. ed. I mean what it does I think is two things; it not only doesn't teach girls that but I think it leaves this lasting fright?

Diana: I think I have exactly the feeling with the high jump over and over again, a million things, and if a teacher had been perceptive enough you might not be having them as badly I think.

Despite or perhaps because of these early experiences most of the women in the study have found pleasure in other forms of movement. In speaking about these pleasures, they provide insights into subjective experiences of physical activity of which those involved in the provision of physical education, recreation and other sites of physical activity need to be cognisant. We have chosen in the next section to focus on two main sources of pleasure, 'sensual pleasure' and 'empowerment', identified from the interviews. These by no means exhaust the possibilities of pleasure in movement described by the women.

SENSUAL PLEASURE: 'I LIKED THE WAY IT MADE MY BODY FEEL'

In one way or another, most of the women talked about the kinaesthetic or sensual pleasure they experienced while participating in physical activity, or the feeling of connectedness, the changed sense of embodiment that was for them an important outcome of physical activity. Given that the field of bodily feelings is not one commonly talked about or developed within any specific discipline of understanding, finding a language to talk about such an area was not easy for the researchers or the respondents. In the translation of the subjective experience of bodily movement into words we have only certain existing discourses and combinations of these discourses to draw upon – this may lend itself to a certain homogeneity of expression which belies the different resonances afforded by different activities with different bodies. Nevertheless, it was clear from the interviews that the kinaesthetic/sensory experiences of movement were important to their pleasure in physical activity. Quite often this was associated with 'flow' and 'rhythm', sometimes in relation to music and sometimes not.

For Cynthia, for instance, the immediate bodily feelings associated with movement were part of her early pleasurable experiences with dance as a child and have since been associated in different ways with all her very different activities:

> I have always loved it. It has always been natural for me to move to music and I just loved everything. I liked the way it made my body feel. I liked what it did to my muscles. I liked the creative aspect. I liked feeling strong. I think that set a tone because I think that it gave me an expectation that movement would be part of my life and a confidence in my body.

And from Carol:

> So that was part of the tap dancing. I guess the other part of it in terms of the rhythm was I really enjoy music and I like to dance but it was music that I had chosen to listen to and to be with and stuff like that so it was easy to get that enjoyment. I guess for the first time in a long time I started to relate to my body again, learning coordination again and things like that, even at a very minuscule level we still had to do that. That was nice too because it was like a rediscovery of some things that had been buried for quite a while, so that was good.

For Claire her bodily pleasure in movement is expressed in the 'feeling' of 'getting her heart rate up' and feeling good about it – that is, the immediate sensory experience rather than the instrumental purposes of weight control and whatever else 'exercise is supposed to be good for'.

> Claire: Hiking is my most pleasurable activity because you get to get the heart rate really up there by ascending or climbing up high and you tend to go for longer.

Alison: So you like the feeling of getting your heart rate up?

Claire: Yeah, getting my heart rate up and getting the fresh air and just not being sluggish; I don't see it as a form of weight control or I'm trying to think what else exercise is supposed to be good for; I see it more as I just enjoy being in the outdoors and I enjoy getting my heart rate up and getting some feeling of well being and I feel good after it, I enjoy all the endorphins or whatever the hell they are, racing through my body.

Alison: Is there a particular feeling that you have in your body that makes it feel good? I know sometimes it's hard to talk about how we move.

Claire: I don't really know; I think that if I don't exercise, like if I go for a couple of days I really miss it and I think what happens then is I feel very sluggish, I feel kind of not heavy but just kind of lumpy and you know, lethargic actually, whereas if I get exercise it really … I feel I sleep better, the feeling within myself, it's spiritual as well as physical is what I would say, it's both and the physical probably gets the heart rate up, you sweat a bit, but I also think there's lot of spirituality to it which is that it feels good to be out looking around seeing even the city, trees, flowers.

Many of the women talk in some way about a sense of connectedness which, for Val, is also tied to being able to 'do things'.

Jan: What is it that motivates you to do that, to walk or to swim; why do you do it?

Val: Because I think it's just a [inaudible word] energy levels as well; you feel cooped up if you're inside a lot; just being outside is important and being in touch with the natural elements.

Jan: Can you say that again? Be in touch with the natural elements?

Val: Yes and just trying to keep fit.

Jan: Why do you want to keep fit? What does it do for you? What does fitness actually mean to you?

Val: I never really thought about it that much but I guess it's keeping healthy; being in touch with your body; being able to do things like run up a flight of stairs; being able to run along the beach, that sort of stuff; it makes you feel really good to be able to do that. I never really understood why.

Jan: What do you mean, 'in touch with your body'?

Val: Well, you know, if you are working hard with your head or thinking too much; it's like you're off in another world and I find physical effort can really bring you back in to yourself and things like that, rather than just being out of your body, when you look into what's in your mind or whatever.

EMPOWERMENT

In different ways the notion of 'power' and 'empowerment' emerged as a major theme from the interviews. Again there was no one meaning associated with these concepts. For instance, for Cynthia, Jenny and Val their sense of power was directly associated with bodily strength and the outward manifestation of muscularity. For Val and Jenny their competence in self-defence was also associated with those attributes of control of space and implied threat that are identified by Connell (1983) in relation to hegemonic masculinity. For those others for whom power was identified as a theme, it was more likely to be connected with the setting and achieving of personal challenges and the ability to perform tasks which require strength or endurance (some of which are traditionally performed by men).

In comparison (though not necessarily totally in contrast) to Connell's readings of power in terms of physical activity and masculinity, for the women power has more to do with changes in personal identity: being in control; identification with body and pride in its/their achievements; having a responsive body which can respond to challenges; is capable and able. This includes physical strength – not expressed so much in terms of prowess or demonstrated as muscularity, but strength as a source of confidence, personal security, the opposite to the vulnerability of patriarchal femininity.

Such a sense of empowerment seems to happen through redefinitions of the body. This empowerment may occur through the realisation of new capabilities when actively pursuing new, more challenging goals or by discovering or rediscovering capabilities when engaging in new or different activities. For some, this may involve overcoming the legacies of feelings of inadequacy left from their early physical education experiences. For instance, when Wendy talked about how she now enjoys chopping wood this has to be seen as a consequence of overcoming the feelings of inadequacy by setting small goals – that is by chopping smaller pieces of wood.

Most of the women spoke of setting themselves challenges or achieving personal goals. The achievement of such goals was in turn linked for some with a deep sense of pride, while for others it seemed to provide meaning to their lives through contributing to their sense of identity or by providing an area over which they had some control.

The setting and achieving of challenges was for Cynthia a strong and recurring motif as she moved into new areas of activity, particularly those where achieving the goal meant pushing through pain, fear or the edge of endurance. Each new activity that she described was characterised firstly in terms of the challenge it provided.

> Swimming was lovely and I took up swimming. That was a similar sort of thing. Number one it was a challenge because when I took it up I didn't even swim with my face under the water. I was a wonderful backstroker but I didn't put my face under the water. I set myself this little challenge that I'm going to be able to swim properly and then I decided I wanted to be able to swim like these people that could go up and down, up and down without stopping. I'm such a determined little bugger. I set this goal that when I turned forty I wanted to be able to do butterfly. So my daughter's coach used to help me and I emptied the pool for weeks, beating everyone round the head.

The connection between knowing what you are capable of and self-identity through being stretched/stretching the body, doing things that you never considered doing, testing how far you could really go if you tried, is made more explicit in Jenny's comments about the exercises she does for her self-defence training.

> Jenny: You don't do [self-defence anywhere else other than there]. You do ten [kicks] left and ten right and it's just so unrelated to anything else. Like you walk or you cycle elsewhere or swim but it's not a thing that a lot of people do.
>
> Jan: All those other things like the swimming and cycling, they are all kind of, as you say, everyday activities and you are using your body in very natural ways. When you describe it, are you saying that you are actually stretching your body, you are actually using it in ways that are quite different?
>
> Jenny: I find that really exciting actually, especially to think that I can do it, because I never thought that you could lift your foot and do a kick above the table – and now I can do all this; without legs and hands. It would be pretty frightening I think, when friends have come to see us and just what we can do and the situations we were able to get out of.

And Tina at 76 takes on the challenge of getting a medal in the various fun runs in which she competes. The meanings however seems to lie less in the simple winning of a medal than that her running and walking now seem to define her to herself more so than her age or perhaps any other aspect of her life. Despite some pain from arthritis she *has* to run/walk.

Jan: So if you describe your pleasure, is your pleasure like the challenge, because it must be hard work?

Tina: It is, it is, it is but I am a real fighter. I know I can do it. It's the challenge.

Jan: And is the pleasure in meeting the challenge?

Tina: Yes, both of them. I can't explain it but still I love to do it. I try to get a place.

Some of the lesbian women talked about the particular spaces which were available for them to feel strong and independent, which were less likely to be available to heterosexual women. For instance, in the following quote, Michelle talks about how it is possible as a lesbian to reject some of the more constraining discourses about femininity and the body.

One of the things that I think, but I'm not really sure, if it's just that it's what I want other than what really is, that having that sense of feeling power and feeling good about your body, is something that traditionally as women we are denied often or only in very circumscribed ways and that one of the nice things about sorta having a sense of ... being a lesbian and trying to reject a lot of that stuff, even though we carry a lot of the baggage with us about fat and about those kinds of things; it's just to allow ourselves a sense of feeling good and strong about our bodies so that you don't need a man up here to chop the wood or to start the boat or to sail fast or those kinds of things, and I just think there's something about allowing yourself to feel that. Your body actually feels physically stronger when you use it, like there is something to it. It actually does feel physically stronger; you're more present in your body, you're more engaged with your body and it works better; you sleep better.

The women's stories are not simply a celebration – the pleasures they now find in physical activity have often been preceded by very negative and alienating experiences leaving residues which continue to colour their relationship with their bodies and physical activity. Moreover, discourses linking health with moral imperatives about exercise, body shape and weight are not totally absent from their stories. Several of the women, some more explicitly than others, refer in some way to participating in physical activity as a way of managing their weight, or creating a body shape with which they feel comfortable.

Living in a western society it is unlikely that such discourses would be totally absent from the women's thinking about their bodies. However, it is clear that such discourses intersect with other ways of thinking about the body, and with bodily experiences, to produce feelings about one's self/one's body which are pleasure-giving rather than debilitating. A sense of embodiment then is complexly woven, as sensory and sensual experiences are linked with body shape, with controlling weight and with health – the interweaving of the sensory and the social.

CONCLUSION

In this chapter we have attempted to describe the ways in which women's participation in physical activity has provided pleasure (and some pain) and to show how participation in physical activity may provide a connectedness which seems to challenge what Bartky (1990: 37) has identified as the 'self-estrangement which lies close to the heart of the feminine condition itself'. We acknowledge that these women, by virtue of their life circumstances – their sexuality, their radical politics or even their age – are able to make different choices about physical activity than is the case for many women. However, we would argue that the articulation of the pleasures they have found in physical activity, by their exception and specialness, helps to confirm the oppressiveness of the dominant discourses which link femininity, physical activity and the body for most women.

In the context of a consumer society, where the body that is valued is 'the young, slim and sexual body' (Shilling 1993: 35), these women are free/have freed themselves from these compunctions by their age, but also by their subjectivities, their positioning in relation to feminist discourses and material conditions. In contrast to the emphasis on pleasure through objective work on the body as machine, rationalised work that has often in some way been purchased, their activities are for the most part free, connected more with natural settings and with collective action than with the pursuit of changes in body shape/image. They provide a window through which we might view alternative ways of thinking about physical activity and movement that challenge the hegemony of traditional games and sport. Their stories also suggest that while social circumstances assist in taking up alternative forms of physical activity which are self-enhancing, participation in physical activities which provide opportunities for empowerment and sensual pleasure may also provide alternative ways of thinking about our embodied selves and so shift our relationship to the social.

References

Bartky, S. L. (1990) *Femininity and Domination: Studies in the Phenomenology of Oppression*, New York: Routledge.

Bordo, S. R. (1989) 'The Body and the Reproduction of Femininity: A Feminist Appropriation of Foucault' in Jagger, A. M. and Bordo, S. R. (Eds) *Gender/Body/Knowledge: Feminist Reconstructions of Being and Knowing*, New Brunswick: Rutgers University Press.

Bourdieu, P. (1986) *Distinction: A Social Critique of the Judgement of Taste*, London: Routledge and Kegan Paul.

Chernin, K. (1983) *Womansize: The Tyranny of Slenderness*, London: The Woman's Press.

Colquhoun, D. (1990) 'Images of Healthism in Health-based Physical Education' in Kirk, D. and Tinning R. (Eds) *Physical Education, Curriculum and Culture: Critical Issues in Contemporary Crisis*, London: Falmer.

Connell, R. W. (1983) *Which Way is Up? Essays on Sex, Class and Culture*, Sydney: George Allen and Unwin.

Dempster, E. (1988) 'Women Writing the Body: Watch a Little How She Dances', *Writings on Dance 3: Of Bodies and Power*, pp. 13–25.

Eccles, J. S. and Harold, R. D. (1991) 'Gender Differences in Sport Involvement: Applying the Eccles' Expectancy-value Model', *Journal of Applied Psychology*, 3, 1, pp. 7–35.

Featherstone, M. (1991) 'The Body in Consumer Culture' in Featherstone, M. Hepworth, M. and Turner, B. (Eds) *The Body: Social Process and Cultural Theory*, London: Sage Publications.

Henderson, K. A. (1990) The Meaning of Leisure for Women: An Integrate, Review of the Research, Journal of Leisure Research, 22, 3, pp 228–243.

McAuley, E. (1992) 'Understanding Exercise Behavior' in Roberts, G. C. (Ed.) *Motivation in Sport and Exercise*, Champaign, IL: Human Kinetics.

Rothfield, P. (1994) 'Performing Sexuality, the Scintillations of Movement'. *Paper presented at the Performing Sexuality Conference, Institute of Modern Art*, Brisbane, Australia.

Scanlan, T. K. and Simons, J. P. (1992) The Construct of Sport Enjoyment in Roberts, G. C. (Ed.) *Motivation in Sport and Exercise*, Champaign, IL: Human Kinetics.

Shilling, C. (1993) *The Body and Social Theory*, London: Sage.

Smith, D. E. (1988) 'Femininity as Discourse' in Roman L. G. and Christian-Smith L. K. (Eds) *Becoming Feminine: The Politics of Popular Culture*, Lewes, U K: Falmer Press.

Tinning, R. (1985) 'Physical Education and the Cult of Slenderness', *ACHPER National Journal*, 107, pp. 10–13.

Young, I. M. (1980) 'Throwing Like a Girl: A Phenomenology of Feminine Comportment, Motility and Spatiality', *Human Studies*, 3, pp. 137–56.

7 Working on the Body: Links Between Physical Activity and Social Power

Sarah Gilroy

Revealing 'insider' information about the research process is an area in which feminist research has taken the lead, but such an approach, whilst demonstrating the rigorous nature of the research, can also put the researcher in a vulnerable position, as it reveals the research as it happened, with all its strengths and weaknesses. Stanley and Wise (1993), however, argue that feminist work ought to be open, even if that openness leaves you vulnerable to criticism. By mapping my biography onto the research story, I am seeking to 'tell it like it was' (and is) rather than providing a sanitised and depersonalised account. In so doing I am seeking to explore both the practical and theoretical problems encountered when researching the links between women's involvement in physical activity and their social power.

The openness advocated in much feminist work and other areas of research is centred around an acknowledgement that in studying social life we are studying ourselves. As researchers we can therefore simultaneously be the researched. In effect, as we develop our understandings of the social world we are changing ourselves, and therefore how we might view the world as researchers. It becomes impossible to totally disentangle the me as 'researcher' and the me as 'I'. There is a recognition that personal experiences are an important source of knowledge which do not need to be rejected as they would if a more positivist approach to social science was being adopted. Personal experiences therefore do not need to be discounted because they do not 'fit' the theory, but rather further theoretical refinement is needed to make sense of experience. However, it is important to point out that whilst feminist research in particular advocates drawing upon the experiential there is some tension between research which 'lets the women speak for themselves' and research which seeks to move beyond that by using theory to analyse what is being said. Like Maynard (1994: 23–24) I believe that: 'Feminism has an obligation to go beyond citing experience in order to make connections which may not be visible from the purely experiential level alone'.

This chapter sets out to explore these issues by focusing on research that I conducted as part of my PhD. Due to the restrictions of space in this chapter, I have drawn selectively from the work in order to provide material to explore some of the problems encountered when researching the links between physical power and social power. It is a personal account of research which critically reflects on the process of the research and considers some of the central methodological and theoretical issues arising out of it. Knowing where to begin the story is not as easy as it sounds, logically it could begin when the research began, but in reality that was not when the ideas that culminated in the research began to form. The trail needs to go further back to include some of my own experiences of being physically active.

As a child and young woman, I led a very active sporting life supported by a middle class background. Although both my parents had been actively involved in sport in their youth, their later involvement was limited to playing with me and my sisters. They encouraged us to be active if that was what we wanted to do so long as we weren't going to come to any harm, and as long as it did not interfere with our school work. A very supportive school physical education (PE) department along with some senior clubs in the area enabled me to develop with the help of specialised coaching. My recollections as a child were of enjoying sport, I liked being outside: it was to me very playful. As I grew older the action became more focused on one sport (hockey) in which I seemed to show most promise. I still enjoyed my sport, but it wasn't so playful: the outcome seemed to matter so much more. Conversely, the other activities which I managed to keep going became possibly more playful – they were light relief, a change from the seriousness of disciplined training. Out of all these experiences I came to develop a sense of physical competence and accomplishment – I could turn my hand to most sports: it felt good. At school my sporting abilities were recognised, I knew I could do something. As I entered my mid-teens I began to sense a change in reaction to my participation: 'wasn't I growing out of these things?' Although this was largely from some adults outside the family I was also aware that fewer and fewer of my female class mates were still as involved in physical activity as I was.

Choosing to train as a PE teacher meant that I moved from a school culture in which I was in the minority to a women's PE college where I was one of the majority: there was no longer any need to justify and explain my involvement in sport. My experiences of being one of a very small number of active young women at school could have been quite threatening: I could possibly have succumbed to the norms for my age and sex and reduced or given up sport – but for some reason I didn't. When I later reflected on my involvement in physical activity, I sensed that at least for me my confidence in my physical competence enabled me to operate in a more confident, if not assertive, manner socially. I was also aware that other women who had had quite different experiences of physical activity may have had a different relation with their bodies and therefore with the world round about them. My interest therefore began to centre around the relationship between physical and social power and whether involvement in physical activity had the potential to empower women socially.

The work of Connell (1987) and De Beauvoir (1979) initially captured my interest, because they touched on the connections between physical and social power and their impact on men's and women's lives:

The social definition of men as holders of power is translated not only into mental body-images and fantasies, but into muscle tensions, posture, the feel and texture of the body. This is one of the main ways in which the power of men becomes 'naturalized', i.e. seen as part of the order of nature. (Connell 1987: 85)

The other [adolescent girl] simply submits; the world is defined without reference to her, and its aspect is immutable as far as she is concerned. This lack of physical power leads to a more general timidity: she has no faith in a force she has not experienced in her body; she does not dare to be enterprising, to revolt, to invent; doomed to docility, to resignation, she can take in society only a place already made for her. She regards the existing state of affairs as something fixed. (De Beauvoir 1979: 355)

These quotations illustrate that the common-sense view of power as being 'natural' is a very strong one. De Beauvoir argues that the adolescent girl who has not been given an opportunity to explore the physical capacity of her body, in effect sees no alternative than to fill the role allocated to her. Connell's point is slightly different as he highlights the point that power (and powerlessness) that is conveyed by the body tends to be seen as natural and so masks the way in which power (both physical and social) is socially constructed. Both these authors discuss the different ways by which men and women may relate to their bodies.

The quotations encapsulated some of the ideas I had been considering, but when I reviewed them in the light of my own experiences and other material that I had read they also raised some questions in my mind. The first major question centred around my unease with the seemingly univer-sal categories of 'men' and 'women'. Was this the case for all men and all women? Clearly whilst my own experiences of physical activity had resulted in my feeling powerful in my body and able to have some impact on the world around me, I suspected that this was not the case for many others. Being white, middle class and able-bodied had, I felt, put me at an advantage when compared to other women. The second question concerned the nature of the connection (or connections if any) between social and physical power. How could it (or they) be identified? To help answer these questions I turned to work written about the body and power.

THEORISING ABOUT THE BODY

Whilst space does not allow me here to fully explore how social theorists have conceptualised power, there are some questions that I feel it is important to discuss about power and the body. When considering the value of theory one of the things I do is test out what is being claimed against my own experience of the world. Does what is being said help me make sense of my situation? In reading about 'power' I became increasingly uneasy about the difficulty I was having in placing myself, as a woman, within the power nexus. By this I mean that the theories seemed too 'grand' and they were often gender-blind (see Knights and Wilmott 1985). It was not that the theories did not make any sense, but rather that they did not help explain how power (and powerlessness) was produced and reproduced at, and through, the level of the individual. Another problem with many of the existing analyses of power is the over-socialised view of men and women that is perpetuated because of the neglect of the fact that although we are social beings we are also physical beings. What I was finding was, as others (Turner 1984; Shilling 1991 and 1993) have found, that the corporeality of the body had been neglected in social theory. It has only been in the last five years or so that we have seen a burgeoning interest in the body in mainstream social theory as well as in the sociology of sport and leisure. Central to this work has been the writings of Foucault and Bourdieu, and it is to some of their work that this discussion now turns.

One of the main attractions of Foucault's work was that, in line with postmodernist thinking, he argued that the body was not 'natural' but that it was produced through power and therefore was a cultural product. To understand the body we need to understand the discourse within which the body is constructed, and then operates. Weedon (1989) concisely outlines the importance of discourse in Foucault's work:

> Discourses are more than ways of thinking and producing meaning. They constitute the 'nature' of the body, unconscious and conscious mind and emotional life of the subjects which they seek to govern. Neither the body nor thoughts and feelings have meaning outside their

discursive articulation, but the ways in which discourse constitutes the minds and bodies of individuals is [SIC] always part of a wider network of power relations, often with institutional bases. (Weedon 1989: 108)

The emphasis on the importance of language (which Foucault shares with many poststructuralists) draws us to seeing the body within the historically specific discourse. For feminists this clear rejection of a biological essentialism was perceived to be particularly useful in terms of its ability to challenge theories which assumed a naturalised body. Linked to this, Foucault therefore saw the body: '... as the point where power relations are manifest in their most concrete form' (McNay 1992: 16). In conceptualising power as being something invested in, and constructed through, bodies, Foucault was also saying something different about how power was distributed, which moved beyond the traditional liberal or Marxist view of power as being something which a group or individual did or did not have. In proposing this alternative, whereby power was seen as being dispersed among people, Foucault's work was seen as being potentially very useful to feminists trying to explain women's power as well as their powerlessness. However, this swing away from seeing power as resting with groups is in itself problematic, as is his view that power does not rest with particular groups and is therefore, in a sense, everywhere. As the back cover to Ramazanoglu's (1993) book asks: 'if this is the case, why don't women exercise more of it' (power)?

Bordo (1990), also drawing upon Foucault, explores women's relation with their bodies by focusing on how they have been represented in the media. Of particular interest to her is the way in which the current obsession with slenderness is represented and internalised by women. In her analysis she draws upon Foucault's notion of the 'intelligible' and 'useful' body to make sense of the way in which women are normalised through body management. Bordo argues that the preoccupation with fat, diet and slenderness may be:

... one of the most powerful 'normalizing' strategies of our century, ensuring the production of the self-monitoring and self-disciplining 'docile bodies', sensitive to any departure from social norms and habituated to self improvement and transformation in the service of those norms. (Bordo 1990: 85)

She argues that what some women regard as power, for example having a slender body which suggests good self-discipline and control of the body, in fact demonstrates a lack of power, in so far as these women occupy very little social space, which contrasts sharply with the amount of space men take up. She also notes that:

> Increasingly, the size and shape of the body has come to operate as a marker of personal, internal order (or disorder) – as a symbol for the state of the soul. (Bordo 1990: 94)

Whilst she contends that it is permissible for even women to have weight and bulk, so long as it is tightly managed, I would argue that the degree of acceptance is mediated by cultural norms. Bordo has fallen into the trap of seeing all women as having the same relation with their bodies regardless of ethnicity, sexuality and able-bodiedness. In terms of class distinctions, Bordo (1990: 94) does suggest that a well-muscled body no longer suggests working-class status, but rather it has become part of yuppie iconography.

Although Foucault has been criticised for not exploring the gendered nature of bodily discipline and control and for presenting a rather passive view of the body, the work of Bordo and others has served to give some indication of the way in which his work may be of value in developing our understanding of the connections between physical and social power.

Although not as frequently drawn upon as Foucault in discussions of the body, Bourdieu's (1992 [1979]) work is of interest because of the connections he explores between social location and bodies. His work primarily focuses on social class and how class is embodied by the way people develop their bodies, how they relate to them and how they produce a certain pattern of physical, cultural and social capital. As Shilling (1993: 128) argues, Bourdieu: '…recognizes that acts of labour are required to turn bodies into social entities and that these acts influence how people develop and hold the physical shape of their bodies, and learn how to present their bodies through styles of walk, talk and dress'. By centring on the body Bourdieu moves beyond Foucault's social constructionist view to develop a more corporeally-based analysis of people's social location. In analysing lifestyles Bourdieu explores the extent to which what the body does and what it consumes is linked to a person's social location. Not only does he argue that the bourgeoisie's sporting habits are different to those of the working classes, but that their taste in clothes and food, among other things, are different. Of particular value for the discussion here on power and physical activity is Bourdieu's view of the way in which the physical capital acquired through involvement in activities such as sport can be converted into cultural, social or economic capital. He argues, however, that the ability to convert this capital is not as great for the working classes as it is for the bourgeoisie. Shilling (1993) develops this idea and offers several examples of ways in which the ability to convert physical capital is often partial and transient for the working classes. Indeed, Shilling goes further than Bourdieu and illustrates some ways in which the conversion of physical capital is gendered. The exchange value of physical capital not only changes over time but it is also differently valued. It is harder for most women to convert physical capital, in terms of sporting prowess, into economic capital. An example of this is the lack of opportunity for women to turn their sporting prowess into a professional career in sport. A recent report about female jockeys highlights some of the problems that women face compared to men when trying to move from 'stable-lad' to jockey (*The Observer*, 20 August 1995).

Although there is not space in this chapter to go into greater detail about Bourdieu's work it is worth raising some of the problems that may be encountered when utilising this work to help make sense of women's experiences of physical activity. Two of the concerns which Shilling (1993) and others have with Bourdieu's work is that firstly, due to the emphasis on social class it is hard to understand the different forms of capital that men and women can develop, and secondly, the degree of agency that individuals have seems lost in '... the corporeal trajectories assigned to them by their social location, habitus and taste' (Shilling, 1993: 146). Finally, I would add that there is little evidence of exactly how people convert their physical capital into any other form of capital.

Work which directly concerns women, their bodies and their involvement in physical activity and considers the question of agency is that by Miller and Penz (1991). In their study of female body builders they concluded that women's colonisation of the pose side of the sport could be seen as a poaching of territory from the men. Women were therefore seen as powerful because they were challenging the legitimacy of men's claims to the sport of bodybuilding. They argue that:

> By giving voice to the suppressed meaning of bodybuilding, women are able to reclaim its female possibilities and hence establish their right to participate in it. (Miller and Penz 1991: 153).

An alternative reading of this script would suggest that women's focus on the pose side of the sport is a form of apologetic, rather than resistance. The pose side of the sport is the more aesthetic and hence the most stereotypically female-appropriate aspect of the sport.

Theberge (1991) also considers the extent to which involvement in bodybuilding can challenge dominant images and interests. To do this she uses the work of Schulze who explores the discourse of bodybuilding in popular accounts as well as through the experience of lesbian bodybuilders. In the media accounts Schulze (cited in Theberge 1991) argues that the potential for female bodybuilders to challenge conventions about gender categories is subverted by the translation of muscle into 'flex appeal'. Similarly, the challenges that the lesbian bodybuilders perceived they made, by shaping their bodies in ways women are not supposed to, were equally regarded by Schulze as being '... a slippery sort of purchase ...' (cited in Theberge 1991: 130). As Theberge comments:

> The confusion of images and meanings – maleness, emphasized femininity, heterosexism, and appeals to conventional notions of fashion – renders the readings problematic. (Theberge 1991: 130)

I would argue that the same could have been said of the Miller and Penz (1991) study, however, both these readings highlight the potential for physical activity to be empowering, even if we still are unsure about the extent to which this happens and how it happens.

ASKING CRITICAL QUESTIONS

These questions concerning the relationship between physical activity and women's power and agency were to be central ones in my research as I began to plan how to conduct the field work. The starting point was to look at where I wanted to get to as a result of the research. At the end of the research I wanted to be able to say something about the contribution that involvement in physical activity made to women's social power or empowerment. Although 'empowerment' is often mentioned in the literature there are few definitions that come to hand. I have regarded empowerment as concerning the process by which women gain more power over their lives. This power enables them to do things for themselves rather than sacrificing themselves to the needs of others. It enables them to resist pressures to adhere to gender-stereotyped notions of what they should and should not do. It also enables them to be more socially assertive. In essence becoming empowered enables women to become more pro-active in terms of what they do with their lives; they become active agents. Whitson (1994:354) uses empowerment in a more specific sense, and sees it as being: '... the confident sense of self that comes from being skilled in the use of one's body ...'. By adopting a wider definition of empowerment I am remaining open to the possibility that women may become empowered through modes other than the physical.

I suspected that for some women their involvement in physical activity would be connected to empowerment, but that for others their involve-

ment may have little impact on existing relations or may actually reproduce relations of relative powerlessness. What needed to be explored was
a range of women's experiences to see if there were any key factors which
contributed to (or inhibited) empowerment. Another problem of which I
was well aware was that even if there was some type of evidence that a
woman had been empowered following her involvement in a keep-fit
class, to what extent was the physical activity itself a contributor as
opposed to the social benefit of getting out of the house and mixing with
others? The area was fraught with methodological problems – how was I
going to 'get at' power, and what was the best method of uncovering the
role that involvement in physical activity played?

One of the first aspects to consider was who to include in the sample,
was it going to be just the women concerned, or was it also of value to
include their partners (if there were any). Pilot interviews were conducted
with women and their partners, both separately and jointly, to explore the
potential for this approach. At that stage of the research I decided that,
interesting though it was to interview couples together, or both parties separately, I found that it was not particularly fruitful in terms of getting at
how the women viewed their involvement in physical activity, what they
felt about their own physical potential. It was very useful, however, in
revealing information about the dynamics of the partnership in terms of
household matters and the woman's leisure. At that stage of the research, I
decided to focus on just interviewing the women and thereby relying more
on their perception of household dynamics, rather than generating other's
accounts as well. Looking back on the research, were I to embark on
similar work, I would probably alter my approach and broaden the source
of data by seeking to interview other household members. In saying this I
am partially acknowledging the value of a broader set of data, but I am
also indicating that as a result of doing the study that I did I would now
shift my focus of attention slightly.

Whilst not having the space here to document in detail how a variety of
women were contacted, it is sufficient to say that some were approached
through their work and some through their leisure activities (both physically active ones and passive recreational hobbies). A questionnaire was
used to make initial contact, after which interviews were conducted with
twenty eight women.[1] I used the questionnaires in two ways. Firstly, the
quantifiable data enabled me to build up a picture of women's leisure
which was not too dissimilar to that illustrated by the Milton Keynes and
Sheffield studies.[2] The main reason, however, was to create a point of
contact with a range of women and to use their questionnaire responses as
a basis for the subsequent interview. Having already gathered data about

their social circumstances and about their degree of involvement in physical activity this enabled me to explore the reasons behind what they had done (or not done).

Following the pilot study, I had intended to interview the women individually, but there were several reasons why this was not always the case. In several instances the women were looking after young children, some had relatives or friends dropping by who stayed in for the discussion, and some had partners returning home who joined in. One woman suggested that I meet with a group of women whom she thought would be interested to talk about their involvement in physical activity. In this sense, this research illustrates the way in which as a researcher you need to remain flexible and open to alternative ways of operating. I had considered group discussions with women about what it meant to them to be physically active, but felt that would lead me to having a less disparate group of women. If they knew each other already, the chances are they would be relatively similar, either in terms of their social backgrounds and interests or possibly even body types. As it turned out, the group of women that I did meet with only knew each other in passing, due to being members of the same fitness gym. Other than their involvement with the gym, they had very little in common, and only came together to meet with me.

The interviews built on each woman's questionnaire response and explored the following general areas: reasons for participation or non-participation in activity and feelings about their body and its capabilities; influence of PE, the impact of work and personal relationships on activity. In addition to this the women were asked to talk about the household arrangements, how these were organised and how these affected their involvement in physical activity.

Although there were many problems that I encountered during the interviews, one of the main problems was that of exploring how the women felt about their bodies and their own physical competence and any sense of power they had, both physically and socially. During the period when I was conducting the interviews I read Haug's (1987) work on the body project, in which she and the collective she worked with wrote about their bodies, and how they felt about particular parts of their bodies, for example their legs and breasts. Whilst I found this work focused on women writing about themselves, I still found it useful insofar as it gave me some ideas about the type of questions I could ask women about themselves and their bodies that would be non-threatening. I also considered the possibility of asking some women to write about themselves if it seemed that that would be a more suitable option. Had I had more time to get to know the women I might have asked them to write about them-

selves, but as I only met with the women up to five times at most I did not
feel that I had built up a sufficient rapport to ask them to do this.

The following sections draw upon some of the data generated through
the research. They are snap shots of the whole which serve to illustrate
some of the complexities of exploring the relationship between physical
power and social power.

DISCIPLINING THE BODY

Several women talked of how they took on board 'feminising' practices
and actively sought to reproduce these ideas, even though they were aware
of their problematic nature. As a result of going to Alexander Technique[3]
classes Sue had come to realise that the best posture for sitting was one
where the legs were loose and apart, but it was a posture she had been
trained to avoid: '... I must admit, although I've been, its been brought
home to me in a sort of conscious way with Alexander Technique, I still
find in company I don't like sitting in a masculine sort of, I mean it
relaxed me but it would be thought of as a masculine way, so I haven't
totally (laughs) been able to ... I still am aware socially that I, I'm supposed to be a lady (laughs)'.[4] Sue clearly felt unable to change what she
was doing, partly because it would mean going against years of socialisation: '... I would feel it's inelegant to sit as a man sits, but that again
would be years and years of behaving or being expected to behave in a
lady-like fashion, and I don't think one throws that aside, you know what I
mean?' In rationalising why she continued to sit with her knees together,
and not challenge this particular construction, despite what she had
learned about a healthy posture, Sue said that society would be too big for
her to take on. Similarly, for this reason she said she would continue to
encourage a certain amount of modesty and restraint in her daughter's
posture. This illustrates the often entrenched nature of many ideas about
physicality and sexuality. It may also be, following Shilling's (1993) discussion of the conversion of physical capital into social and cultural
capital, that Sue felt that maximum social and cultural capital could only
be gained by developing a certain type of socially acceptable physical
capital. This raises the possibility that it may be easier to challenge certain
bodily practices when older, and possibly less reliant or less concerned
about the conversion value of personal physical capital.

Ideologies about femininity and masculinity continue to be reinforced
through a variety of means throughout women's lives. Several women
from the group I interviewed reported that people had tried to warn them

off weight-training by saying that they would get great big muscles, and that as they got older and stopped doing the weights, their muscles would sag. The message behind these comments was that such changes in their bodies would be unfeminine, and generally therefore things that women should avoid. One of the women said that people considered them 'butch' because they weight-trained. That is perhaps why one of the women said that she never told anyone she was going to do weights, she just talked of going to the gym, a much more innocuous, and therefore appropriate-sounding activity for a woman. What this means in terms of women's bodies being disciplined is that it is both men and women who are disciplining women's bodies. A body which breaks the boundaries of what is acceptable for men or for women is a threatening body because it challenges the status quo and questions the validity of the norms that many people have lived their lives by. It is clear from what some of these women have said that they were aware of the price they paid for revealing what they did, that is by saying they did weight-training, as opposed to saying they went to the gym.

In discussing the ways in which women discipline their bodies, I have explored some of the ways by which women struggle with notions about what they 'should' do with their bodies and what they want to do with their bodies. In the following section I argue that, for these women, disciplining the body is invariably about reshaping the body.

RESHAPING THE BODY

A common theme in the interviews was a desire on the part of the women to change their body shape and possibly also lose weight. Several saw their bodies as being the wrong shape and therefore they wanted to remodel them. Jenny for example wanted to: '... get rid of my fat stomach ...', whilst Hazel wanted to: '... lose weight off my backside (laughs) that's where I've always got it ...'. These and other women seemed to be striving to achieve their 'ideal' shape: '... you've got this image of women, you know, we say, you've got this image haven't you, of women. I think I've learned to accept it now that I'm not never going to be a sort of size eight, but you do get this craving to be small and dainty'. For Jo it had not been at all easy: '... I was always very conscious of it [her weight], and like going to dances and sitting there, I always envied my slim friends and I remember trying desperately, trying to slim...'.

It is important not to forget that 'shape' is closely linked to 'look', as Jo's comment reveals: '... its always nice again, like if you've got an appreciative husband you know, so and the fact that if you've got someone who notices what shape you are or (laughs) I mean if you can get into your bikini and still look good, I mean that pleases me (laughs)'. 'Look', however, is not just about body size and being trim or flabby, it is also about displaying certain impressions of yourself. 'I think I am fairly feminine and I would like to look feminine ... I mean I don't worry about conforming to the norm in most respects, you know socially and that sort of thing doesn't bother me, but I must admit, I would like to be slimmer and maybe taller, although you know I accept myself as I am ...' (Jane).

In these accounts there seems to be a recognition of the unreal nature of the norms about female body shape and size, but there also seems to be a desire to strive towards these norms. It seems that the problem for many of the women lies not in the existence of a stereotyped norm, but in terms of the unattainable nature of it (that is, a size eight). The desire to lose weight or change body shape was often coupled with a desire to get fit. Many of the women felt that the best way to eventually lose weight and shape up was through some kind of physical exercise. As Anna put it: '... when you diet you don't lose weight where you want to, whereas with exercise you have a chance that something might work'. As with Miller and Penz's (1991) study, the mirrors both at home and in the gym seemed to be used for 'rational' rather than 'contemplative' reasons, to help women identify how their body-work was going as opposed to admiring themselves. As Carol's comments illustrate, mirrors were not the only means that were used to identify how well the body was shaping up: '... now I go in the gym and I look in that long mirror and I think yuk, that's got to come off, but at the moment I am nearly okay in proportion. I think if you, you know if you look at yourself and you see the bits. Also if you jump up and down, the bits that wobble need to come off (laughs) ... you can usually see the bits round the waist, the top of the thighs, and know that those bits should go'. As Bordo (1990) reminds us this is all part of 'bolting down' the body and making it tight. Clearly, having body parts that wobble is not part of the look that Carol is pursuing, yet by the same token she does not want to '... look like Mrs. Universe. You know I want to be, I want to have a sort of profile, but I don't want to be big and muscley'.

Clearly then there are some contradictions in discourse of the body as espoused by Carol. She wants to have a 'bolted down body', but not one which is 'too much' so. It seems that either to bolt the body down 'too much' and develop a well-muscled physique or to be 'too flabby' is equally powerful in terms of the ability to resist dominant ideologies about what women's bodies should be like. It could be argued therefore that shaping the body and resisting through the body is related to the degree of shaping and the extent to which it challenges dominant ideologies about what it is to be a woman or a man. Bordo (1990) however, would argue that 'bolting down' the body fulfils the pattern of gender normalisation and leads to the creation of a 'docile' body. However, as Shilling's (1993) discussion of physical capital reminds us, notions of gender normalisation must surely be mediated by class and, I would add, ethnicity, age, sexuality and disability. In challenging dominant gender ideologies, women are also invariably challenging dominant ideologies relating to age, class and ethnicity.

There are some contradictions, therefore, in the reshaping of women's bodies. Whilst on the one hand the shaping of a female body into a well-muscled body can be seen as challenging, it can also be seen (as Bordo's work outlines) as leading to gender normalisation and the creation of a 'docile' body. In making sense of this, I turn to Bourdieu's work and consider what type of capital women can gain from (re)shaping their bodies. As was argued earlier the exchange value of women's physical capital is very limited. Women prostitutes have a limited time span before their bodies lose their exchange-rate value. In a similar way it could be argued that female gymnasts have a limited period of currency. As they begin to mature and develop secondary sex characteristics, so they lose their currency in the world of sport. One key point to emerge from these examples is that having the ability to convert physical capital does not necessarily mean that those concerned are also empowered. To answer the question about empowerment means that we have to look at the social context of the activity as well as the activity itself.

PHYSICALITY AS A SOURCE OF POWER

My questioning therefore attempted to probe whether empowerment was linked to physicality, or to other aspects of the activity, such as its location. In essence what I was exploring was not only the extent to which we could argue that there are different routes to empowerment, but also whether there seemed to be anything particular about empowerment generated through physicality. Linked to this was the question of whether the type of physical activity had an impact on the potential for women to become empowered. I explored whether it was the activity per se that was crucial, or whether it was the experiences that a woman has within that context that was important.

Several of the women's stories are of help in clarifying this problem. Claire felt strongly that doing physical activity offered something that was unique:

'... if you do a physical activity it does somehow boost your confidence, I think particularly if it is anything that involves speed or accuracy or skill, if you know you can hit the target in archery, or be a good tennis player it just washes over the rest of your life. Also, you can't do anything like playing tennis which is competitive and driving without being quite assertive and it probably, just if you are used to asserting yourself on court, it's much easier to put double-glazing sales-men in their place off court'.

Jo's confidence grew again when she took up windsurfing in her forties. This confidence came partly from developing new skills, but also from being the oldest woman out on the lake. These stories illustrate Bourdieu's point about the potential for the conversion of physical capital into social capital. It also raises a common feature of involvement in physical activity; the acquisition of skill. In the competitive situation that Claire describes, she sees competitive sport as being particularly useful in helping women become more assertive. Clearly, though, many other leisure activities involve learning new skills, as Lucy did when she went to upholstery classes. However, there was little evidence of women using the skills, or capital gained through those activities, in other areas of their lives.

Not all the experiences of physical activity were positive, indeed for some the negative experiences served not only to close off a possible avenue for future enjoyment, but also led to a lower self esteem and to dis-empowerment. Whitson (1994) moreover questions whether it is possible for empowerment through activities such as traditional team sports where much is based on force and domination.

CONCLUSION

This chapter has sought to explore some of the practical and theoretical problems I encountered during the research about women's involvement in physical activity. In so doing I have illustrated that research is a living thing – it changes as do we, the researchers, in the process of researching. As I stated in the introduction research is spiral in nature and generates new avenues for further work.

In considering the role of physical activity in the empowerment process the research generated as many questions as it answered. Although there is some support from my research for it to be argued that involvement in physical activity can empower women socially, there are still many questions to be asked. The following areas need to be explored further: under what conditions does the process of converting one form of capital into another become possible; to what extent is the nature of the activity and the context within which it takes place important; is the experience of empowerment and how it manifests itself different at different stages in women's lives; and, finally, under what conditions can involvement be disempowering?

Notes

1   Questionnaires were distributed to 334 women, of whom 172 returned them. They were mostly white and aged between 16 and 66. Social class was difficult to assess as there was only a 52% response rate to the question on household income. Of the 172 women who returned their questionnaires, 51 said they would be interested in talking further about their involvement in physical activity. Of this number 28 women were finally interviewed.
2   The Milton Keynes and Sheffield studies conducted by Deem (1986) and Green et al. (1987) respectively were both large-scale studies into women's leisure which involved the gathering of data through questionnaires and interviews.
3   Alexander Technique is a form of movement education.
4   The names of the women have been replaced by pseudonyms.

References

De Beauvoir, S. (1979) *The Second Sex*, London: Penguin.
Bordo, S. (1990) 'Reading the slender body' in Jacobus, M., Keller, E. F. and Shuttleworth, S. (Eds) *Body/Politics: Women and the Discourses of Science*, London: Routledge.
Bourdieu, P. (1992[1979]) *Distinction: A Social Critique of the Judgement of Taste*, London: Routledge.
Butler, S. (1987) 'Revising femininity? Review of Lady, Photographs of Lisa Lyon by Robert Mapplethorpe' in Betterton, R. (Ed.) *Looking On*, London: Pandora.
Connell, R. W. (1987) *Gender and Power: Society, the Person and Sexual Politics*, Cambridge: Polity Press.
Deem, R. (1986) *All Work and No Play*, Milton Keynes: Open University Press.
Green, E., Hebron, S. and Woodward, D. (1987) *Leisure and Gender: A Study of Sheffield Women's Leisure Experiences*, London: Sports Council and ESRC.
Haug, F. (Ed.) (1987) *Female Sexualization: A Collective Work of Memory*, London: Verso.
Knights, D. and Wilmott, H. (1985) 'Power and identity in theory and practice', *Sociological Review*, 33, 1, pp. 22–46.
McNay, L. (1992) *Foucault and Feminism: Power, Gender and the Self*, Cambridge: Polity Press.

Maynard, M. (1994) 'Methods, practice and epistemology: the debate about feminism and research' in Maynard, M. and Purvis, J. (Eds) *Researching Women's Lives from a Feminist Perspective*, London: Taylor & Francis.

Miller, L. and Penz, O. (1991) 'Talking bodies: female body builders colonize a male preserve', *Quest*, 43, pp. 148–163.

The Observer, 20 August 1995.

Ramazanoglu, C. (Ed.) (1993) *Up Against Foucault: Explorations of Some Tensions Between Foucault and Feminism*, London: Routledge.

Shilling, C. (1991) 'Educating the body: Physical capital and the production of social inequalities', *Sociology*, 25, 4, pp. 653–672.

Shilling, C. (1993) *The Body and Social Theory*, London: Sage.

Stanley, L. and Wise, S. (1993) *Breaking Out Again: Feminist Ontology and Epistemology*, London: Routledge.

Theberge, N. (1987) 'Sport and women's empowerment', *Women's Studies International Forum*, 10, 4, pp. 387–393.

Theberge, N. (1991) 'Reflections on the body in the Sociology of Sport', *Quest*, 43, pp. 123–134.

Turner, B. (1984) *The Body and Society: Explorations in Social Theory*, Oxford: Basil Blackwell.

Weedon, C. (1989) *Feminist Practice and Poststructuralist Theory*, Oxford: Blackwell.

Whitson, D. (1994) 'The embodiment of gender: discipline, domination and empowerment' in Birrell, S. and Cole, C. (Eds) *Women, Sport and Culture*, Champaign, IL: Human Kinetics.

8 Élite Women Wheelchair Athletes in Australia

Tanni Grey

Élitism in disabled sport is still a relatively new concept. Many people in both the sporting and academic worlds do not fully understand the changes disabled sport has gone through in the last fifty years in moving from a method of medical rehabilitation to truly competitive sport. Over this period of time Adapted Physical Education and Adapted Physical Activities have increased in popularity as academic subjects within Further and Higher Education, but they have only tended to portray sport for disabled people from one of its distinct angles – the mostly non-competitive participation level. The élite end of the spectrum has been given little exposure academically. This is particularly so for women athletes. In track and road racing improved methods of training and technology have all contributed to new levels of achievement in disabled sport, where an extensive international competitive circuit exists alongside Paralympic and World Championship Competition (Banks 1992). Since wheelchair racing first developed in the 1950s, it is now a suitable time in the development of the sport for the changes that are occurring to be tracked, so that sport can be further developed for the future for all levels of ability. As a consequence of my being awarded a Winston Churchill Fellowship, I was able, in 1993, to investigate wheelchair track and road racing in Australia.

AIMS OF THE PROJECT

As both a student and a wheelchair athlete, I decided for my Churchill Scholarship to look at the provision available for wheelchair athletes in track and road racing at an élite level. A central aim of the Churchill Scholarship Scheme is to enhance not only the knowledge of those who qualify but also their overall learning experience, thereby looking to the development of the research process as much as the actual findings. Australia was chosen as the location for the study for several reasons. Since wheelchair racing is still developing, there are few centres of excellence in the world. In recent years the standing of Australian athletes has improved markedly, with high world rankings for both male and female competitors, and I wanted to examine the reasons for their successes. This has been achieved partly by reformulating the system of coach education, but also by providing more opportunities to enable athletes to progress from the grass-roots level to the top of the athletic pyramid. As a result of the broad parameters of the scholarship, the goal that I set was to get a feel for how élite athletes found the system that they were operating in. By looking at the overall system and the solutions that the Australian Wheelchair Athletics Section found to some of their developmental obstacles, it was hoped that some new ideas could be put back in to the British system to ultimately improve available provision. From the perspective of a competing athlete, the scholarship also provided the opportunity to train with a squad of athletes and compare the training schedules that Australian coaches and athletes utilised to those which are generally accepted in Britain. I spent the majority of my time in Perth, not just because of the extremely hospitable weather in Western Australia during the British winter months (although that admittedly played a part), but because the wheelchair squad and coaches that were based there at that time enabled me to set up a base from which to carry out my work.

METHODS

Since there is a lack of literature on the structure of the National Disability Sports Organisation (NDSO) around the world, virtually all of the research had to be carried out by interviewing and discussing issues and themes with athletes and administrators to build up a picture of this working system. Athletes were randomly selected, and interviewed at training or competition venues. As the study progressed the focus turned more towards female athletes. All athletes had competed in international competitions, some as part of the official Australian team. A small percentage were 'club' standard athletes who had competed overseas because they had self-funded their attendance at those events. The questions which the athletes were asked were wide-ranging, and designed to allow the athletes to talk about issues that they felt were important to their own sporting careers, such as the initial problems that they had encountered when getting into the sport, current issues such as financing and sponsorship, employment or studying and training, and how they would like to see the sport develop for the future.

THE RESEARCH PROCESS

During the research process every individual researcher is affected and directed by their own personal experiences as well as their beliefs and attitudes. I am influenced by the basic facts that I am female, use a wheelchair for daily life, as well as sport, and am a student. As such it is hard, in each specific area of research that I look at, to always be able to differentiate what affects the work that I carry out. The most significant effect on my work, which is common to all my research, is that as a competing athlete sport is a central part of my life, and I place a high priority on training and competition schedules. However, sport for people with disabilities is perhaps unusual compared to able-bodied sport, in that not only are many of the athletes actively involved in managing, or contributing to the administration of, their sport, as well as organising their own individual schedules, but more often than not competing athletes actually fill the majority of the positions in the governing bodies. Whether their involvement is an advantage in the running of sport, or is detrimental, is open to a wide range of arguments. It is certainly not ideal for competing athletes to either be in this position or involved in carrying out research because of the time commitment involved. At the moment it is still seen as necessary because of the organisational structure of the movement. While the sporting movement is still growing the needs of the athletes should have a high priority within the organisational structure, and ideally sport should be put before any political manoeuvring – although this is not always the case. Encouragingly, demand for athlete empowerment is coming from both the athletes and the administrators. Governing bodies of sport have increasingly seen the need for the athletes' mandate if they are to move forward, but this brings additional problems in that there is increased demand on the athletes' time. In previous years athletes have been reluctant to put forward their ideas for a variety of reasons. Some are just not interested in any political aspects of sport, while some athletes by choice wait until their career is over before becoming involved. As with able-bodied women, those that compete in sport have other commitments, such as a family and/or a career, that understandably makes other involvement difficult. On a personal level, at times it is extremely difficult to be involved at different levels of either research or working in sports development, but I continue to feel a responsibility to attempt to increase the profile of the sport, and work to develop better opportunities for athletes. In Britain, as in many countries around the world, the majority of the work undertaken is done by volunteers, and I feel that it should be possible for the athletes themselves to have a stronger voice in guiding and developing their future. If athletes are empowered to take a standpoint, then it is likely that everyone will benefit from the closer working relationship.

Studying in Australia for three months gave me the opportunity to break away from many of the commitments that I face at home and enabled me to concentrate solely on the theme of the scholarship and setting training goals. Travelling extensively through the competitive season (which lasts for approximately eight months of the year) means losing a permanent base, which can sometimes have a positive effect, but realistically has an adverse effect on studying. During my school and college years, with the inevitable clash between exams and the competitive track season, I got used to carrying a pile of books with me. I have always found it a challenge meeting academic deadlines while trying to complete a training schedule, aiming to achieve personal best performances and competitive goals. Attending competitions can make study sometimes near impossible, due to communal living, team commitments, or just the fact that in preparing for an event concentration and work seem harder to achieve. On the positive side, being an athlete has provided me with opportunities (such as the scholarship) that I would not have come across if I was purely a student. It enables me to have a fair degree of freedom to plan my time and occasionally being away from the distractions and commitments at home can help my studies. As a considerable amount of time is spent in airports or in transit, this time can be utilised, thanks to modern portable computer technology.

In the case of looking at the development of disabled sport in Australia, being an athlete actually provided an advantage all the way through my research as it saved much valuable time establishing contacts. Through previous international events, I met and became friends with many of those whom I wished to interview. As a result of this, it was possible, prior to the formal commencement of the study, to carry out some basic research at European events which in turn made the research process easier once established in Perth. Perth also offered a large population of wheelchair athletes who, though rather dispersed geographically, were able to come together to form reasonable early morning training groups to beat the heat of the day. These sessions provided wide access to those whom I had not previously met through international competition.

Many of the athletes involved in my research had experienced similar types of conflict with their racing careers. As with able-bodied sport, for the vast majority of wheelchair athletes there is not the prize money or sponsorship to make it possible to afford to make racing a career. Most relied on work (full- or part-time), or other non-regular commitments (for example, public speaking) in order to subsidise their sport. Those who were not in full-time employment were taking college courses at varying levels, in order to give flexibility to their time, and give them increased potential for a career once their competing days are over. At the same time many athletes were also involved in programmes to increase general participation in wheelchair racing, which added to their commitments, but fulfilled a sense of responsibility that they felt to the sport.

HOW THE USE OF A WHEELCHAIR AFFECTS THE RESEARCH PROCESS

Using a wheelchair for daily life makes its mark on the work that I do, although for me it doesn't necessarily make the work any harder. I was born with spina bifida, and although I could walk when I was young, by the time I went to school my ability to walk had deteriorated to the extent that I had to use leg callipers and a wheelchair to aid my mobility. I came to see using a wheelchair as something very positive, because for the first time it gave me freedom to charge around the playground with my peer group. While being raised in a non-disabled environment was excellent for my education, it did not teach me to be aware of my disability in a social context or consider long-term effects of using a wheelchair, nor how people outside my own school and home environment considered 'disability'. However naive, I didn't realise that people considered being in a wheelchair to be so bad. I just thought that I was the same as everyone else, but just did some things differently! As I come into contact with more disabled women, and also become aware of more disability research, I realise that not everyone has been provided with the same tools to successfully ignore these negative expressions, and that in fact my view of being in a wheelchair may be atypical. In many cases women believe that they cannot set goals, or that social and environmental barriers will bar their success (Buscaglia 1994). Many women experience real barriers to overcome to renew their self confidence and get on with their life, competing or working in an academic arena, but this is true of any woman, not just those with a disability.

While having a disability affects the way that women are treated in society, female athletes are also affected to a large degree by society's perception of disability sport. While some form of participation has been recommended for many years to aid the 'medically infirm', competitive sport for people with disabilities only really began this century. Prior to the 1930s the life expectancy and quality of life of spinal-cord injured was expected to be extremely low, due to the medical complications associated with such a disability. Many were told that after their injury they would never recover to any form of 'normal' life, whatever that might be. The Second World War resulted in a large number of spinal-cord-injured veterans returning to Britain and the USA. This drove the advances in medical science and care, which in turn resulted in increased life expectancy in newly-injured paraplegics and tetraplegics. Stoke Mandeville Hospital (in Buckinghamshire, England) was originally opened to deal with some of those who were injured in the war, but became the centre where wheelchair sport began, and indeed today the sport still has many of its roots there. Sir Ludwig Guttman, a doctor at the hospital, recognised that sport provided an extremely effective tool for the rehabilitation of his patients. He also discovered that those with a spinal-cord injury wanted, and more importantly could exhibit, the same trends of competitiveness as those that were considered able-bodied or non-disabled. People's previous assumption of a disconnection or incongruity between competitiveness and those with a disability competing in sport, as recognised by this 'discovery', set many of the negative attitudes that are still prevalent today. Certainly the image of disability sport is changing, and the growth in numbers of participants and level of competition increases as the years pass on. Some athletes felt that in the past society has considered them to be 'brave' or 'courageous', because of competing with a disability. This attitude is starting to change. Merklinger has stated that 'the ultimate experience in competitive sport is the quest for an Olympic medal. Athletes with a disability are no different' (Merklinger 1993: 3). Athletes who were asked to consider the initial barriers they had to overcome when becoming involved in wheelchair racing did not feel that discrimination was as much of a problem as finding relevant information on obtaining chairs and advice, or the monetary hardship with buying equipment (especially when an athlete has no proven track record to help in obtaining sponsorship or Government funding). Many of these findings were identified in the Loughborough University of Technology Survey (Williams and Taylor 1992) carried out for the British Wheelchair Racing Association (BWRA). While in Britain there has been increased awareness of disability sport, and the attitude of those outside sport has been seen to be far more encouraging, there is still a long way to go in terms of gaining support and recognition from the able-bodied governing bodies. Although recognition is not essential to the continuation of disabled sport, being seen and accepted as an athlete is a goal of many, including myself. Sport in fact has a positive role to play and can do much to enhance society's perception of disability. Part of the reason for the new image of disability sport is due to increased success on an international level, and this has been brought about by to choose from. Quite simply it is expected that wheelchair users want to utilise the same facilities for training and studying as non-disabled athletes. I was able to experience at first hand the very positive attitude shown towards wheelchair athletes, and the media coverage that they received, which was very encouraging. In the period of time that athletes had been competing at an international level, many felt that the attitude towards disability sport has changed quite considerably. Since public recognition of wheelchair racing has increased, more people understand that it is possible to be an athlete if you use a wheelchair. This attitude means that people view me very differently. I and other athletes are no longer seen to be merely 'having a go' at Paralympic competition, and there is far less stigma attached to being a disabled athlete as society's level of understanding has changed considerably. Today, when asked about racing, the question is less likely to be 'Do you train?', rather, 'What phase of your training are you in?'. As I have always seen myself as an athlete first, using a wheelchair as the tool of my sport, rather than a 'disabled' athlete, this change is very much welcomed. This increased understanding has ensured that studying certain areas of the athlete's training and/or coaching is less difficult. For instance, studying élite athletes in Australia gave me insight into not only the work that was being done, but showed me how differently the athletes are treated, and the benefits of continuing to work to develop the sport. Undoubtedly one of the catalysts for change was the 1992 Barcelona Paralympics, which received in Australia perhaps the most encouraging amount of media recognition in the world, with wide daily coverage in all forms of the media which dramatically increased the profiles of the athletes and their sport. The Sydney Paralympics (in the year 2000), and the environment in which the Games will be held, should do even more to raise the profile of an already prosperous sport. If Britain is to consider further bidding for major championships then there is much to learn from the Australian model for integration.

ISSUES CONCERNING WOMEN IN THE RESEARCH PROCESS

While for many years the ability and aspirations of women to participate in sport have been targeted as an area of concern by administrators and academics, the area of women with disabilities has only been considered more recently. As those who compete in disabled sport are small in number compared to those who are able-bodied, the number that compete at an élite level is even less. It is perhaps understandable that in the past

changes in the organisational structure. In the post-Seoul Paraly
many countries, including Australia and Britain, sought improvei
the organisational structure of wheelchair racing to improve futur
chances. Previous problems that had been encountered in both c(
and the new ideas that were formulated were put back into the s
grass-roots level to ensure that support would be given at a wide ra
levels and that more people would be encouraged to compete. Cl
occurred with the internal restructuring of the Wheelchair Atl
Association in Australia when athletic bodies (for all disability gi
made moves for recognition within the non-disabled governing body
move has done much for wheelchair athletics by focusing on the ath
sporting ability rather than on the disability. The Australian Institu
Sport now accepts participation by disabled athletes in its sports trai
programme in Canberra.

At other levels the Australian Sports Commission has recogn
accreditation courses for coaching disabled athletes which is part of
non-disabled scheme. The courses were developed by those that w
within the wheelchair division to ensure that an accurate picture of whe
chair racing was provided. The Australian Coaching Council runs a cou
for high-performance coaches which is the highest level of accreditati
available and is only accessible to coaches that are internationally reco
nised as being the best in their field. The first coach for disabled athletes l
be accepted for this course is a wheelchair racing coach, and also
woman! On a pragmatic level these moves provide increased understand
ing to all those involved in non-disabled athletics, and will enable th(
attraction of further expertise. This in turn will increase the credibility,
and aid the development, of the sport, creating a more integrated network.
The athlete then becomes the main beneficiary. Experienced and well-
trained coaches are always an important part of any sports growth and
wheelchair racing is no different. There are differences in the way that
wheelchair athletes train (in racing this means that a wider range of distance can be covered), but many principles are the same, and some adaptation is required. All athletes that took part in the study felt that these
moves were on the whole very positive, and wanted further work to be
carried out so that this potential could be maximised. Australia quite possibly provided a near perfect environment in which to work and carry out
my research. Using a wheelchair provided few barriers in a society where
many of the social and environmental barriers restricting access for everyday living are removed. In a practical sense, because everyone I interviewed was either in a wheelchair or employed by a wheelchair governing
body, all interviews took place in accessible areas, and there were plenty

disabled women's concerns and issues have been considered less often. If anything, élite female disabled athletes are caught in the middle of several movements. Jenny Morris has repeatedly pointed the finger at feminist research, stating that it has failed to properly address the needs of disabled women (Morris 1993) and that disabled women have in fact been caught between feminist research and disability campaigning (Morris 1991). In the same vein, the disability movement has failed to look at the changes in disability sport, or the positive role it has had in gaining more public recognition for those with disabilities. What is important to remember is that disabled women cannot just be added on to existing research in the hope that their needs will be served, or their demands properly addressed. However, their concerns remain extremely valid in the changing world of sport and as a competing female athlete I feel that the need to study other women is one of the only ways that changes can be made to improve provision at the entry levels. Disabled female athletes must be considered not only from a feminist perspective, to understand their needs as women, but from a disability standpoint as well to ensure they do not continue to remain invisible (Henderson et al. 1995).

As women are looked at more closely, it appears that there are many negative connotations associated with having a disability. Barton (1993), Morris (1991), and Buscaglia (1994) have suggested that those with a disability may be conditioned by society into a perception of inferiority, due to the negative opinions associated with using a wheelchair for daily life. It has even been suggested that women with disabilities experience a double disadvantage in trying to achieve in today's world. However, I certainly cannot remember a time when I personally have felt this to be the case. Although being a woman in disabled sport bears little effect on what I am, or feel I am, able to achieve, it does cause me to look at certain areas more closely. Researching in Australia did give me the opportunity to spend a lot of time with female athletes to find out what they felt about the issues that affect them, but with no pressure of having to prepare for a competition. It taught me to consider a whole range of other opinions, and to look for solutions to questions that are being asked in Britain about the future of women's sport. It was useful to see the positive way that not just women, but all disabled athletes are treated and also what can be achieved if there is a concentrated effort to change structures and attitudes. Above all it taught me more about disabled women in sport, and the way that others are perceived that was so different to my own experience of being a woman in a wheelchair.

One concern, when examining the participation of disabled women in sport, is that the combined numbers of men and women who compete in the recognised disability groups at élite level competitions are identified rather than the actual numbers of women competing at this level. This alone should be cause for considerable concern, but it also affects women who are involved in sport. At the 1972 Paralympics Games in Heidelberg, Germany, 27 per cent (273 out of 1004) of the athletes were women (Labanowich 1989), although no mention is made of their physical disability groupings even though that is how the sport is organised. In other sports such as basketball (the largest wheelchair sport in Britain), only 7 percent of those registered in the National League are women (Perry 1994).

In both the UK and Australia the percentages (and number of women regularly competing) are fairly similar and this allows favourable comparisons to be made. Before the number of women competing can be increased, the ways in which women currently come into the sport need to be understood. A high percentage of those that compete on a worldwide base are injured as a result of a spinal-cord injury, and therefore generally begin later in life. Women are also involved in fewer of the activities which have been found to result in paraplegia in men, such as contact sports, motorcycling and working in manual industry. The female-to-male split of people coming through spinal units has been estimated as approximately one in five (Ellis 1994), so the available population to compete in sport is far smaller than that for men. Out of the smaller number available for competition, not all will want to compete. A cause for concern in all countries is the lack of junior (under 18) athletes coming through, and the lack of athletes with congenital disabilities wanting to participate. This must lead us to question the provision of physical education at school level, and also the work that the governing bodies are doing to ensure that those who wish to compete have the opportunity to do so. Because the number of women competing is smaller than for men, the ladder of progression is very different to that which men go through. Some would argue that if athletic promise is shown then 'the top' can be seen to be reached far more quickly for women than for men, with all the benefits that this entails, such as team selection, sponsorship and media coverage. It can however often work the other way and discourage some women who show less initial improvement but may have higher long term potential. They feel that they will never be able to compete with those at the top. However in both Australia and the UK there are large gaps between those that compete at a recreational level, serious competitors, and those that are considered élite. It is especially hard on younger athletes who develop at different rates, and have different levels of disabilities. The International Paralympic Committee is moving to protect women's sports by introducing a quota system to guarantee places at major games. Although this should protect the sport, on a personal level I do not believe that this is the answer. All development should be done outside of the Paralympic Games to ensure that they remain élite and all national groups should take more responsibility for encouraging women and providing the opportunities for them to compete and improve. Most females will welcome the policy of looking to ensure that women's interests are guarded. However it could also be seen that favouring women in this way could indeed become some form of positive discrimination, which would also need to be held in check.

The majority of women interviewed would like to see the depth of competition increase. It would add increased validity to the sport and also make the competition more meaningful. However, even though there is an unequal number of men and women competing in wheelchair racing, many other areas of the sport appear equal. In road races where prize money is paid, in the majority of cases the structure is equal. Many disabled women in wheelchair racing also receive good media coverage compared with the disabled men who compete, and comparable if not better sponsorship deals (although in both cases not in the same league as nondisabled athletes). This leads us to question whether this is indeed the correct way to encourage women to compete, as it will be only the few who benefit. There are certainly very mixed views as to how this will effect the athletes who are competing. On one side it could be said that because there are less women to compete for equal prize money they are in fact advantaged over the men's division. This contradicts the idea that women with disability experience a double disadvantage over men. For there to be greater rewards it is recognised that the level and especially the breadth of competition needs to be improved. However, some women athletes feel that by encouraging more women to compete they may reduce their own chances of maintaining the level of reward they currently achieve. This may be a 'Catch 22' situation. Because of the disparity in the breadth of competition between the men's and women's divisions, some feel that a larger proportion of the prize money should go to the men's division in order to maintain the same level of reward for the same performance. For example, there is a race in the UK in which, in 1994, fifty men and three women competed. Is it considered to be fair that the first three placings in both men's and women's divisions were awarded prize money? Because of the small numbers of women in the race, it could be considered that there was a prize for coming last in the women's division! Many women feel that the first place should be of equal value, and then prize money should be more dependent on the number of athletes competing in the different divisions. This is an interesting way forward.

Although the immediate concern of attracting more women into sport must continually be addressed, there also need to be efficient systems in place in order to be able to develop those women to their full potential. In this area there is still much work to be done in order to achieve this aim. A good nationwide structure must be in place to be able to support the women who come into the sport, and using current athletes at a local level will not only provide much-needed role models, but their experiences can be used to guide the sport.

CONCLUSION

When I applied for the Churchill Scholarship, it was under the category of Young Sports' Leaders. As well as aiming to gain benefit from the high level of training I was able to experience in Australia, my academic aim of investigating ways in which wheelchair racing in Britain could benefit from the study of the organisational structures of other countries was facilitated. Once the Scholarship began I also became interested in looking more specifically at the needs of women in disabled sport, and women élite athletes' view of the sport that they are involved in. It was found that women have strong opinions about the way their sport is changing but need to feel able to express these opinions more fully, and need to be empowered to play a fuller part in the way their sport is developing. This research highlighted a number of key issues, but it was clear that it was only scratching the surface, and that further work needs to be done to assess more fully the needs of women in other countries and other sports.

References

Banks, J. (1992) 'Maximising Athletic Performance at the 1992 Paralympics', *Stagecoach*, July - September, pp. 18–24.
Barton, L. (1993) 'Disability, Empowerment and Physical Education' in Evans, J. (Ed.) *Equality, Education, and Physical Education*, London: Falmer Press.
Buscaglia, L. (1994) *The Disabled and Their Parents: A Counselling Challenge*, New Jersey: SLACK Incorporated.
De Pauw, K. P. (1986) 'Research on Sport for Athletes with Disabilities', *Adapted Physical Activity Quarterly*, 3, pp. 292–299.
Ellis, R. (1994), Superintendent Physiotherapist at Pinderfields Spinal Unit. *Personal communication*, September 1994.
Henderson, K. A., Bedini, L. A., Hecht, L., and Schiller, R. (1995) 'Women with Physical Disabilities and the Regulation of Leisure Constraints', *Leisure Studies*, 14, pp. 17–31.

Labanowich, S. (1989) 'The Paralympic Games: A Retrospective View', *Palaestra*, Summer Paralympics, pp. 9–52.

Merklinger, A. (1993) 'Equity for Athletes with a Disability'. *Paper presented to the International Paralympic Committee Athletes Committee*, Manchester, England.

Morris, J. (1991) *Pride Against Prejudice: Transforming Attitudes to Disability*, London: The Women's Press.

Morris, J. (1993) 'Feminism and Disability', *Feminist Review*, 43, pp. 57–69.

Perry, G. (1994), Development Officer for the British Wheelchair Basketball Association. *Personal communication*, September 1994.

Scruton, J. (1979) 'Sir Ludwig Guttman: Creator of a World Sports Movement for the Paralysed and Other Disabled', *Paraplegia*, 17, pp. 52–55.

Steadward, R. (1990) 'Excellence – The Future of Sports for Athletes with Disabilities, in Williams, T., Almond, L., and Sparkes, A., (Eds) *Sport and Physical Activity: Moving Towards Excellence*, The Proceedings of the AIESEP World Convention July 20–25, Loughborough University.

Swain, J., Finkelstein, V., French, S., and Oliver, M., (Eds) (1993) *Disabling Barriers – Enabling Environments*, Milton Keynes: Open University Press.

Williams, T. and Taylor, D. (1992) *Wheelchair Racing: Disability Sport Participation Studies*, Loughborough National Sport Development Centre.

9 Sexual Harassment and Sexual Abuse in Sport
Celia Brackenridge

'Monsters don't get near to children – nice men do'. This quotation comes from a television interview in 1993 with Ray Wyre, Director of the Gracewell Clinic for the rehabilitation of sex offenders. It sums up neatly the myth surrounding sexual harassment and abuse, that such behaviours are the result of *stranger danger* when, in reality, just the opposite is the case. It also reminds us that myths or expectations can mislead or distract us and that research about what we think we know is just as important as research about what we think we don't know. This chapter draws on my own experiences of carrying out preliminary research into sexual harassment and abuse by sports coaches: in particular, it explores the methodological and ethical difficulties faced when researching such sensitive and emotive topics. My intention is to challenge some of the traditional approaches to research and to demonstrate that there is a rich vein of material to be tapped by those who are brave enough to 'enter the field' in this way (Whyte 1984). Most importantly, the chapter argues that, as feminists, we should be willing to work in difficult areas of research, to ask difficult questions and to voice unpopular messages if we wish to make a positive contribution to the betterment of women's experiences of sport and physical activity. Throughout this chapter, following the advice of Kirby and McKenna (1989), I refer to those who assisted in interviews as participants and not as subjects or interviewees since I have tried to recognise the shared process of the research. Oakley (1981) has also urged us, as women researching women, to avoid the hierarchical relationship which often arises between the interviewer and the interviewee. All engaged in this research have been changed by the experience and some participants have kept in regular contact since we first met, either to seek reading or further help or to offer advice, contacts and ideas. Arguably, then, the research is collaborative, even though I am the named 'researcher'.

WHOSE PROBLEM IS IT ANYWAY – WHY STUDY SEXUAL ABUSE?

There is a view that sexual abuse is just another moral panic and that, if ignored, it will go away. There has also been a backlash against the child protection movement (see Finkelhor 1994) stimulated by those, including aggrieved parents and falsely-accused teachers, who are worried that the rights of the child have become highlighted too much. However, Finkelhor suggests that the backlash, which he likens to 'social problem fatigue', is not sustainable since the issue of child welfare has an enduring moral authority. He also suggests that the child protection movement will be strengthened by the rise of women in the workforce, the growth of feminism as a social movement and the fact that the rights of the accused are now also on the research and professional agenda, which has effectively taken some of the steam out of their criticisms.

In sport, far from being a new problem, sexual abuse almost certainly has been around for centuries but, until recently, has been ignored. As feminism has permeated sport so the research agenda has started to shift to embrace questions of gender equity, gender power relations and sexual violence in sport. Since sexual abuse is a form of sexual violence it was only a matter of time before it came to the attention of sport researchers. One might almost argue then that this research arose at a point of historical and political necessity. Indeed, researchers in several different countries began, quite independently, to study sexual harassment and abuse in sport; for example, Tod Crosset in the USA (1986), Celia Brackenridge in England (1987; 1990) and Helen Lenskyj in Canada (1992). From these overviews there has now begun a differentiation of studies into more specific questions about the nature of sexual harassment and abuse, which sports or individuals might be most susceptible, what role parents, administrators and the law might play in child protection and how sexually abusive behaviour is linked to other abuses like nutritional control or physical violence in sport.

My motives for starting this research were clearly articulated from the start. After more than ten years of researching and writing about women and sport, I felt that I had failed to make any real impact upon the experience of discrimination which women in sport face. Moreover, a kind of immunity to women's issues had begun to develop amongst the media and many sport organisations as the backlash against feminism felt in the 1980s (Faludi 1991) started to permeate sport in the early 1990s. Investigating sexual abuse in sport was not only a logical progression for me as a feminist researcher but it also helped to revive media interest in the general issue of sex discrimination in sport. Sexual abuse is a pernicious social crime which has attracted widespread media and academic attention in the 1980s. I had little doubt that the exposure of this problem in sport would not only shock but also stimulate the attention and moral repugnance of the particular publics I was trying to reach. My tactic was to get these publics to admit that, if sexual abuse in sport was morally wrong and should be stopped then, logically, the same should apply to sexual harassment and sexual discrimination. In other words, I adopted an overtly political approach in choosing to do this research. On this basis, it might be argued that I was myself guilty of exploiting the victims of abuse who participated in the work since I was using them to further a broader feminist agenda. However, I would refute that since I regard those who helped me as collaborators 'from the margins' (Kirby and McKenna 1989), that is they were marginalised in terms of their power to change the structures and processes of sport and needful of alliances to help them in this task. Whether the work has had or will have any greater positive impact on sport than my earlier projects, such as those concerning women in team sports (Brackenridge 1985) or women in coaching (West and Brackenridge 1990), remains to be seen.

TACKLING TABOOS – DEFINING THE PROBLEM

Any study of sexual behaviour inevitably encounters a set of social taboos about the body in our society. These include irrational fears about such things as contamination and menstruation (see Clarke and Gilroy 1992), the sexual identity crisis or so-called role conflict of the female athlete (see Allison 1991), the sexual confidence of the male athlete (Klein 1990) and so on. Taboos are not helpful to us when they block research access but they are fascinating because they reflect ways in which society has tried to come to terms with and rationalise dissonance in social behaviour (see, for example, Douglas 1970; Hearn and Morgan 1990; and Shilling 1993). Some of the myths which have influenced this research are that sport is a morally pure category of behaviour, that the authority of the coach is inviolable and that sexual behaviour, of any kind, is outside the normal discourse of sport (Brackenridge 1994). Whilst most of us might agree that *sexual harassment* occurs in sport, just as in other areas of life, there seems to be a deep reluctance to accept that *sexual abuse* of children could possibly occur in the sports setting or that there is a need to do anything about it.

Table 9.1 offers a working model of what I have called the sexual discrimination/sexual abuse continuum which attempts to show the relationship between sex discrimination, sexual harassment and sexual abuse. This model is based on the assumption that sexual discrimination, sexual harassment and sexual abuse are all discriminatory behaviours which include both *institutional* and *personal* components. The model is intended

Table 9.1   The Sexual Discrimination /Abuse Continuum

Sex Discrimination	Sexual Harassment	Sexual Abuse
INSTITUTIONAL...............................PERSONAL		

'the chilly climate'	*'unwanted attention'*	*'groomed or coerced'*
– vertical & horizontal	– written or verbal abuse	– exchange of reward or
– job segregation	or threats	privilege for sexual
– lack of harassment	– sexually oriented	favours
policy and/or officer	comments	– rape
or reporting channels	– jokes, lewd comments or	– anal or vaginal
– lack of counselling or	sexual innuendoes, taunts	penetration
mentoring systems	about body, dress, marital	by penis, fingers or
– differential pay or	situation or sexuality	objects
rewards or promotion	– ridiculing of performance	– forced sexual activity
prospects on the	– sexual or homophobic	– sexual assault
basis of sex	graffiti	– physical/sexual
– poorly/unsafely	– practical jokes based on sex	violence
designed or lit	intimidating sexual remarks,	– groping
venues	propositions, invitations or	– indecent exposure
– absence of security	familiarity	– incest
	– domination of meetings,	
	play space of equipment	
	– condescending or patronising	
	behaviour undermining self-	
	respect or work performance	
	– physical contact, fondling,	
	pinching or kissing	
	– vandalism on the basis of sex	
	– offensive phones calls or	
	photos	

to offer a clear, semi-objective but flexible approach towards defining what is a very unclear, highly subjective set of experiences. By listing behaviours associated with each of the 'categories' I have been able to test out the usefulness of the model with participants in the research, and to ask them to point out inaccuracies, ambiguities and gaps.

Sexual discrimination, frequently defined as 'less favourable treatment on the basis of sex', is evidenced in organisational settings where women have a tougher time than men – what the Canadians call the chilly climate (Lenskyj 1994). For example, women generally occupy lower status positions, do lower status jobs and receive less pay than men (Lovenduski and

Randall 1993). Sexual harassment, usually defined as unwanted behaviour or unwelcome advances on the basis of sex, is rather more personal in nature but is facilitated by an institutional climate which permits, rather than sanctions, such behaviour. Sexual abuse is a direct attack upon a person's sexual being by another, on the basis of the abuser's greater power. Both abuse and harassment constitute what I call *invasion without consent*. Sexual abuse may be same- or cross-sex but always involves interpersonal relations and is usually perpetrated by a figure having, and/or desiring, power. It usually arises from a carefully groomed situation in which the perpetrator gradually wins the confidence and co-operation of the victim. Table 9.1 gives examples of each type of behaviour on the continuum. My purpose in proposing this model is to point out that (a) discrimination and abuse are linked and (b) it is not possible simply to dismiss sexual abuse as the ravings of sexually depraved individuals. By failing to prevent abuse, institutional cultures are responsible, in effect, for giving permission for abusive relations in sport: therefore, sport organisations have an important role to play in regulating and preventing such behaviours. This model was refined through a number of stages and is still under review. It began from a combination of my own knowledge and hunches and from my reading of social work literature and was developed with the help of my research participants, indirectly through their own stories and directly through feedback about it in and/or after interviews.

HOW DO YOU KNOW THAT YOU KNOW – WHAT COUNTS AS KNOWLEDGE?

I could have chosen to start my research by using a survey of clubs, athletes or coaches to see what was 'out there'. However, in my view, the questionnaire survey is a doubtful research method for this kind of topic – like taking a blunt instrument to unpick a delicate and tangled set of issues. It might also have caused untold harm by raising fears or compounding the pain of abuse which some athletes had already suffered. I therefore started my empirical investigation with athlete interviews and intend to interview coaches and parents of athletes at some future point in order to triangulate my data (see for example McFee 1992). My interest is in the interpersonal relationships between these various actors and how they define their situation in different ways. I have also employed a research student to study the organisational aspects of child protection in sport through an investigation of governing bodies of sport and other major sports agencies. Selecting the right individual for this post was, in

itself, an exercise in deconstructing power since research students are traditionally subordinate to their supervisors: we have attempted to negotiate
this issue together by agreeing to adopt as open a communications style as
possible, by promising mutual critique on whatever we write and by taking
different but complementary perspectives on the research theme. My own
work focuses more on the interpersonal aspects of sexual abuse in sport
and hers more on organisational cultures and attitudes towards child protection. Within a couple of years we hope to have a fairly comprehensive
map of the issues and be well-placed to work practically with organisations wishing to strengthen their child protection policies and practices.

Prior to interviewing athletes, I felt it was important to develop a
working definition of sexual abuse but this needed to be problematised.
For example, some studies of child abuse have included looks and gestures
in their definition whilst others include only physical contacts: some
studies include sexual abuse by same-age individuals, whereas others only
count abuse where there is a minimum of five years difference in ages
between the abuser and the abused (see Fisher 1994 for a discussion of
definitions). So we can see immediately that measurements of the incidence or prevalence of sexual abuse will vary depending on precisely
which definition is adopted. My working definition, as presented in Table
9.1, was based on a review of relevant literature from the cognate fields of
sociology and social work and was tested against the experiences of my
participants. Even before starting to read or arranging any interviews I
spent time talking with an experienced child protection specialist who was
able to outline the issues and point me towards key material. This proved
to be an invaluable move: it helped me to select which questions to begin
with, alerted me to likely problem areas in the practical management of
interviewing and accessing data and, most important of all, gave me a
mainstream account into which I could begin to fit my sport-specific work.

I have returned to my notes of this encounter again and again and, each
time, feel more strongly that sport science has much to learn from its professional partners and its discipline roots. What I brought to the research
was a deep knowledge and understanding of sport with an applied knowledge of sport psychology and sport sociology. What I lacked, and what I
was able to compensate for in some measure by this approach, was knowledge of the child protection and social work systems in which most
research on sexual abuse has been done.

In addition to problematising both my definition of child abuse and my
research approach to it, I also had to discard my previous conceptions of
what counted as 'data' in this study. For example, notes from a telephone
call from an anguished parent, or cases of abuse reported in the media or

Table 9.2   Sexual Harassment in Sport – Risk Factors

COACH VARIABLES	ATHLETE VARIABLES	SPORT VARIABLES
– sex (male)	– sex (female)	– amount of physical handling required for coaching
– age (older)	– age (younger)	– individual/team sport
– size/physique (larger/stronger)	– size/physique (smaller/weaker)	– location of training and competitions
– accredited qualifications (good)		
– rank/reputation (high)	– rank/status (potentially high)	– opportunity for trips away
– previous record of SH (unknown/ignored)	– history of sexual abuse (unknown/none)	– dress requirements
– trust of parents (strong)	– level of awareness of SH (low)	– employment/recruitment controls and/or vetting (weak/none)
– standing in the sport/ club/community (high)	– self-esteem (low)	– regular evaluation including athlete screening and cross referencing to medical data
	– relationship with parents (weak)	– education and training on SH and abuse (none)
– chances to be alone with athletes in training, at competitions and away on trips (high)	– medical problems especially disordered eating (medium/high)	
– commitment to sport/national coaches association codes of ethics and conduct (weak/none)		– use of national and sport-specific codes of ethics and conduct (weak)
– use of car to transport athletes (frequent)		– existence of athlete and parent contracts (none)
		– climate for debating SH (poor/non-existent)

(Note: Comments in brackets indicate emerging trends from interview data.)

sports literature, all became data for me. Indeed, it proved so difficult to find people who were prepared to speak out and be interviewed about experiences of sexual abuse in sport that I resolved to collect cases from any available source to expand the range and depth of my material. I catalogued cases in two ways: the first was a list of direct cases comprising those with whom I had personally conducted interviews and the second a list of indirect cases comprising those culled from the media, books or articles, with all sources carefully recorded. In this way my total list of cases grew fairly quickly.

What is clear from the work done so far is that conventional notions of 'sampling' go out of the window with this kind of research. Because of this, it would not be feasible to pursue research questions about incidence and prevalence, nor to seek to establish any descriptive statistics about child abuse in sport. This means that the 'evidence' base may look somewhat thin. However, the first question I am always asked by the media and by major sport authorities is 'How widespread is it?'. The point of my interviews was to check out with participants whether the emerging model of risk factors, shown in Table 9.2, resonated for them and whether the discrimination/abuse continuum proved to be a useful organising framework. The analysis of risk factors is certainly tentative at this point: it will be expanded and adapted as the research progresses and will also need to be verified repeatedly in order to develop its predictive power.

GETTING IN TOUCH – FINDING SOMEONE TO INTERVIEW

Victims of sexual abuse do not simply step forward from nowhere. Finding individuals to interview was the first practical problem. My first breakthrough came through a friend working in leisure management who knew of my research interest and also knew someone who might be prepared to talk with me. My friend acted as mediator and, after protracted and carefully planned negotiations, made a rendezvous for a meeting between me and the contact.

Further interviews were set up after a telephone help line which followed the BBC TV *On the Line* programme in August 1993 about sexual abuse called 'Secrets of The Coach': from the 91 callers another 12 people volunteered to talk to me, some only briefly by telephone and others during in-depth interviews. From there I used the snowball technique (Arber 1993), often used in research on marginal populations (Lee 1993), which involved asking each contact to let me know if he or she had any further ideas about who might have information for me. This served me well for about a year and generated another handful of possibilities but the response eventually dwindled and many such potential interviewees failed to come forward.

BEING HONOURABLE – ETHICAL GUIDELINES

Kirby and McKenna (1989) stress the importance of being honourable when doing research with the oppressed, in other words being completely open and honest at all times and not doing anything which might compound the marginalisation of the oppressed group, such as using subterfuge in order to get at data. This principle might present some difficulties for those doing participant observation but for my work it fitted perfectly. With a topic of this sensitivity it was important to give the participants as much control over the interview as possible. Some pulled out of telephone calls or meetings through sheer fear or panic. In the absence of any clear guidelines (thanks to a colleague, I later discovered those of the Social Research Association which would have helped enormously (Wearmouth 1994)), I established my own parameters for the interview process. Each person was given my name and address through an independent third party and invited to get in touch. If and when they chose to do so I replied, offering to meet at a time and venue chosen by them. At the start of the interview, they were assured that they could leave at any time or ask me to refrain from using their story. Complete confidentiality was assured and the process of rendering anonymous and securing the data from the interview was outlined. In addition, my background as an athlete and coach was sketched out to help establish common ground and, I hoped, put the participants at their ease.

There is no doubt that the most difficult aspects of my research arose from the ethical dilemmas which confronted me. Whilst I was able to protect my participants from recognition by rendering anonymous all the interview material, I also had to bear in mind that their identity, or more likely the identity of the coaches they were discussing with me, might be revealed if I described their sport. For this reason I decided to anonymise both the individual *and* the sport when transcribing the notes from interviews. In doing so, something of the context was lost but I felt that this was a necessary sacrifice in order to protect the participants and their coaches. I also 'lost' some data by choosing to work with notes rather than a tape recorder but this was a deliberate decision as I was certain that audio equipment would have scared away some of my participants. With hindsight I could have used a recorder with certain participants and I may consider doing so in the future.

I spent a considerable amount of time studying ethical codes for research from the British Psychological Society (1978), the British Sociological Society (1984) and from various universities. I was disturbed to find that neither of the institutions which employed me during my research had human consent forms or ethical committees. Seeking to change this became, in itself, a supplementary task. It is indeed ironic that a study about ethical behaviour should have been carried out without any institutional ethical guidelines! In the absence of these I had to set my own boundaries and use self-censorship (Lee 1993: 189). The process of monitoring these boundaries became a regular one. Almost like remembering to turn on and off a switch when using the computer, I had to turn on and off my ethical gaze each time I worked on the project.

Additional ethical pressures arose from the media who, at times, were hungry for results. Their insistence on statistics, names, places and precise details had to be carefully deflected not only to protect the identity of individuals and organisations but also to avoid preempting the findings of the work. Although publicity was important since it helped to generate more cases it was not always worthwhile. After the making of the BBC programme, during which the programme researchers, interviewers and camera crew behaved in exemplary fashion, I refused certain media interviews because of fears of exaggeration or sensationalisation of the issues.

KEEPING TRACK – THE RESEARCH DIARY AND OTHER RECORDS

For me, engaging in feminist research meant that I kept a record of the process as well as the content of the research (Kirby and McKenna 1989). This then helped me to see how my ideas changed over time and how my 'results' developed. Keeping a diary also helps enormously with contingency planning, for example moving to a different source of data if access to one source is blocked. I made the mistake of starting the diary for this research very late on and had to draw on memories rather than contemporary events and impressions for much of it. On reflection I think this may have happened because this was not a formal 'project' as such, with funding and a definite start and end date, but an ongoing investigation to which I kept returning whenever I had the time. However, once I got started I wrote using almost a stream-of-consciousness style since the ideas flowed so fast: the diary became long and intricate but now, when interrogated, shows clearly how issues like entering the field, overcoming inertia and building the trust of participants have been dealt with.

Separate from the diary were my files, one for correspondence with outside agencies, professional and academic contacts, one with all the data from interviews and correspondence with participants and several more with newspaper clippings, articles and other relevant documents. The file of participant data was always kept separately from the rest, in a locked drawer, to optimise confidentiality. Once notes from each interview had been transcribed I could safely make them public. I tried to ensure confidentiality by substituting pseudonyms for every person, place and sport mentioned. I indexed each transcript, listing and numbering each statement on a separate line and then undertook an analysis across the various transcripts. As a theme or issue emerged it was checked against the table of risk factors to see whether it was consonant with what was there or not, drawing theory out of practice (Glaser and Strauss 1967). There was a certain amount of trial and error with this stage of the analysis, testing out the degree of fit between different themes and different combinations of statements but, overall, the mapping exercise proved remarkably easy as the data seemed to tumble out of the transcripts. Any uncatalogued items were kept to one side to be checked as possible lines of further enquiry. Nothing was discarded.

HELP OR HINDRANCE – WHOSE SIDE ARE YOU ON?

The people willing to be interviewed for my research frequently revealed that they had suffered emotionally, psychologically and often also physically. On the other hand, I found that, once the initial fears and anxieties of being interviewed had been overcome, participants were determined to make their stories heard and only too willing to talk to someone who took them seriously and wanted to do something about the problem. Almost all the participants I talked to recognised that they were helping to safeguard the future of others in sport and that their own history, however painful, had to be heard in order to achieve this end. As a researcher I recognised that there was an element of the counsellor in me: participants occasionally broke down in the middle of an interview and needed reassurance and comfort. This required extremely sensitive handling in order not to compromise my role as researcher, violate the trust that I had established or take me into realms of professional behaviour which were beyond my own expertise. It was vital for me to remember at all times that I was not a qualified counsellor or psychiatrist and that, with the best will in the world, I could not offer those specialist skills to someone in a research interview. However, the comfort level established at the start of the interview was vital if I was to maximise trust in the relationship and get the most from the conversation.

I prepared for the eventuality of 'victim dependency' by securing a copy of a national directory of counselling and support agencies and offering to refer participants who wanted specialist help to their nearest agency. In several cases, participants tried to draw me into their struggle to obtain redress against abusing coaches. However, I knew that my credibility as a researcher would be jeopardised if I became involved in any individual's case and that my prospects of gaining access to interview coaches later in the research would be seriously undermined if I was seen in any way to 'take sides'. In reality, of course, I *was* taking sides because the whole research project was about empowerment for the disempowered. I gave participants as much information as I could about mechanisms for reporting abuse and I gave advice, where it was requested, about how to document experiences and where to seek redress but I did not intervene directly with any sport organisation on behalf of my participants. The handling of what Fetterman calls 'guilty knowledge' (cited in Miles and Huberman 1994: 294) was, and will continue to be, my most difficult ethical dilemma.

Many of my participants have continued in correspondence with me. I may return to them for further discussions as the framework for the research emerges and the models of abusive relationships become clearer. In the meantime it is also likely that these individuals might wish to make contact with each other to form their own support group. Should this happen then confidentiality would be maintained by contacting each individual to ask whether they wished to be put in touch with anyone else. I would, initially, act as a conduit for replies and would then withdraw from the group, unless asked specifically by members to take an advisory or advocacy role.

There is always a balance to be struck in working on an issue like this, between seeking to explore and understand the experiences of those who are 'victims' of child sexual abuse and trying to represent those who might be accused falsely of perpetrating such a crime. The progress of my research would have been much easier had I received support from the major sport authorities in this country, not just financially but in terms of opening doors, encouraging debate and demonstrating commitment. As it was, not only could I not raise research funding but, for several years, met with obfuscation and denial from key sport organisations. I would classify this type of resistance as *inertial* (Finkelhor 1994); that is, arising from absence of co-operation, delay, apathy and bureaucracy, rather than *oppositional*; that is, through systematic, organised blockage. Examples of inertial resistance to my research included: failure to reply to letters (sometimes after two or three had been sent), assurances that 'something was being done' when no action was evident after several months, and rejection of requests for funding on the grounds that the work was too controversial. The fear of a witch hunt was so strong that I was 'cooled out' by certain sport organisations who thought that I was making blanket accusations about coaches. I recognised that I needed access to these groups in order to develop the research so my strategy to deal with this difficulty was to offer detailed information about my work together with constant reassurances that it would benefit coaches as well as children.

WITCH HUNTS AND MORAL PANICS – CONCLUSIONS

There is no such thing as proof in this kind of research. The best that can be hoped for is repeated confirmation of hunches or expectations to the point that reasonable confidence may be placed in the predictive power of any speculated models. Although there are theoretical accounts of sexual harassment and abuse in the literature of sociology, psychology and psychiatry, the most compelling accounts of sexual harassment and abuse perpetrated by males on females in sport come from pro-feminist or feminist analyses of patriarchal power (Crosset 1986; Brackenridge 1994; Burton Nelson 1994). Despite the appeal of these explanations there remain some important puzzles. Social work research (see Morrison et al. 1994) indicates that abuse by females, of both females and males, *does* occur. So even though there are currently very few recorded cases in sport, the question of female-on-female and female-on-male abuse must be addressed at some future point. The confounding issues of sexuality and sexual preference of the abuser also need careful examination, particularly in view of the widespread myths about homosexuality, especially lesbianism, in sport which are exacerbated by media revelations such as those by Mewshaw (1993). We simply do not know yet what the facts are. Rather than starting new moral panics, or fuelling old ones, we should be prepared to engage in research which challenges not only what we once took for granted but also how we think about the world.

WARNING

Whilst I have tried in this chapter to encourage qualitative research by women with women I am acutely aware of the problems that 'lifting stones' can cause. I prefer to err on the side of caution and advise that researchers should not move into this field of enquiry without very clear advice and guidelines from experienced tutors. As a further safeguard, I also advise that any researcher wishing to do work on sexual harassment or sexual abuse in sport works, as I did initially, in collaboration with a qualified social worker or therapist.

Editors' Notes

The Times (28 September 1995) reported on its front page that:

An Olympic swimming coach was jailed for 17 years yesterday for raping and abusing girls who trusted him to make them stars.

Paul Hickson, the British team coach at the 1988 Olympics in Seoul, was sentenced after a judge described his assaults on 11 swimmers, including two rapes, as dreadful and filthy. He had denied abusing girls aged 13 to 20 between 1976 and 1991, while he was coaching in Norwich and Swansea.

References

Allison, M. (1991) 'Role Conflict and the Female Athlete: Preoccupations with Little Grounding', *International Journal of Applied Sport Psychology*, 3, pp. 49–60.

Arber, S. (1993) 'Designing Samples' in Gilbert, N. (Ed.) *Researching Social Life*, London: Sage.

Brackenridge, C. (1985) 'The Place of Psychological Consultancy in Women's Team Games: Help or Hindrance?' in Graydon, J. (Ed.) *Women, Psychology, Sport*, Proceedings of a one day conference of the British Society of Sport Psychology, Polytechnic of North London, BSSP.

Brackenridge, C. (1987) 'Ethical Concerns in Women's Sport', *Coaching Focus*, 6, Summer, Leeds: National Coaching Foundation.

Brackenridge, C. (1990) 'Cross Gender Relationships: Myth, Drama or Crisis', *Coaching Focus*, 16, Spring, Leeds: National Coaching Foundation.

Brackenridge, C. (1994) 'Fair Play or Fair Game: Child Sexual Abuse in Sport Organisations', *International Review for the Sociology of Sport*, 3, pp. 287–299.

British Psychological Society (1978) *Ethical Principles for Research with Human Subjects*, BPS Annual General Meeting: York.

British Sociological Association (1984) 'Statement of Ethical Practice', *Network*, 43.

Burton Nelson, M. (1994) *The Stronger Women Get, the More Men Love Football*, New York: Harcourt Brace.

Clarke, G. and Gilroy, S. (1992) 'This Bloody Business: Menstrual Myths and Periodic Leisure' in Brackenridge, C. (Ed.) *Body Matters: Leisure Images and Lifestyles*, Eastbourne: LSA No. 47.

Crosset, T (1986) 'Male-coach/female-athlete relationships'. Paper presented to a conference of the Norwegian Confederation of Sport on 'Coaching the Top Level Athlete', Sole, Norway, 15–16 November.

Douglas, M. (1970) *Purity and Danger: An Analysis of the Concepts of Pollution and Taboo*, London: Penguin.

Evans, J. (Ed.) (1993) *Equality, Education and Physical Education*, London: Falmer Press.

Faludi, S. (1991) *Backlash: The Undeclared War Against American Women*, New York: Anchor.

Finkelhor, D. (1994) 'The "Backlash" and the Future of Child Protection Advocacy: Insights from the Study of Social Issues' in Myers, J. E. B. (Ed.) *The Backlash: Child Protection Under Fire*, London: Sage.

Fisher, D. (1994) 'Adult Sex Offenders: Who Are They? Why and How do They Do it?' in Morrison, T. Erooga. M. and Beckett, R. C. (Eds) *Sexual Offending Against Children: Assessment and Treatment of Male Abusers*, London: Routledge.

Glaser, B. G. and Strauss, A. L. (1967) *The Discovery of Grounded Theory*, New York: Aldine.

Hearn, J. and Morgan, D. (Eds) (1990) *Men, Masculinities and Social Theory*, London: Unwin and Hyman.

Kirby, S. and McKenna, K. (1989) *Experience, Research, Social Change: Methods from the Margin*, Toronto: Garamond.

Klein, A. (1990) 'Little Big Man: Hustling, Gender Narcissism, and Body Building Subculture' in Messner, M. and Sabo, D. (Eds) *Sport, Men and the Gender Order*, Champaign, IL. Human Kinetics.

Lee, R. L. (1993) *Doing Research on Sensitive Topics*, London: Sage.

Lenskyj, H. (1992) 'Sexual Harassment: Female Athletes' Experiences and Coaches' Responsibilities', *Sport Science Periodical on Research and Technology in Sport*, Coaching Association of Canada, 12, 6, Special Topics B-1.

Lenskyj, H. (1994) *Women, Sport and Physical Activity: Selected Research Themes*, Ontario: Sport Canada.

Lovenduski, J. and Randall, V. (1993) *Contemporary Feminist Politics*, Oxford: Oxford University Press.

McFee, G. (1992) 'Triangulation in Research: Two Confusions' *Educational Research*, 34, pp. 215–219.

Messner, M. and Sabo, D. (Eds) (1990) *Sport, Men and the Gender Order*, Champaign, IL: Human Kinetics.

Mewshaw, M. (1993) *Ladies of the Court: Grace and Disgrace on the Women's Tennis Tour*, London: Warner Books.

Miles, M. B. and Huberman A. M. (1994 [2nd edition]) *Qualitative Data Analysis: An Expanded Sourcebook*, London: Sage.

Morrison, T., Erooga, M. and Beckett, R. C. (Eds) (1994) *Sexual Offending Against Children: Assessment and Treatment of Male Abusers*, London: Routledge.

Myers, J. E. B. (Ed.) (1994) *The Backlash: Child Protection Under Fire*, London: Sage.

Oakley, A. (1981) 'Interviewing Women: A Contradiction in Terms' in Roberts, H. (Ed.) *Doing Feminist Research*, London: Routledge and Kegan Paul.

Shilling, C. (1993) 'The Body, Class and Social Inequalities' in Evans, J. (Ed.) *Equality, Education and Physical Education*, London: Falmer Press.

Social Research Association (undated) *Ethical Guidelines* [kindly provided by Hazel Wearmouth, Leeds Metropolitan University, 1994].

West, A. and Brackenridge, C. (1990) *Wot! No Women Coaches? A Report Relating to the Lives of Women as Sports Coaches in the UK 1989/90*, Sheffield: PAVIC Publications.

Whyte, W. F. (1984) *Learning from the Field: A Guide from Experience*, London: Sage.

10 Time and Context in Women's Sport and Leisure

Margaret Talbot

The use of time profiles in researching the relationships between time and context in women's involvement in sport has been negligible. However, its use is described here as an aspect of a larger piece of research (Talbot 1991), where the major data source was interviews with forty Yorkshire women. Twenty were league club hockey players and twenty were 'casual' players of badminton, all recruited from the same sports centre in West Yorkshire where they played on a Thursday evening. All the women were white. The age ranges of the hockey players (between 18 and 41 years) and badminton players (between 21 and 43 years) were similar, but the distributions of ages differed, with the majority of hockey players aged between 25 and 33, while the ages of the badminton players stretched fairly evenly between 28 and 43. The family situations of the two groups of players were markedly different, with more of the badminton players' families in the 'later establishment' stage of the family life cycle (Rapoport and Rapoport 1975). Of the badminton players, fourteen were married (all but one with children), three were single and three were divorced with children. Two of the three single women lived with their parents and one lived alone. Eleven of the hockey players were married or in stable heterosexual relationships, only four with children: none was divorced. Only one woman lived alone; four lived with parents, one with a woman friend and her father, one with a female tenant and two with female partners. Of the badminton players, four were full-time mothers and houseworkers, eleven had part-time jobs and five were in full-time paid work. Only one of the hockey players was a full-time mother and houseworker; three had part-time jobs; and sixteen had full-time paid work, seven as physical education teachers.

TIME

The overall research focused on the women's own retrospective accounts of their participation in sport and leisure, in relation to their work and family activities. However, in order to provide a contemporary context for

142

the women's sports activities, it was desirable to find some way of eliciting and recording their patterns of time use, and the shape of their routines. *Time* is one of the two crucial currencies for women's out-of-the-home leisure, the other currency being personal money (Pahl 1989). I have identified elsewhere the flaws in the commonly-used residual definitions of leisure as 'time free from work' (Talbot 1979a, 1979b, 1990).

The purpose of the research was to situate the women's physical activities in their temporal and social contexts. It was therefore not felt that detailed analysis of time use, such as that produced by time diaries, was appropriate. Quite apart from the fact that keeping a diary in itself changes time use (Szalai 1975), it is also very time consuming: a research instrument which would take as little time as possible to administer, and which would not endanger the relationships between the women and their sports activities, was required.

A further consideration was that the women lived very different lives, with a range of time, work and family commitments: to construct a time-use schedule which would have allowed any comparability would have been difficult, if not impossible. Rather, the intention was to situate the women's activities in context – to understand the constraints and relationships framing the activities, their *meaning* (Talbot 1979a, 1988), rather than comparing patterns of time use. Therefore, the women were being asked to generalise their own patterns of time use, rather than having imposed upon them categories and time slots by which they should describe their lives. The hope was to avoid categorising by activity, so often used in questionnaires and interview schedules, and which so many respondents find irrelevant, meaningless, or irritating, because their experiences fail to 'fit' researchers' models.

WEEKLY TIME PROFILES

Piloting confirmed that most women did have, despite elements of unpredictability, mental weekly schedules which they routinely used to cope with the competing pressures for their attention and time, and to accommodate other family members' needs and schedules. From discussion with the women who helped with the piloting, a very simple, one page form (see Figure 10.1) was developed so that the researcher and the women interactively could record *weekly time profiles*, outlines of time use during a 'typical' week. It was clear from the discussions that the women saw the week as a recognisable and useable unit of time, distinguishing weekdays from weekends, and with aspects of a relatively predictable routine distinguishing one day of the week from another. Women almost always, when asked to talk through the shape of their weeks day by day, defined their days by the time they got up in the morning and when they went to bed, and these times were often what distinguished one day from another. The time profile form therefore allowed for recording these times at the beginning and ending of each day. Space for each day was divided into morning, afternoon and evening, which accommodated both distinctive and transitional parts of the day and uses of time. Most important, the forms allowed for recording multiple uses of time during any section of the day or week.

The women were also asked to indicate the extent to which the weekly patterns they had described were predictable. In the event, the only adaptation which was needed was to allow for winter and summer seasonal schedules. This seasonality stemmed mainly from hours of daylight and the weather, which were in turn translated by the women into the opportunity or chance to 'get out', other than being at work or performing essential chores like collecting children from school. The hockey players also saw their lives in two distinct winter and summer seasons, corresponding to their playing and closed seasons, in which their time schedules were very different, even if they were involved in other, summer activities. The back of the form was therefore used to record the relevant season, and the variations of time use cited by the women between the two seasons. The use of a matrix format without hourly categories, but using hours of the day as markers, allowed for flexibility and accuracy in recording the women's descriptions of their activities. The weekly time profile forms were easily completed, easily augmented or qualified with the women's comments, and 'user-friendly' because of the way they were completed interactively, between respondents and the researcher. The intention was to ensure the active participation of the women who were research partners in this process, by placing the form between us during the conversation. While I actually filled in the form and led the questioning, my research partners were able to shape the construction of their weekly time profiles, by pointing to omissions, adding qualifications or changing entries. The process was an iterative and interactive one, with me as researcher dependent on my research partners for the information which constructed the profiles, and they being able to review the overall shape of the profile to check that it represented their 'typical' weekly time schedule.

The information obtained from these weekly time profiles turned out to be far richer, and to offer far more possibilities for further use and application, than had been anticipated. They had been intended to be used

Figure 10.1 WEEKLY TIME PROFILE

Given Name:_____
Code No: _____

	Morning				Afternoon						Evening			
	8 9	10	11	12	1	2	3	4	5	6	7	8	9	10	11
Monday															
Tuesday															
Wednesday															
Thursday															
Friday															
Saturday															
Sunday															

as a backcloth of time use and distribution – a temporal context for the
women's accounts of their current lives. But the detail and level of information which were provided, in my research partners' determination to
ensure that I properly understood the nature of their weekly routines, was
an unexpected bonus.

FAMILY OBLIGATIONS AND SOCIAL NETWORKS

The time profiles provided an unexpectedly rich picture of the interrelationships of family members' uses of time and their influences on each other. The centrality of many of the women to the nexus of family life came through in their own time profiles; but the way the women refined, delimited, qualified and allocated their own time use also implicitly indicated their concern for, and responsibilities within, their households and beyond, into the extended family. There is exciting potential for employing this simple instrument with all the members of a household or family group, so as to understand better the nature of these relationships, the background to the negotiations which go on in all such groups, and the ways individuals perceive the same event or time slot (see Finch and Mason 1993). This would allow more sensitive collection of information about the way different family members define and experience common activities within time slots, and help to show how inappropriate is the use of the term 'family leisure', without regard for the distinctions between different family members' experiences (Scraton and Talbot 1989).

While patterns of kinship and friendship may vary (Allen 1979), the time profiles clearly indicated that women depended on their social networks, and that they were depended upon by others. This was especially the case for the less formal, non-institutionalised activities which seemed to represent commitments as firm as more formal activities, even when allocation of particular time slots to them was more variable. Indeed, the way time slots were allocated to visiting parents revealed their priority. Precious weekend time, sometimes whole or half days, were allocated to family visits, especially when elderly parents lived some distance away or were beginning to have problem with mobility. Taking mothers to get their shopping in the car was a common way in which these women, often heavily time-committed, helped to extend their mothers' mobility and support them in ways which would be valued and acceptable. Several women allocated time, usually part of an evening or weekend, simply 'spending some time with my mother' or 'his father'. While parents-in-law were less often alluded to than own parents, it was clear that in-laws still did figure in the women's itineraries of family commitments and obligations, and accounted for very considerable time slots when they lived a distance away.

These types of commitment were not only extended, but dominated women's lives when elderly members of the family were ill or in hospital. Shirley (43, married with two children) qualified all the entries on her weekly time profile, by telling me that this routine had been re-established

quite recently. While she had begun to play badminton six years previously, the time profile led her to qualify this by referring to her uncle's
stroke which had virtually suspended her usual routine for two years. She
had done all his housework, washing and shopping while he had been well
enough to be at home, which meant very large blocks of time spent in his
house; after he was taken into hospital, she still kept his house 'aired and
dusted' and visited him twice every day, and organised the rest of the
family's visits to him. This underlines the importance of using the time
profiles with some reference to the period of time for which routines are
established, and highlights the impact of some overwhelming family
obligations, which are so often seen as women's responsibilities, on their
leisure opportunities.

Sometimes, the timetabling demands of formal activities meant that the
time slots of visits to family members or other informal activities were
dependent on the timing of the formal activity. Joan (28, single, living
alone), for example, allocated Monday and Tuesday evenings in tandem
with basketball and going to do her father's washing. The specific night
for each depended on when basketball matches were, but the allocation of
these two obligations to those two time slots did seem to be absolute. This
emphasises the centrality and utility of the concept of *relationality* (Bella
1989) to women's leisure. Relational perspectives require researchers to
take more account of hegemonic relationships between the genders,
between different social and economic groups, and of the different ways
they frame work, leisure, free time, sport and recreation. This relates not
only to interpersonal relationships influencing women's leisure, but also
the trading-off of different times and activities for commitments which
may be differently valued but nonetheless important in their own right.
The concept of relationality, used with this kind of information, may help
researchers to understand better how overloads and conflicts are resolved.

Similarly, allocations of time slots were made, not just to 'outings', but
as Carol (25, single, living with parents) said, to 'taking my mother out
because otherwise, because of her arthritis she can't get out'; not just to
family visits, but as Linda (28, single) reported, to 'spending some time
with my friend's father, even though we live with him'. Despite their adult
status and the demanding nature of their jobs and sport commitments,
those women who were living in their parents' home also recorded time
slots into which they fitted chores and other contributions. These reflected
the reciprocity which seemed to be built into these patterns of time use,
like Sue (30, single, living with parents) doing the ironing for the family
on Wednesday or Tuesday evenings to free her mother. The single women
mentioned activities with their mothers most often, with the use of time

qualified and defined by that form of companionship or service. This emphasises the importance to women of their relationships with their mothers and was supported by women's accounts of the devastating effects on them when their mothers died (Talbot 1991).

THE INFLUENCE OF OTHERS

Many of the players' recorded activities were framed, not by where they were taking place, but with whom and in what form. Christine (31, married, no children), for instance, referred to the Thursday evening badminton with her sister, followed by going to the pub 'with the girls' – the other badminton players and their sisters or sisters-in-law. Similarly, Pat (36, married with two children), who played badminton twice a week, described her Thursday evening badminton as 'with friends' and the Monday evening badminton as 'at the club which I run myself', although both activities took place in the same sports centre. In this case, both her companions and the nature of her relationships with the activity – the type of experience and the level of her involvement and role in it – defined the activity as both different and similar.

Many of the hockey players made the same kinds of distinctions between the different occurrences of their participation, between, for example, mixed hockey which they saw as not serious, and the Saturday afternoon match, which was always the hockey commitment which was most absolute. However, the distinctions with regard to different types of hockey did tend to refer more to characteristics of the activity itself, or the women's own relationships with it, than to the people with whom they played. Pauline (26, married, no children, physical education (PE) teacher) filled the whole of her Saturday afternoons in her profile sheet with hockey, because she felt she had to arrive early and leave last for all matches because she was club Chair. However, when the hockey players were helping me to construct their time profiles with reference to activities other than hockey, then they did often refer to the same kinship – or friendship – defining contexts as the badminton players used. Kay's (28, married, no children) Monday evenings were spent playing league darts with her husband, while Margaret's (30, married, no children, PE teacher) early Wednesday evening swim was 'with a few of the staff from school – not all the PE department, just people who'll come along'.

The number and centrality of references to *others* (people with whom the women had some kind of dependency relationship), in these women's weekly time profiles provided unexpected insights into women's activities (see Table 10.1). In future research, more systematic application of this instrument with the companions with whom, or with reference to whom, people allocate time, could provide enhanced understanding of interacting individuals' perceptions and definitions of leisure activities. However, in the context of this research, the degree of 'otherness' was even more striking, because it had not been directly sought. The data was illuminating, for example, in terms of the domination by young children of their mothers' free time and accountability, and the ways in which informal activities were themselves defined by the people with whom they were undertaken.

'Others' figured not only in activity terms, such as the traditional female role of servicing others' activities (Morris 1990; Talbot 1979b, 1989; Thompson 1990) by driving children to their classes, clubs and teams, watching them and/or waiting for them to bring them home, but also in *thinking for others*. Examples are Iris (43, married, two teenage daughters) 'getting the girls' things ready for school' on Saturday mornings; and Pat (38, married, three children) setting aside most of Mondays for washing, not only as a matter of routine, but because her husband and both her sons each played two rugby matches during the weekend and there would be no way she could 'catch up' if she did not do. Table 10.1 shows the instances and totals of time allocations referenced by *others*. Research using this instrument with a larger sample should produce identification of some patterns of *otherness* among different women (for example, at different stages of the family life cycle, or with different family groupings), and possibly some bases of comparison between them. While this sample was small, the frequent references by the full-time houseworkers to other people to punctuate their routines support the observations made by many

Table 10.1 References in Weekly Time Profiles to 'Others'

	Badminton	Hockey
Children	62	40
Husbands	43	37
Whole family	5	6
Friends/kin	31	46
Parents	12	16
Parents-in-law	5	2
Boyfriends	13	8
Babysitters	14	8
TOTAL	**185**	**163**

researchers, from Hannah Gavron (1966) to Erica Wimbush (1988) about women's expressed needs to identify markers in the day to make some kind of structure for their time when they are at home, when their activities are relatively undifferentiated or fused.

HOUSEWORK AND SHOPPING

The time slots allocated to housework by the women who were full-time houseworkers differed markedly, as would be expected, from those allocated (when they were even mentioned) by women with full-time paid jobs. Whereas details about cooking were given by several of the women who did not work outside the home, those women with full-time jobs, especially those who had children, would mention meals and food only in relation to someone else relieving them of the responsibility for the evening meal. Meals were necessary events for which they had to cater, but the work involved was hidden in the weight and rush of other commitments which they bore. Similarly, none of the women with full-time jobs mentioned routine gardening and none of the older women set aside the mythical whole evening to wash their hair: only a few of the younger, single women did that. Clearly, the weekly time profiles provided evidence that for many of the women, chores were marginal, even though recognised as necessary.

The larger number of hockey players having full-time jobs, and the number of them who were teachers, was represented in the hockey players' time profiles. These showed more formalised activities, and more time related to their paid jobs, with chores, especially for the single women, relegated to weekday evenings, as Karen (22, living with male partner) put it, 'to keep the weekends free for hockey'. Shopping, except where it was defined by companions (usually children or female relatives), was much more likely to happen on their way to another commitment, rather than as a separate activity.

Shopping was one activity which the time profiles showed taking on a number of forms and purposes, depending on the ways it was framed, with whom and in which time slot. Contrary to popular myth, only one of the women said that she routinely went shopping on Saturday afternoons with her husband. But 'shopping' featured in a variety of ways: taking mothers shopping, or going shopping with older daughters; clothes shopping, always with a friend, mother or sister; shopping to get out of the house, usually by women at home with young children, and always accompanied by their children; routine daily, or several times a week, shopping for specific types of consumables (especially by the women who tended to spend more time cooking); shopping on the way elsewhere or as convenient, usually for food, as a matter of urgency and alone; the 'weekly shop', depending on a car, and sometimes accompanied by husbands and children, or freed to go alone by husbands looking after children; and 'snatched moments' of free time, for the women with the use of a car who could 'slip into' town or city. The variety of experiences expressed by these women illustrated the range of possible relationships between them and their activities and shows how problematic is the labelling of activities as either 'leisure' or 'chores'. It also highlights the ways in which the presence of others can transform and redefine activities.

THE INFLUENCE OF CHILDREN

There are clear patterns of *others* dominating weekly time profiles, particularly those of the women with very young children. Three individual examples will illustrate the richness of the data represented by individual time profiles, especially when they are used in relation to the context of the stage of life cycle and social/cultural position of the women concerned.

First, the time profiles provided examples of the way the demands of young children intersect and dominate the lives of their mothers, preventing any allocation of block time during the periods when they are solely responsible for them. Sandra's (33, married) weekly time profile shows how, in weekdays, her life was ruled by her two children (ages one and three), and that she depended on her husband to relieve her from these pressures. During all five weekdays, time was cut across by 'taking Richard to play school', 'playing with Edward', 'collecting Richard from play school', 'Richard's sleep', 'going out for a walk', 'husband home for meal', 'bath and bedtime – husband helps', 'story for elder child', and feeding both children three times each day, before she could negotiate for 'free' time at home, or for commitments outside the home.

This pattern framed her evening and weekend hockey commitments (Monday evening selection committee, Wednesday hockey training, Thursday indoor hockey, checking the pitch on Saturday mornings and Saturday and Sunday afternoon matches). Her time use was a triumph of organisation and a reflection of the amount of support provided by her husband through helping and babysitting. It also clearly demonstrates the strength and depth of her commitment to hockey. Other women played or contributed to their clubs as much as Sandra, but none did so within the framework of this kind of commitments and demands on their time.

At a practical level, the weekly time profile form allowed for vertical recording across several days, as in the case of Sandra, whose weekdays were so shaped by her children's needs. Sandra was one of the three hockey players to list no other leisure activities. Her time profile explains why. Discussing it also extended her list of commitments to include committee work; since she had not mentioned this in that part of her interview relating to activities, the time profile provided a useful checking device for understanding the range of her commitments.

THE INFLUENCE OF SPORT

Beryl's (41, married, four children aged 10 to 18) time profile form, on the other hand, illustrates the well ordered slots of time during different days of the week which accrue from an established family routine, where family members have similar, and even shared, interests. It shows the importance of sport in the lives of Beryl and her family: sport permeated their whole week, and her family's relationships were reciprocally reinforced and framed by sport. Merely listing the same instances during the week when sport and members of the family or the whole family related, is to appreciate the salience of sport in this family's life and relationships, which could not have been illustrated as simply or vividly without the weekly time profile.

Plotting the week from Monday, Beryl's 'leisure' time slots were as follows:

Monday: 6–7 p.m. jogging with the whole family, sometimes with Beryl's brother's family as well, followed by tea with her brother's family, followed by television at home.

Tuesday: 7–8 p.m. hockey training, followed by drink in the bar while selecting teams, until around 9.45 p.m.

Wednesday: 3.30–5 p.m. squash with a friend; evening spent ironing and watching television at same time.

Thursday: 5.30–7.30 p.m. takes Tracey (daughter) to athletics training, other side of city; 7–9.30 p.m. every third week, indoor hockey.

Friday: 6.30 p.m. onwards visiting friends with husband.

Saturday: 9–10.30 a.m. watching, with husband, Neil (son) play football for school; 10.30 a.m.–12 noon (husband stays watching Neil) watching Tracey and Gill (daughters) play hockey for school; 2.30–5.30 p.m. play hockey match (daughters in same team), or watch Gill when schools county or territorial match; evening 'night in', including 'Match of the Day'.

Sunday: morning, jog as family; most afternoons play hockey match (with daughters), or family car outing, or family visit to sports centre; evenings may watch television.

Beryl's other commitments included a part-time paid job two days per week. She was determined that she would always 'be there' for her family when needed; but the way in which she had enmeshed those family members' needs with her own and her husband's sports interests was remarkable.

In contrast, Angela (21, single, living with parents) spent much more time at her paid job working in her father's shop, which left her 'free' all day on Mondays, Saturday afternoons and alternate Sundays or afternoons, and evenings from Tuesday to Thursday. Her allocations of time slots were just as shaped by the needs of relatives as Beryl's, but were very different in character and in terms of the place of sport in her week.

She was still in the process of working out her *Mondays*, only having had four Mondays off up to that point, but she listed her uses of that day as shopping, day trips to Bridlington or the Dales, or staying at home, with no companion mentioned; 5–6 p.m. squash with a friend; after evening meal, 8.30–11 p.m. paid babysitting for a friend she met playing squash.

Tuesday: 6.30 p.m.–12 midnight television at home with boyfriend, or watching him play squash, or go out with him in his car for a drink.
Wednesday: evenings (alternate weeks) watching television at home with boyfriend, or paid babysitting for someone who knows her 'through the shop';
Thursday: 6.30–8 p.m. badminton with sister, then 'out' with old school friends including squash partner;
Friday: 8.30–11 p.m. babysitting with boyfriend;
Saturday: morning shopping (personal) with mother, and eating lunch out together; evening after work play squash, or watch friend or boyfriend play, followed by pub with boyfriend and other friends.
Sunday: alternate half days, out for the day if weather good, or watch or play squash, or stay at home; evening bath and watch television before going out for drink with boyfriend.

Angela's week shows squash threading through her life and other activities, even introducing her to clients for babysitting, as well as extending her and her boyfriend's network of friends. Her Thursday badminton with her sister was part of the routine, as were her Saturday mornings and lunches with her mother. But it is striking how often and in how many different ways she managed to spend time with her boyfriend. Unlike many young women who lack leisure activities of their own, and have little choice but to support those of their boyfriends (see, for example, Green et al. 1990; Griffiths 1988; Leonard 1980), Angela had established that *she* was a squash player and, although she watched her boyfriend play, she certainly had not stopped playing herself. Having met him playing squash, her identity as a player was established. She does not record, however, that *he* watched *her* play! Her mention of her boyfriend's car as a crucial factor in some of her commitments does illustrate how boyfriends can actually extend young women's mobility, albeit within a dependent relationship.

BADMINTON AND HOCKEY PLAYERS

The weekly time profiles suggest that the hockey players generally appear, especially in their relationships with their sports activities, to have been markedly less 'other-directed' than the badminton players. More of the badminton players had dependent children and this offers a partial explanation. Although the hockey players collectively made a total of forty-six references to friends and kin, fifteen more than the badminton players, these refer not to their hockey but to the more informal activities revolving around families, like visiting parents, babysitting and spending evenings with friends. Furthermore, the profiles demonstrate that, even for the same person, the term 'playing sport' encompasses a wide range of degrees of formality, commitment and relationships to 'others'.

The *distribution* of references to 'others' was remarkably similar for both badminton and hockey players, except, as might be expected given their different family circumstances, in regard to husbands and children. The badminton players made between them sixty-two references to children in both weekly and daily time slots; the younger the children in the family, the more frequently did they shape women's time allocations. The hockey players made only forty references to children between them, almost all from those women with their own children. The demands on women are indicated by the routine way mothers set aside time for children's meals, naps, bedtimes and journeys to and from school or play school, which were repeated every weekday. As Rowena (34, badminton player, married, with two boys aged five and thirteen) put it, 'You're much more tied when they're at school'. She was referring to the lack of flexibility in the allocation of her time which school hours (which differed for her because of the boys' age difference) imposed on her; school holidays at least allowed her to plan her days with more variety and flexibility.

This is a significant point, because it questions the belief that sending children to school 'frees' mothers to undertake their own activities. The popular programming of public sports facilities during school times for mothers of young children may not be as appropriate as it seems to the sports facility managers who are trying to make such provision. This research indicates that the times when more women are actually free to participate in sport is when other people, usually male partners, are available to take over child care for the block time required for sports playing – in the evenings, during peak times.

The time profiles of the other women who had pre-school-age children graphically showed the intermittent nature of their time commitments. Times of children's waking, napping and sleeping, as well as feeding, taking them to and fetching them from play or nursery school, constituted landmarks in the day and were liberally, albeit routinely, scattered across these women's days, with respite apparently only at weekends and on the evenings when they had commitments to play their chosen sport. The accountability of these women during the times (most of their waking hours) and places they were responsible for young children was accompanied by lack of any other activities, even housework – let alone 'leisure' activities – recorded in the spaces between these intermittent commit-ments: neither the blocks of time available, nor the place they were located, nor the level of vigilance or physical control required for these young children, allowed women to programme or even 'steal' other activities into these times.

This is borne out by findings from other studies about the effects of young children on mothers' leisure opportunities (Oakley 1974; Wimbush 1988). Even though national and local policies (Sports Council 1988, 1993) have identified women with young children, first as being a 'target group', and then as having special needs, it is doubtful that public providers really appreciate sufficiently the nature and effects of these time and place constraints to enable them to cater adequately or sensitively for women and their children.

WORK AND FAMILY

Intermittent distribution and use of time was also a marked feature of the profiles of those women who had part-time jobs, and who balanced more finely family and work commitments. When there were also small children, or even primary school age children who had to be fetched from and taken to school, the punctuation of the women's days was even more frequent and invasive.

Women's accountability to their families for much of the time was also demonstrated by those women's time profiles which recorded certain of their husbands' evening activities which took them outside the home, with the result that the women were 'stuck' at home to look after the children. But it has to be said that the references to husbands in relation to the women's allocation of time were more complex than that, with support in childminding and feeding being among the most valued forms of help from male partners.

There were also instances of women making these restrictions into something more positive. Sylvia (41, hockey player, married with two children) described how two out of three Thursday evenings were her husband's 'night out with the boys', when she was responsible for the children; she used that time for 'my own things – writing letters, washing my hair and so on'. It is also relevant that every third Thursday was her indoor hockey night, which took precedence over the 'boys' night out'. Some women used their husbands' night out with the boys as a parallel, or legitimation, of their 'nights out with the girls', often with their mothers babysitting. Another response was to plan deliberately for these slots, 'getting on' with essential chores which apparently irritated their husbands, for example using the sewing machine.

The badminton players made a total of forty-three references in their weekly time profiles to husbands, while the hockey players mentioned them only thirty-seven times: those hockey players who were married but without children accounted for more of these references than those who did have children, and there were far more references to joint (couple) activities during the week than there were among the badminton players. This pattern may well be related to the later age of marriage of the hockey players, and the fact that some had met their partners through their interests in sport. There may thus have been later (and longer) periods of joint leisure – an example of the distinction between the influences of age and life cycle stage.

Reference to husbands also affected the time allocated to the evening meal by several of the women: because of lack of predictability about husbands' return home, time slots of between two and three hours could be allocated, with alternative uses of time limited. The women obviously felt that they had still to be there, just as they were when children came home from school, with the meal ready or almost ready, and not doing anything else. This was a time of day when husbands apparently expected attention and service, which their paid jobs 'earned' them (Green et al. 1987, 1990). This time of the day, however, is also one of the times when there is most leisure or sport opportunity available.

It was noticeable that on the evenings when they were committed to playing badminton or hockey, the allocations of time to meals by women were markedly less, sometimes because on those evenings husbands would expect to feed themselves and in some cases the children as well, or to have arranged to eat a cooked lunch at work, or were playing badminton with their families and delaying a meal until afterwards. The women had in these cases negotiated or bargained for time and space for their activities, helped by their regular commitment.

Husbands' activities affected or influenced both their wives and their families in a variety of other ways. Pat (36, hockey player with two children) allocated one evening each week to doing the books for her husband's business, an example of the way Finch (1984) has described women's support of their husbands' work. Christine (26, hockey player, no children) spent at least one evening each week on activities related to being a member of her husband's football club social committee, a formalised form of the general servicing of men's sport by women (Talbot 1979b, 1989; Thompson 1990). Like the runners researched by Barrell et al. (1989), the activities of husbands could also become, or act as a focus for, a whole family activity. Where the family is not directly involved, the location of husbands' activity becomes the starting point or location for other activities by the family. Jean (36, two children) mentioned the Sunday morning outings for her husband to go fishing while the rest of the family went for a walk along the canal path. And there were occasions for some of the badminton players, as on the regularly programmed Thursday evenings at the local sports centre, when the whole family shared the same activity, consciously planned for that purpose.

The need for couples and families carefully to organise their weeks to spend time with each other was a recurrent theme, although it was managed in a variety of ways. There were several references to 'spending time together' as couples or families, or 'keeping time free' for the children. The research was completed before the term 'quality time' was in common currency; but it was clear that these women and their families not only aspired towards it, but planned carefully for it in their busy schedules. There were several instances of women saying, somewhat defensively, that 'these days' it was important to 'work at' having enough free time together. Iris's routine Sunday evening ironing was the context for an opportunity to talk with her husband without being interrupted while the children finished their homework. The single women, too, spoke about the need to keep a few, precious time slots 'free'.

SUNDAYS

The weekly time profiles showed Sundays, whatever the family or house-hold circumstances, to be a day when time could be set aside for more diffuse purposes, often also related to the extended family. Sunday appeared to be a day of relative lack of busyness and an opportunity for regrouping or regeneration for the week ahead. There were repeated references, especially by the women with young children, to 'peace', 'being all together', 'relax-ation'. For the married women who allocated time to church on Sundays, attendance was always qualified by whether they went alone or with other members of the family; even then, they recorded on their time profiles what the rest of the family were doing while they were at church. The two single women for whom church activities were very important referred not only to attendance at Sunday service, but to other church commitments during the week, like the local synod of which Linda (28, hockey player, single) was a member, but which she had not mentioned in her descriptions of her work/family/leisure commitments; and the need of Irene (40, hockey player, single), as a lay preacher, to prepare her address in advance of Sunday. The time profiles thus provided useful additional information about the women's non-sport commitments and relationships.

Sunday was the only day during the week for which newspapers were recorded on the profiles: that is not to say that Sunday was the only day when newspapers were read, but it was the only day when the activity became worthy of mention. The specialness of Sundays was apparent, but still tempered by the ways in which domestic ideologies and unequal share in domestic chores impinged on the women's time and opportunities. Jean qualified the allocation of Sunday afternoons for family outings by record-ing that it always took her as long to prepare for and clear up after them as the time spent on the outing. The notion of Sundays as the 'leisure day' of the week is questioned by the differential experiences of different members of the same family or household (Morris 1990; Scraton and Talbot 1989, Talbot 1979b).

SATURDAYS

Saturday nights were also clearly seen as special. There was almost a moral imperative to be out on Saturday evenings and, if not, alternatives or their rationales were recorded. This was particularly the case among the young, single women: Saturday nights were set aside, although activities could vary. As Beverley put it, 'no set routine, but always out', whereas

Joan, only three years older but with her own home, said: 'If I stay in any night it's Saturday', when she had friends round to play cards, watch television and have a drink. Jennifer referred to 'being committed to going out', and Mary qualified the occasional Saturday night badminton with her husband with the availability on the same evening of her parents for babysitting and a badminton court at the sports centre. Married women without children would be out with their husbands, usually in pubs or clubs, and often with other couples. Roz (28, married, badminton player), a publicity manager with her own house, somewhat apologetically claimed to have spent Saturday nights for the last year decorating.

TELEVISION

Television did figure in the Saturday night time allocations, even among the women who went out: several aimed to be home in time for 'Match of the Day', and several used the programme as a focus for inviting friends to share the evening. Even though many of these women had very congested weeks, given the domination of television in time budget and leisure surveys (BBC 1994, Dixey with Talbot 1982), it was surprising how little use of television was indicated by the weekly time profiles. Obviously, the more time slots allocated to activities outside the home, the less likely it was to see significant amounts of time being allocated to television. These women appeared either to use it to accompany or enliven boring activities like ironing, or in very selective ways, as in 'Match of the Day'. Otherwise, television was most likely to be used by women on their own in the evenings, usually when husbands were out and they were responsible for children who were in bed; even then, most mentioned simultaneous activities like sewing or knitting.

Women's so-called 'dependence' on television is questioned by work (Brunsdon 1981; Dixey with Talbot 1982, Wimbush and Talbot 1988) which shows that they are by no means uncritical of what is offered to them. The interest in sport among the women in this research is certainly not reflected in the scheduling of sport on British television, in which women's sport accounts for less than 5 per cent (Women's Sports Foundation 1994). David Morley's research (1986) on family members' television watching confirms the differential experiences of different members of the same family, even of the same programme. Valerie's reference to 'occasionally joining my husband watching the second half of the rugby league' on Sunday afternoons implies, not only a different relationship with that activity, but also a different framing of obligations around that time slot. Andrea used television in a variety of contexts and with a range of companions during the week (with her boyfriend, on her own, with her parents, with friends and to accommodate her boyfriend's patterns of free time associated with his shiftwork).

ROUTINES AND COMMITMENTS

The weekly time profiles, then, provided rich insights. They clearly illuminate some of the nuances of routines and are sufficiently flexible, if undertaken interactively, to allow research partners to provide contexts for their activities, and to contrast, say, winter and summer schedules. The profiles outlined by these women indicated four broad degrees of routineness: activities which were firmly committed into a particular time slot and which appeared to have primacy over other activities, like Saturday afternoon hockey matches; activities for which women were dependent on others, such as for babysitting or booking a court, like Thursday evening badminton; activities which were more or less frequent, less regular than weekly, but nonetheless firmly committed, like dramatic societies; and activities whose time allocation was flexible but to which there was firm commitment – activities for which families and couples in particular 'made time', like family visits or outings together. The weekly time profiles showed the interrelationships of activities, both pleasurable and obligatory, which women grouped together within the same time slots, and the ways commitment could be absolute, qualified, conditional or relative. The centrality of skills and autonomy needed for the management and organisation of time in this process of coping with home, work and family, confirms the need for leisure researchers and sport providers to understand better the background for women's choices, setting priorities and allocating time (Talbot 1988).

FURTHER USES OF TIME PROFILES

The time profiles provide further illustration of the need to take account, not merely of the percentage participation so beloved by the Sports Council (1993) and General Household Survey (1994), but of the salience and significance of activities in people's lives, by having regard also to frequency and intensity of participation (Veal 1979) and to the barriers which people overcome to participate. The ways in which these patterns might change if viewed and interpreted differently offer an exciting application of the use of time profiles in research replicated some years after the initial research; in comparing patterns of time allocation for different cohorts of people at the same age; or in comparing groups of people with a range of characteristics (age, social class, ethnic and cultural background, sex and so on).

The time profiles were used within more extensive in depth interviews, and were not developed as free-standing research instruments. In order to interpret the information provided, they would need to be supplemented by other information, such as the circumstances of the people whose time use is being recorded. The importance of the data relating to context and the incidence and significance of *others* underline the importance of such supplementary information.

With regard to the relationships between women and leisure and sport, the time profiles offer a wealth of information about relationality and the nature of perceived freedom – a central concept in leisure theory. I have argued elsewhere (Talbot 1979b, 1991; Wimbush and Talbot 1988) that it is necessary to distinguish between 'time free from' and 'time free to': but the time profiles add a further dimension – 'time free for'. So often, the women used this phrase with reference to 'others' taking on a responsibility, so that they themselves could 'get on with' something, or choose an activity. In these cases, freedom is relative in both senses.

References

Allen, G. (1979) *A Sociology of Friendship and Kinship*, London: Allen and Unwin.

Barrell, G., Chamberlain, A., Evans, J., Holt, T. and Mackean, J. (1989) 'Ideology and Commitment in Family Life: a Case Study of Runners', *Leisure Studies*, 8, 3, pp. 249–262.

Bella, L. (1989) 'Women and Leisure: Beyond Androcentrism' in Burton, T. and Jackson, E. (Eds) *Understanding Leisure and Recreation*, Philadelphia: Venture Publishing.

Bott, E. (1957) *Family and Social Network*, London: Tavistock.

British Broadcasting Corporation (1994) *The People's Uses of Time*, BBC.

Brunsdon, C. (1981) 'Crossroads: Notes on Soap Opera', *Screen 22*, 4, p. 2.

Central Statistical Office (1994) *Social Trends*, London: HMSO.

Dixey, R. with Talbot, M. (1982) *Women, Leisure and Bingo*, Leeds: Trinity and All Saints' College.

Finch, J. (1984) "It's Great to have Someone to Talk to": The Ethics and Politics of Interviewing Women' in Bell, C. and Roberts, H. (Eds) *Social Researching: Politics, Problems, Practice*, London: Routledge and Kegan Paul.

Finch, J. & Mason, J. (1993) *Negotiating Family Responsibilities*, London: Routledge.

Gavron, H. (1966) *The Captive Wife*, Harmondsworth: Penguin.

General Household Survey (1994) London: HMSO

Green, E., Hebron, S. and Woodward, D. (1987) *Leisure and Gender*, London: Sports Council/Economic and Social Research Council.

Green, E., Hebron, S. and Woodward, D. (1990) *Women's Leisure, What Leisure?*, Basingstoke: Macmillan.

Griffiths, V. (1988) From 'Playing Out' to 'Dossing Out' in Wimbush, E. and Talbot, M. (Eds) *Relative Freedoms: Women and Leisure*, Milton Keynes: Open University Press.

Griffiths, V., Humm, M., O'Rourke, R., Batsleer, J., Poland, F. and Wise, S. (1987) *Writing Feminist Biography 2: Using Life Histories*, Studies in Sexual Politics, Sociology Department: University of Manchester.

Leonard, D. (1980) *Sex and Generation: A Study of Courtship and Weddings*, London: Tavistock.

Morley, D. (1986) *Family Television: Cultural Power and Domestic Ideology*, London: Comedia Press.

Morris, L (1990) *The Workings of the Household*, Oxford: Polity Press/Blackwell.

Oakley, A. (1974) *The Sociology of Housework*, London: Martin Robertson.

Pahl, J. (1989) *Money and Marriage*, Basingstoke: Macmillan.

Rapoport, R. and Rapoport, R. with Strelitz, Z. (1975) *Leisure and the Family Life Cycle*, London: Routledge and Kegan Paul.

Scraton, S. and Talbot, M. (1989) 'A Response to "Leisure, lifestyle and status: a pluralist framework for analysis"' *Leisure Studies* 8, 2, pp. 155–158.

Sports Council (1988) *Sport in the Community: The Next Ten Years*, London: The Sports Council.

Sports Council (1993) *Women and Sport: A National Strategy*, London: The Sports Council.

Szalai, Z. (1975) 'Women's time: women in the light of contemporary time budget research', *Futures*, 7, 5, pp. 227–281.

Talbot, M. (1979a) 'Meanings in Physical Activity: a Speculative Discussion', *Momentum*, 4, 2, pp. 28–33.

Talbot, M. (1979b) *Women and Leisure*, A State of the Art Review for the Joint Panel on Recreation Research, Sports Council/Social Science Research Council: London.

Talbot, M. (1988) 'Understanding the Relationships Between Women and Sport: The Contribution of British Feminist Approaches in Leisure and Cultural Studies', *International Review for Sociology of Sport*, 23, 1, pp. 31–41.

Talbot, M. (1989) 'Family Diversity: women, physical activity and family life' in *Better Family Life Through Physical Education and Sport*, report of 11th Congress of International Association of Physical Education and Sport for Girls and Women, Bali, Indonesia.

Talbot, M. (1990) 'Leisure Studies – All Things to All Men and Women?' *Elsie McFarland Lecture*, University of Alberta, unpublished.

Talbot, M. (1991) '"It Means a Lot to Me": An Investigation of the Place of Sport in Women's Lives and Leisure'. PhD Thesis, University of Birmingham.

Thompson, S. (1990) 'Thank the Ladies For the Plates: the Incorporation of Women into Sport', *Leisure Studies*, 24, 1, pp. 135–143.

Veal, A. J. (1979) *Sport and Recreation in England and Wales: An Analysis of Adult Participation Patterns in 1977*, Centre for Urban and Regional Studies: University of Birmingham.

Wimbush, E. (1988) 'Mothers Meeting' in Wimbush, E. and Talbot, M. (Eds) *Relative Freedoms: Women and Leisure*, Milton Keynes: Open University Press.

Wimbush, E. and Talbot, M. (Eds) (1988) *Relative Freedoms: Women and Leisure*, Milton Keynes: Open University.

Women's Sports Foundation (1994) *Media Pack*, London: Sports Council/ Women's Sports Foundation.

11 Gender Relations in Physical Education Initial Teacher Education

Anne Flintoff

Like many other feminist research projects, mine grew from the links I began to make some years ago between my experiences and concerns as a lecturer in initial teacher education (ITE) in physical education (PE) and my developing understanding of, and commitment to, feminism.[1] Access to feminist theories as part of my Master of Arts studies in 1984 helped me to understand the processes by which gender inequalities are reproduced in and through schooling. Importantly, I was also alerted to the critical role teachers can play in challenging and resisting these processes, and as a result began to question my own role as a teacher educator. Without an awareness and understanding of gender relations and how these may be transmitted through schooling and PE, students will be unable to adopt strategies to challenge these in their own teaching. Certainly my own training in the late 1970s had not included any attention to these issues! I began to question the extent to which my own institution of higher education was raising these issues with students, given that there is now over a decade of feminist research and writing on education and schooling on which it is possible to draw. However, as well as recognising *what* intending teachers were taught – the curriculum *content* – I was also very conscious of the ways in which gender was influencing and structuring classroom *interactions* at ITE level, including those in my own teaching groups. I became increasingly aware that many of the processes characteristic of coeducational school classrooms, such as boys dominating the teacher's time and attention (see, for example, Mahony 1985), were often happening in my own classes.[2]

This chapter aims to discuss some of the methodological issues and problems I encountered when undertaking my PhD research which explored gender relations in ITE PE. It shows how feminist research which focuses on men and institutions, as well as women, raises quite different issues and questions to research which focuses on women alone. In doing so, I hope this chapter will provide practical help for those planning research in similar settings, as well as contributing to the debate about what it means to do feminist research.

164

The overall aim of my research was to investigate the extent to which teacher education institutions constructed, confirmed or contested gender identities in PE. I was interested in both the ITE curriculum *content* – what counted as legitimate, professional knowledge – as well as the *process* of teacher education. My interest in exploring both these aspects, together with what I felt to be limitations of existing research on teacher education, directed me towards an ethnographic study.[3] It involved an in-depth study of two case study institutions, chosen as typical of those currently involved in the training of intending secondary PE teachers, and reflecting the separate and distinct historical development of PE (see Fletcher 1984). Hence the institution I have called 'Brickhill' had been a former women's PE college, and 'Heydonfield' a former men's PE college. I spent a term in each institution, observing the formal aspects of institutional life – lectures, workshops, practical sessions – but also parts of the informal culture too – the students' sports clubs or the bar, the staff common room and so on. I also interviewed the key decision-makers such as the heads of departments and the course leaders, since they would be in powerful positions to either support or resist equal opportunities initiatives. Analysis of course documentation and other institutional literature formed the third method of data collection used.

A *FEMINIST* ETHNOGRAPHY

From the outset, I was clear that the research would be feminist, although at first, this raised more questions for me than it solved. As I will show later, in many ways my research questioned rather than simply confirmed many of the characteristics commonly associated with doing feminist research (see also Barbara Humberstone's Chapter 13). It was only towards the end of the project, and subsequently, that I have been able to be clearer about where my research 'fits' in relation to the now wide-ranging and well-established debates on feminist research. Whilst actually doing the fieldwork, I experienced considerable uncertainty about what I was doing or where I was going! Reassuringly, this is not an uncommon situation for beginning researchers (see Skeggs 1994).

Before starting the fieldwork, I read everything I could find which explored the process of *doing* social research, and particularly ethnographic research. There were two main types of material: firstly, accounts of educational ethnographies which, although not feminist, had useful points to make about how the empirical work had been conducted and some of the difficulties encountered (see, for example, Ball 1984); and secondly, feminist literature on research. In the main, the latter consisted of theoretical discussions about research, raising questions about what makes research feminist and how this might be different from other kinds of research (see Bowles and Klein 1983; Stanley and Wise 1983). There *were* a few empirically based accounts which had explored aspects of young women or girls' schooling (see Davies 1985; Griffin 1985; Scraton 1989) but none of these included a study of men and men's experiences, as well as those of women – a disconcerting omission given that this was something my study was clearly going to involve.[4] Smart's (1984) reflective account of the methodology used in her study of the law and marriage in England was a key exception, and reading this raised a number of crucial questions for my own study.

Smart's study involved the use of a number of different research methods, including documentation and interpretation of the historical legislation on marriage, divorce and the family, but also in-depth interviews with solicitors and magistrates, few of whom were women. Several of the orthodoxies of feminist research which had been suggested in my reading so far were questioned by her research. For example, although she claimed that her research was feminist, and aimed at improving the lives of women, it was not necessarily *about* women's views or their experiences. It included quantitative data as well as qualitative, and saw a place for both (much feminist writing at that time inferred, if not actually stated, that quantitative methods had little to offer in an exploration of women's lives). Finally, she questioned the ideas about the power relationship the researcher holds over the researched and the extent to which the researcher ought to make herself 'vulnerable' in the process of the research. She pointed out that when interviewing powerful males, as she did, the power dynamics were reversed, and making herself more vulnerable (sharing her own experiences and thoughts for instance) would have presented her with huge problems.

Whilst this account reassured me that mine was an appropriate context for feminist enquiry, it also alerted me to the potential difficulties of conducting feminist research on men, and in male-dominated institutions. It highlighted the possible effects this might have – not just in terms of the kinds of data I would be able to collect, but also for my experience of actually doing the research.[5] What follows is a reflective account, written retrospectively, which describes some of the issues and problems raised in my research. As Kelly et al. (1994) note, there has been very little debate about what feminist research on men should entail, or how the research practice might differ, if at all, from that in studies which have only included women; this account aims to contribute to this area of feminist debate.

Research on, by, and for Women?

The question of what makes research feminist has been central to the development of feminist scholarship. A simplistic answer might suggest that feminist research is that which recognises women's inferior position in society, and is committed to the production of knowledge which is useful in improving that position. Feminist research is fundamentally linked to politics and its primary aim is to create change and improvement in women's lives. However, this kind of response fails to reflect the important and in-depth debates and questions with which feminists continue to struggle: namely, what kinds of feminist knowledge do we need; how best can we produce this, and how can this knowledge be used to bring about change in women's lives for the better?[6]

Few would dispute that feminist research should be about making women's lives and experiences central. As Roberts (1981: 15) suggests, 'feminism is in the first place an attempt to insist upon the experience and very existence of women'. However, as debates about what makes research feminist become increasingly sophisticated, the principle that it is research 'on, by and for women' no longer suffices. Whilst there is no agreement among feminists about the extent to which we should be involved in researching men and masculinity, I share with Smart (1984) and Kelly et al. (1994), the view that to research women's oppression necessarily involves the study of men and male-dominated institutions. As Kelly et al. (1994) have noted, while much feminist research does focus on women, and on creating knowledge about their experiences, if we are to understand women's oppression we must also research how this is structured and reproduced. Women's accounts cannot provide us with everything we need to know about the strategies and practices which men use to maintain their power. Nevertheless, as they and others (see, for example, Canaan and Griffin 1990) argue, there needs to be a very clear aim to any research specifically to do with men and masculinity:

> While studying the construction of masculinity is of key importance, what needs to be explored is not so much how men 'experience' this, or explicating different 'masculinities', but ... the connections between the construction and practice of masculinity and women's [and children's] oppression. (Kelly et al. 1994: 34)[7]

My research was not exclusively 'on' women, but involved working with both men and women, as well as analysing the gendered policies and practices in two very different, but nevertheless male-dominated institutions.[8] As well as researching individuals' attitudes and practices,

I was involved in building up a picture of the 'gender regimes' of these institutions.[9] This necessarily involved researching the attitudes and behaviours of men as well as women. For example, detailed and extensive observation in both the fieldwork settings enabled me to build up a picture of the strategies male students used in their gender identity 'work' in PE, and how these operated to control and limit the experiences of both women staff and students (see Flintoff 1993b).[10]

Whilst institutional ethnographies provide detailed, 'rich' accounts, they can, nevertheless, only present partial pictures, and my focus on men and masculinity, as well as women and femininity, meant that there were very clear areas of institutional life which I could not research. Early in the fieldwork I realised that there were important aspects of male PE culture I would not be able to observe – for example the interactions between male students in the changing rooms. As Curry's (1991) study shows, the male locker room is one of a number of important, male-only, sites where important 'gender work' predominates, and where more research is needed.[11]

Another important aspect of male student life which I could not observe was the initiation ceremony for new male students at the beginning of the academic year at Brickhill. This event was to take place in a pub some miles out of town, where the students had hired an upstairs function room to ensure privacy. Short of posing as a member of the bar staff (unethical and, I suspect, something I would not have been able to cope with anyway!) I was left with little choice other than to conclude that here, too, was another aspect of male PE culture which would have to be left to a male researcher to document and analyse. Skelton's recent (1993) biographical account suggests such initiation ceremonies form essential contexts for the reproduction of an informal, but nevertheless extremely powerful, male PE culture, which can operate to undermine formal course philosophies. Importantly, he also notes how the informal male *staff* culture might encourage, rather than challenge, such processes.

Beyond Experience, Towards Interpretation

Ethnography aims to produce an in-depth study of one or a small number of cases, with the researcher often spending lengthy periods of time 'in the field'. As Willis (1981) notes, ethnography allows the researcher to learn about 'the cultural viewpoint of the oppressed, their "hidden" knowledge and resistances as well as the basis on which their entrapping "decisions" are taken in some sense of liberty, but which nevertheless help to "produce" structure' (Willis 1981). I was interested in the ways in which gender relations impacted on the lives and experiences of women students and staff in ITE in PE, and how they negotiated an identity within PE ITE culture. Data collection in ethnographic research usually involves a range of techniques, but particularly those which enable the actors' meanings and interpretations of situations to be understood (Hammersley and Atkinson 1983; Hammersley 1989). In this sense, ethnography as a theory of research shares aspects of feminist research: in both, there is an attempt to build up theory which is 'grounded' in people's everyday experiences and lives, through the use of appropriate methods. In both kinds of research, the issue of *interpretation* is critical, and in feminism particularly, there have been extensive debates about this issue. As Maynard (1994) notes, some feminists have argued that to do anything but let women 'speak for themselves' would constitute violation. Feminist research must be *more* than simply a description of women's lives. Whilst women's experience might constitute a starting point for the production of feminist knowledge, it is not sufficient for understanding the processes and practices through which this is organised. It is the ways in which women's lives are *interpreted* by *feminists* (rather than simply *by women*) which allows feminist knowledge to be built up; by using theory to interrogate practice.

One of the key features of feminist research is the acknowledgement that the production of knowledge is a social and political process, in which the researcher herself plays an important part. As Holland and Ramazanoglu (1994: 131) argue,

> Each researcher brings particular values and particular self identities to the research and has lived through particular circumstances. While these values, identities and experiences do not rigidly determine particular points of view, they do give researchers variable standpoints in relation to subjects of the research.

In this sense, they suggest that the process of interpretation is always a site of struggle. The researcher must be open to continual reflection about her standpoint, and to the possible silences and absences in her data.[12] Current disagreements amongst feminists about what kind of feminist knowledge is needed, and how best this should be created, centre on the way in which *some* women's standpoints and experiences have been ignored or silenced (see Stanley and Wise 1990). The on-going struggle for feminists is to produce knowledge which adequately accounts for the differences *between* women, and yet does not lose the overall goal of challenging women's *shared* oppression.[13]

The process of reflection is not a static one, and very often constitutes a learning process for the researcher. Kelly et al. (1994) for example, recount how their understanding of research was radically altered as a result of working with women with disabilities. Changes in our political understanding and commitments, they argue, influence 'what we notice, what we take account of, and what we see as needing to be accounted for' (Kelly et al. 1994: 30). Similarly, in my own research there were changes in the process (both in interpretation and focus) as a result of both my expanding theoretical understanding, and my on-going observations in the field. One example of this interrelatedness between theory and data is my eventual analysis of 'masculinity' within PE. Observing the ways men used homophobic comments as a form of 'put down' to one another led me to read a whole new area of theory around the social construction of masculinity (see Brittan 1989; Connell 1987). As a consequence, I began to appreciate the central role which heterosexuality plays within gender relations. The production of all social research involves interpretation; whilst this is not their sole prerogative, feminists try to make explicit the process of decision-making which produces that interpretation.

Power in the Research Relationships

An early assumption of feminist research was that it sought to minimise or eliminate power relationships between the researcher and the researched (see, for example, Oakley 1981). Oakley argued that it was impossible to get to know about the lives of pregnant women if the researcher adopted an 'objective', distanced stance. She argued that the personal involvement of the researcher in the interview process should not be viewed as 'dangerous bias', but rather the 'condition under which people come to know each other' (Oakley 1981: 58). However, these early debates about the importance of minimising power within the *researcher-researched* relationship ignored the power differentials which can exist between women (McRobbie 1982; Stanley and Wise 1990). Differences between women in terms of their age, class, race or sexuality, for example, may be far more significant that their 'shared femininity' (McRobbie 1982). Most feminists would now agree that what is essential is to *acknowledge* power and differences between women, and to show how these are influential in the research process. Rather than abdicating the responsibility for the ethical and political concerns of the research 'subjects' by writing the 'self' out of research reports – thereby creating the illusion of 'objectivity' – the researcher must be prepared to situate herself *reflexively* in the research account, and provide an analysis of the social relations underpinning the research process (Harding 1987; Stanley and Wise 1983).

However, when the research focuses on men or institutions, the issue of power in the research process raises quite different issues and problems. As Kelly et al. (1994) note, in this situation, it is often a case not of 'sharing it [power]' but of 'how to limit its potential use against us, and how to conduct a study which reveals its surface and hidden forms in relation to the research question/topic' (Kelly et al. 1994: 38). My position in the research was very similar to that of Smart (1984), who has suggested that while feminism necessarily influenced the direction of her research and structured the questions it asked, it could not enter into the *practice* of the research. As she goes on to note, whilst it is generally recognised that the researcher has an obligation to the *reader* to reflect on her position in the production of the research, this has very different consequences from the suggestion that feminist researchers should make themselves open or vulnerable to the *subjects* of the research. Whilst feminism did enter into the practice of my research, I could not say that this was in any consistent or substantial way, and it played very little part in the majority of the interviews I conducted.

As with Smart's study of the legal system, a large percentage of my research involved spending time with men, in this case, male lecturers. For a large part of the time in interviewing these staff about equal opportunities, I too, found myself in the frustrating position of having to 'hide' my feminist values and opinions, and listen to overtly sexist (and sometimes racist) views. However, I experienced similar frustrations in my interviews with most of the women lecturers too, since few showed a commitment to, or an understanding of, feminism either. Far from having to make myself 'vulnerable' in the interview process I found that in all the interviews except two, the control was very much with the interviewees, rather than with me. For example, both heads of department 'talked' around questions and gave me little opportunity to intervene and ask questions at all. With some, it took me a long time just to summon the courage to ask for an interview at all.

I made a considerable effort to make the interview as relaxed and as unthreatening as possible – for example, by memorising the questions to help spontaneity; thinking carefully about the time and location of the interviews, and how to minimise the impact of the tape recorder. Looking back on this now, I realise that this may well have had a significant impact on the interview process – but not necessarily in ways which I had intended. It may have reinforced my *lack* of status and control over the interview process. I very quickly became aware of the limitations of semi-structured interview schedules, as I struggled to stop staff avoiding the question, or talking around it. I was surprised to find (perhaps naively on my part) that the presence of the tape recorder in no way inhibited the expression of some extremely sexist views and opinions by some men, no doubt again a reflection of status differentials between us. The two interviews in which I felt most at ease, where I did feel I was able to adopt the more open and sharing manner prescribed by Oakley (1981), were both with women, one of whom had become one of my 'key informants', and the other who had shared her feminist views early in the interview.[14]

Research which Improves Women's Lives

Feminist research practice could also be said to be distinctive in terms of its insistence on its political nature: it aims to challenge patriarchy and improve women's lives, and in this sense is often described as research *for* women. However, as Maynard (1994) notes, there are several different kinds of change which might result from a feminist research project. Whilst women taking part in the research might be empowered, including the researcher herself, there is also the possible longer term impact which the research could make to policy or legislation, and therefore to other women's experiences in the future. Bringing about change is, however, not a straightforward process, nor necessarily something over which the researcher has full control. Consciousness raising has been suggested as an important part of including women as subjects in the research process (see Cook and Fonow 1986), but can prove problematic in practice. Certainly in my own research it was only towards the end of the fieldwork, and only with some staff and students, that I felt able to interact with them in ways which might facilitate any kind of consciousness raising. Whilst ethnography is a style of research which allows for intense relationships to be built up, within my fieldwork it was only possible to do this with some of the individuals working there. Although I generally felt more comfortable spending time with women rather than men staff, I made a conscious effort to avoid being seen to be spending too much time with one individual or group, in an attempt to see as broad a picture of the institution as possible. Nevertheless, I developed good friendships with several of the women who invited me to their homes for meals on occasions. As with other ethnographies (see Ball 1981; Whyte 1955) I found I acquired 'key informants' in each institution who were invaluable in helping me with the research. Both these individuals were women, although neither would describe themselves as feminists. It was with Anne, one of these women, that I felt I was most able to work in ways which could be called feminist practice.[15] For example, we had long discussions in which we swapped stories about our experiences of working in male-dominated PE settings. However, looking back, the extent to which being involved in the research had a positive, empowering impact on Anne is debatable. Whilst it may have given her the opportunity for supportive discussions, it did little to change the oppressive environment in which she (and the other women) had to work. I was very conscious that at the end of the fieldwork I was simply leaving her to it, and that I had probably benefited more than she from our relationship.

There were many occasions during the fieldwork where I did not feel able to raise feminist issues. In fact, like Scraton (see Scraton and Flintoff 1992), I often specifically chose *not* to intervene when I observed sexist comments or practices, unless this was in a very general way and I could make comments which would not threaten individual staff. Despite this, there was a sense in which I felt that I needed to be relatively open about my feminism, because in the small world of ITE PE, I knew I was likely to interact with these people in the near future, and I considered it unethical to present a view of myself which was totally false. Like Greed (1990) I felt that I could not indulge in what she has called the 'hit and run' mentality of some research, since I knew I was likely to continue to live and work amongst these people after the research had ended. Nevertheless, finding some kind of 'balance' was extremely difficult, and I tended to vary this, depending on how confident or comfortable I felt with the individuals or the context. On some days, I was just too tired to engage in challenge, and chose to stay quiet, conserving energy for later situations where I judged I might be able to make a better impact.

On one occasion at Heydonfield I was directly accused, by a male member of staff, of 'staying too much on the sidelines', and of being in danger of 'raping' (his word) the research setting, and taking information without contributing anything in return. Concerned that my research practice was scarcely matching the principles of collaborative, consciousness-raising feminist research, I volunteered to present some of my observations and analysis about a particular aspect of the PE course at one of their training days. I found the process of presenting the findings to a mainly male group extremely daunting, particularly as I was aware that I was questioning one of the established practices of the department. The result was a very cursory dismissing of my findings by the male head of PE, who disagreed with my analysis, and who later attempted to discredit the work by suggesting that it no longer reflected the contemporary practice of the department. At the time, I remember feeling totally dejected about the whole affair, feeling that I had done little to raise anyone's consciousness about anything! However, looking back at this incident now, whilst I might not have been immediately influential in changing the department's practice, what I did do was to raise questions and offer an alternative analysis. The whole process was a good example of male dominance and sexism within the department.

PRACTICALITIES AND ETHICS IN FEMINIST ETHNOGRAPHY

This final section deals with some of the practical and ethical issues of doing an *ethnographic* research project. Whilst the general points raised here will not be new to those familiar with this kind of research, I also point out some of the specific issues raised by doing ethnography in a *PE* context, an area of social life often excluded from other educational ethnographies.[16]

The Selection of Case Study Institutions and Gaining Initial Access

A major difficulty in the selection of the case study institutions and of gaining initial access was explaining the purposes and intentions of the research to gain 'informed consent'. I needed to explain the research in a meaningful and open way, but at the same time in a way which would not jeopardise my chances of having the proposal accepted, or affecting the way in which people acted once I arrived. It is very easy to become labelled as a feminist and therefore dismissed as 'biased' from the beginning, simply by revealing that you are interested in gender (see Griffin 1985). It was for this reason that my initial introduction of the project was in the broad terms of 'how ITE courses prepared students to take on board issues of equal opportunities in their teaching'. Significantly, one course leader at Brickhill interpreted the fact that I was interested in equal opportunities to mean that I would only want to talk to women staff and students.

The role of 'gate keepers', more often men, in determining whether research into particular contexts is sanctioned or funded is often crucial. Although I had a clear list of criteria for the kinds of institution I would have preferred for the research (including for example, institutions which had both undergraduate and postgraduate courses in PE; different kinds of institutions, ideally with a different historical background, and so on) the selection process was always one of negotiation and compromise.[17] It was important that staff were responsive and generally supportive of my research if observation and data collection was to proceed smoothly. Six institutions were approached by letter with a very broad outline of the research, with a follow-up visit made to five (one institution did not reply to my letter). Staff in four of the institutions welcomed me and seemed supportive of the research, but in one they made it clear they were uneasy about the possible involvement of their department. The immediate concern of the head of PE was one of confidentiality – that my research might lead to future developments in course design being 'leaked'. Since a course leader, a few moments earlier, had assured me that they didn't have a problem with equal opportunities because they had recently got mixed changing rooms (!) I felt another plausible explanation for his reluctance might have been to do with concern over what the research could reveal about the department's practice in this area. Reluctantly, I decided not to choose this institution for the research.

An Observational Role?

'Gaining access' to the many different groups and social situations I wanted to observe was never simply a question of getting the initial per-mission and acceptance of the official 'gate-keeper', in this case the head of department. It was always an on-going process which was never com-pleted and needed continual attention. Factors such as the importance of the researcher's appearance and dress, and being 'placed' by the research subjects, have been identified as important aspects in gaining access to research settings (see, for example, Benyon 1983; Finch 1984).

Since I wanted the fieldwork to be sufficiently flexible to allow me to learn about both staff and students' views of institutional life, I chose to adopt an observational rather than a participative role, declining offers to be involved in any teaching.[18] By distancing myself from the authority structures of the staff, and declining to participate actively in the practical activities in which the students were engaged (as a 32-year-old, a PE student's timetable, once so attractive, appeared quite daunting) I avoided much of the role conflict which can be a major factor in choosing to adopt a participant-observer role (see Woods 1986).

However, it soon became clear that it would be impossible to simply observe. My presence in classes always had an effect on both the lecturer and the students, even though I tried to be as unobtrusive as possible.[19] Like other educational ethnographers, I ended up manufacturing a 'special' role within the institutions for myself, where, to the students, I became an informal counsellor, chatting over issues, or suggesting ideas to help them plan lessons, and to the staff, the emergency helper, occasionally agreeing to help out with the interviewing of prospective stu-dents, or supporting students on teaching practice.

Nevertheless, there were ethical issues which arose from adopting this kind of role, particularly because I was able to move between the two quite separate groups. Whilst I chose to introduce myself to student groups as a postgraduate research student, rather than as a lecturer from Leeds Polytechnic, as some got to know me better they were keen to know more about my background – whether I had been a PE teacher and so on. On a one-to-one or small-group basis, I felt more able to be open about my involvement in teacher education, yet doing this meant they would then invariably ask me to comment on what I thought of their course, and how it compared to those at Leeds! Similarly, staff would ask me how students were responding to particular aspects of their course, and I found I had to become very good at giving rather vague answers, or talking around the question.

Dress

The importance of the correct dress in PE culture has been noted elsewhere (Scraton 1989), and it was important in my fieldwork too. For example, I deliberately wore a skirt rather than my more usual trousers for the one day initial visits, very conscious of the initial 'image' I was presenting. During the fieldwork, the different research contexts necessitated a particular dress, and this sometimes posed problems for me as I moved from one research setting to another. For example, a day's programme might involve me in observation of a practical soccer session on the fields in the rain, a course-planning meeting in the staff room, and a session in the swimming pool. Few accounts mention the necessity of a thermal vest for ethnographic study in PE contexts, or how being chilled to the bone can have a negative effect on one's ability to concentrate!

Since a large percentage of the observation focused on student lectures or seminars, I wore a rather conservative track suit which was both appropriate for the context, and allowed me to 'blend in' with the student body as I tried to be as unobtrusive as possible. However, since staff at both Heydonfield and Brickhill wore formal dress except when they were teaching practical sessions, I had to change dress if I knew I would be working mainly with staff. On more than one occasion, the importance of correct dress was made explicit to me. For example, when arriving to observe an indoor athletics session, the lecturer commented to me 'at least you bothered to get changed, not like our previous visitor who turned up late, in tatty jeans and outdoor shoes!'. The staff toilet became an important and well visited venue for me, not just for scribbling down field notes unobtrusively, but also for frequent dress changes.

Heterosexuality in the Research Process

Feminists have argued that the researcher must make open the processes involved in data collection as a crucial part of the research itself. However, these accounts rarely address issues of heterosexuality. Warren (1988) has suggested that given the lack of credibility often attributed to women's research, it is perhaps not surprising most women choose to deliberately conceal such fieldwork problems. On a number of occasions, I had to deal with difficult situations in this respect. More often, it was a 'relatively harmless' comment, or 'only a joke', or a touch on the knee. For example, one male member of staff, despite not knowing me very well, felt able to make a comment about my bra size; another asked me whether I would like a 'dirty weekend' away with him, waiting to see my embarrassment before adding that he meant a weekend with staff and students on an outdoor education venture. On another occasion, I had to change my planned schedule of observations, for several days, to avoid the attentions of a particular male member of staff. So much for 'objective' research!

Whilst these were annoying and irritating incidents – which I suspect few male researchers have to deal with – twice I was reminded of the possibility of more significant hazards of doing research as a woman. During the fieldwork, I often stayed late at the university to use the library, a practice I reconsidered as a result of two specific incidents. Walking to the station from Heydonfield one night, I was struck on the cheek by a piece of chalk thrown from a van full of men who jeered and clapped as the missile successfully reached its target. Later that week, a woman student was assaulted in the same area. As a result of these two incidents, I felt pressurised into bringing my car back to the fieldwork in order that I might feel safer travelling at night.

CONCLUDING COMMENT

This chapter has described some of the issues and problems associated with doing a feminist ethnography of PE ITE within two institutional, male-dominated, settings. It has been argued that doing feminist research in male-dominated settings raises quite different issues and questions to those which focus on women and women's lives alone. Adopting a feminist research practice which, for example, may include consciousness raising, or attempting to reduce the power differentials between the researcher and the subjects of the research, become much more problematic and questionable when researching men. If we are to understand women's oppression more fully, we do need much more critical research which focuses on men, masculinity, and their institutional power. What I hope this chapter has done is make a contribution to on-going debates about how such research might develop.

Notes

1   Whilst recognising the diverse ways in which the term feminism has been used and defined, I am using the term here to describe a political practice which places women's experiences as central, and which seeks to challenge and change their oppression by men.

2   I am using the term PE 'classroom' broadly to include practical sessions in the gymnasium, on the playing field, and so on, as well as theoretical sessions in lecture rooms.

3   The EOC's (1989) study, for example, relied heavily on data gathered from a structured questionnaire, and could not capture the ways in which gender can influence classroom practice, and the specific ways in which this might happen within ITE in physical education.

4   But see Humberstone's work (1986; 1990) which has explored the impact of gender within coeducational outdoor activity settings.

5   I also read two other accounts of doing feminist research with men – Scott (1984) and Stanley and Wise (1979) both of which raise similar points to Smart.

6   See Ramazanoglu (1989) for an excellent discussion of these questions.

7   I cannot do justice to feminist critiques of the emerging new field of 'Men's Studies', and concerns that this may simply become yet another area of academic life dominated by men (see, for example, Canaan and Griffin 1990).

8   The two institutions were very different in terms of the gender profiles of staff and students. Nevertheless, even at Brickhill, where these were skewed in favour of women, the ethos remained male-dominated – see Flintoff (1993b).

9   Kessler et al. (1987) have used the term 'gender regime' to describe the process by which particular kinds of masculinity or femininity become hegemonic within an organisation.

10   Brittan (1989) uses the term 'work' to stress that gender identity is never something which is achieved, but has to be continually worked at in every social situation.

11   There is now a developing body of research which is beginning to explore the social construction of masculinity (masculinities) through and within sport (see, for example, Messner and Sabo 1990; Messner 1993).

12   It is only recently that I have been able to reflect, in any great detail, about the production of my research knowledge, and its epistemological position. There is no space here to explore the different epistemological positions which feminists may adopt (see, for example, Harding 1986; 1987; Stanley and Wise 1990).

13   Postmodern critiques, of course, question the very existence of women's *shared* oppression: see Weiner (1994) for a good overview of the develop-

ments and shifts in feminist theories in education, and Scraton (1994) for a discussion of postmodernism and leisure.

14   Ethnographers often acquire a 'key informant' to help them with their research – someone who can help the researcher understand the organisation of the institution, provide knowledge and information on specific areas, and who is generally supportive of the research.

15   This name, like others in this chapter, is a pseudonym.

16   Ball (1984), for example, notes that he specifically excluded PE from his observational schedules.

17   Practicalities such as cost or ease of travel have also to be taken into account when choosing the research locations.

18   At Brickhill, I was asked whether I would like to teach the second year unit of work on equal opportunities.

19   Comments from lecturers such as 'I don't know what you think Anne', or 'I'm sure you would do this differently Anne', suggested that I had quite a significant effect on the research setting.

References

Acker, J., Barry, K. and Esseveld, S. (1983) 'Objectivity and Truth; Problems in Doing Feminist Research', *Women's Studies International Forum*, 6, 4, pp. 423–435.

Ball, S. J. (1981) 'Case Study Research in Education: Some Notes and Problems' in Hammersley, M. (Ed.) *The Ethnography of Schooling*, Nafferton: Driffield.

Ball, S. J. (1984) 'Beachside Reconsidered: Reflection of a Methodological Apprenticeship' in Burgess, R. (Ed) *The Research Process in Educational Settings: Ten Case Studies*, London: Falmer.

Benyon, J. (1983) 'Ways In and Staying In: Fieldwork as Problem Solving' in Hammersley, M. (Ed.) *The Ethnography of Schooling*, Driffield: Nafferton.

Bowles, G. and Duelli Klein, R. (Eds) (1983) *Theories of Women's Studies*, London: Routledge and Kegan Paul.

Brittan, A. (1989) *Masculinity and Power*, Oxford: Basil Blackwell.

Canaan, J. and Griffin, C. (1990) 'Men's Studies: Part of the Problem or Part of the Solution?' in Hearn, J. and Morgan, D. (Eds) *Men, Masculinities and Social Theory*, London: Unwin.

Connell, R. W. (1987) *Gender and Power*, Cambridge: Polity Press.

Cook, J. A. and Fonow, M. M. (1986) 'Knowing, and Women's Interests; Issues of Epistemology and Methodology in Feminist Sociological Research' *Sociological Enquiry*, 56, 1, pp. 2–29.

Curry, T. J. (1991) 'Fraternal bonding in the locker room; a profeminist analysis of talk about competition and women', *Sociology of Sport*, 8, pp. 119–135.

Davies, L. (1985) 'Ethnography and Status: Focussing on Gender in Educational Research' in Burgess, R. G. (Ed.) *Field Methods in the Study of Education*, London: Falmer.

Equal Opportunities Commission (EOC) (1989) *Formal Investigation Report: Initial Teacher Education in England and Wales*, Manchester: EOC.

Evans, J. (1989) 'Swinging From the Crossbar: Equality and Opportunity in the Physical Education Curriculum', *British Journal of Physical Education*, 20, 2, pp. 84–87.

Fletcher, S. (1984) *Women First: The Female Tradition in English Physical Education, 1880–1980*, London: Athlone.

Finch, J. (1984) 'Its Great to Have Someone to Talk to: The Ethics and Politics of Interviewing Women' in Bell, C. and Roberts, H. (Eds) *Social Researching: Politics, Problems and Practice*, London: RKP.

Flintoff, A. (1993a) One of the Boys? An Ethnographic Study of Gender Relations, Coeducation and Initial Teacher Education in Physical Education'. Unpublished PhD thesis, School of Education, Milton Keynes: Open University.

Flintoff, A. (1993b) 'One of the Boys? Gender Identities in Physical Education Initial Teacher Education' in Siraj Blatchford, I. (Ed.) *Race, Gender and the Education of Teachers*, Milton Keynes: Open University.

Greed, C. (1990) 'The Professional and the Personal: A Study of Women Quantity Surveyors' in Stanley, L. (Ed.) *Feminist Praxis: Research, Theory and Epistemology in Feminist Sociology*, London: Routledge.

Griffin, C. (1985) *Typical Girls? Young Women From the School to the Job Market*, London: Routledge and Kegan Paul.

Hammersley, M. and Atkinson, P. (1983) (Eds) *Ethnography: Principles in Practice*, London: Tavistock.

Hammersley, M. (1989) *The Dilemmas of Qualitative Method: Herbert Blumer and the Chicago tradition*, London: Routledge.

Harding, S. (1986) *The Science Question in Feminism*, Milton Keynes: Open University.

Harding, S. (1987) 'Is There a Feminist Method' in Harding, S. (Ed.) *Feminism and Methodology*, Milton Keynes: Open University.

Holland, J. and Ramazanoglu, C. (1994) 'Coming to Conclusions: Power and Interpretation in Researching Young Women's Sexuality' in Maynard M. and Purvis, J. (Eds) *Researching Women's Lives from a Feminist Perspective*, London: Taylor and Francis.

Humberstone, B. (1986) 'Learning for a Change: A Study of Gender and Schooling in Outdoor Education' in Evans, J. (Ed.) *PE, Sport and Schooling – Studies in the Sociology of Physical Education*, Lewes: Falmer.

Humberstone, B. (1990) 'Warriors or Wimps? Creating Alternative Forms of Physical Education' in Messner, M. and Sabo, D. (Eds) *Sport, Men and the Gender Order: Critical Feminist Perspectives*, Champaign, IL.: Human Kinetics.

Kelly, L., Burton, S. and Regan, L. (1994) 'Researching Women's Lives or Studying Women's Oppression? Reflections on What Constitutes Feminist Research' in Maynard, M. and Purvis, J. (Eds) *Researching Women's Lives from a Feminist Perspective*, London: Taylor and Francis.

Kessler, S., Ashenden, D., Connell, B. and Dowsett, G. (1987) 'Gender Relations in Secondary Schooling' in Arnot M. and Weiner, G. (Eds) *Gender and the Politics of Schooling*, London: Hutchinson/Open University Press.

Mahony, P. (1985) *School for the Boys? Coeducation Reassessed*, London: Hutchinson.

Maynard, M. (1994) 'Methods, Practice and Epistemology; The Debate About Feminism and Research' in Maynard M. and Purvis, J. (Eds) *Researching Women's Lives from a Feminist Perspective*, London: Taylor and Francis.

Maynard, M. and Purvis, J. (Eds) *Researching Women's Lives from a Feminist Perspective*, London: Taylor and Francis.

McRobbie, A. (1982) 'The Politics of Feminist Research; Between Talk, Text and Action', *Feminist Review*, 12, pp. 46–51.

Messner, M. (1993) *Power at Play: Sports and the Problem of Masculinity*, Boston: Beacon Press.

Oakley, A. (1981) 'Interviewing Women; A Contradiction in Terms' in Roberts, H. (Ed.) *Doing Feminist Research*, London: Routledge.

Ramazanoglu, C. (1989) *Feminism and the Contradiction of Oppression*, London: Routledge.

Roberts, H. (1981) 'Women and their doctors; power and powerlessness in the research process' in Roberts, H. (Ed.) *Doing Feminist Research*, London: Routledge.

Scraton, S. (1989) 'Shaping up to Womanhood: a Study of the Relationship between Gender and Girls' PE in a City Based Local Education Authority'. Unpublishd PhD thesis, Milton Keynes: Open University.

Scraton, S. (1994) 'The Changing World of Women and Leisure; Feminism, Postfeminism and Leisure', *Leisure Studies*, 13, 4, pp. 249–261.

Scraton, S. and Flintoff, A. (1992) 'Feminist Research and Physical Education' in Sparkes, A. (Ed.) *Research in Physical Education and Sport: Exploring Alternative Visions*, London: Falmer.

Scott, S. (1984) 'The Personable and the Powerful: Gender and Status in Social Research' in Bell, C. and Roberts, H. (Eds) *Social Researching: Politics, Problems and Practice*, London: Routledge and Kegan Paul.

Skeggs, B. (1994) 'Situating the Production of Feminist Ethnography' in Maynard, M. and Purvis, J. (Eds) *Researching Women's Lives from a Feminist Perspective*, London: Taylor and Francis.

Skelton, A. (1993) 'On Being a Male Physical Education Teacher; The Informal Culture of Students and the Construction of Hegemonic Masculinity', *Gender and Education*, 5, 3, pp. 291–303.

Smart, C. (1984) *The Ties that Bind: Law, Marriage and the Reproduction of Patriarchal Relations*, London: Routledge.

Stanko, E. (1994) 'Dancing with Denial; Researching Women and Questioning Men' in Maynard, M. and Purvis, J. (Eds) *Researching Women's Lives from a Feminist Perspective*, London: Taylor and Francis.

Stanley, L. and Wise, S. (1979) 'Feminist Research, Feminist Consciousness and Experience of Sexism', *Women's Studies International Forum*, 2, pp. 359–374.

Stanley, L. (Ed.) *Feminist Praxis: Research, Theory and Epistemology in Feminist Sociology*, London: Routledge.

Stanley, L. and Wise, S. (1983) *Breaking Out*, London: Routledge.

Stanley, L. and Wise, S. (1990) 'Method, methodology and epistemology in feminist research' in Stanley, L. (Ed.) *Feminist Praxis: Research, Theory and Epistemology in Feminist Sociology*, London: Routledge.

Stanley, L. and Wise, S. (1993) *Breaking Out Again; Feminist Ontology and Epistemology*, London: Routledge.

Warren, C. A. (1988) *Gender Issues in Field Research*, California: Sage.

Weiner, G. (1994) *Feminisms in Education: An Introduction*, Buckingham: Open University Press.

Westcott, M. (1979) 'Feminist criticisms of the social sciences', *Harvard Educational Review*, 49, 4, pp. 422–430.

Whyte, W. F. (1955) *Street Corner Society*, Chicago: University of Chicago Press.
Willis, P. (1981, 2nd ed.) *Learning to Labour: How Working Class Kids Get Working Class Jobs*, Farnborough: Saxon House.
Woods, P. (1986) *Inside Schools: Ethnography in Educational Research*, London: Routledge.

12 The Sporting Lives of Women in European Countries: Issues in Cross-national Research
Sheila Scraton

The project which is discussed here has been underway for three years and our collective experiences of the research process have been exciting, stimulating, at times frustrating, but above all have raised important questions for the whole research team about doing research into women and sport. This chapter discusses some of the methodological, practical and personal challenges encountered in engaging in a cross-national research project into the experiences and meanings of sport in the lives of women in England, Germany, Norway and Spain.

These questions revolve around research into sport that is *feminist*, *qualitative in methodology* and *cross-national*. This chapter focuses on the *process* of doing the research rather than a discussion of the research findings. The research is still in progress and it is the process that has provided the research team with many challenges, both political and personal.

BACKGROUND TO THE PROJECT

The research team came together through contacts and networks in the 'world' of women and sport with a co-ordinator in each of the four participating countries. The first meetings involved intense discussion and the sharing of experiences as we progressed, from the initial broad aim of wanting to look comparatively at the experiences of women who participate in sport to the following key areas of attention:

1 An exploration of the ways that women integrate sport into their lives.
2 Their experiences of physical activity and the effect sport has on their body image, their concept of self and their social relations.

The sorts of questions we were raising included:
- What role does sport play in the lives of women?
- How does sport influence women's lifestyle?
- How does lifestyle influence women's sporting involvement?
- How do women's sporting experiences relate to their experiences and understandings of their body, physicality and sexuality?

These questions emerged from a sharing of our own understandings and experiences of sport and a 'brainstorming' around ideas. The research team are not only academic researchers committed to the theoretical and practical analyses of women and sport but also are, or have been, active participants in a range of physical activities, some to a highly competitive, representative level and others through participation in their recreation and leisure time. As women who are, or have been, active sportswomen, we wanted to know more about the positive experiences that we feel we have gained through being physically active as well as to identify the barriers that we have had to hurdle in order to play, compete or share in sporting activity. In line with Bredemeier et al. (1990: 4) we were enthusiastic to 'explore and describe "women's ways of knowing" ... their ways of ascertaining and verifying truth ... in the domain of physical activity'.

Traditionally research in sport has been dominated by the natural sciences such as medicine, physiology, biomechanics and so on. Although work in the social sciences has gained increasing importance it has been primarily androcentric, concentrating on men's sport from the perspective of male researchers (Hall 1988). It is only during the past two decades that women's involvement in, and experience with, sport has been critically addressed (see Hargreaves 1994). Much of the early empirical work on women and sport focused on sex-role differentiation, dispelling the myths of women's physiological inferiority in relation to sport (Dyer 1982; Ferris 1978) and the historical development of women's sport (Hargreaves 1994). The emphasis in much of this work was on the constraints women face in the world of sport and their experiences of discrimination and prejudice. It is only more recently that research has begun to explore the positive gains that sport and physical activity can bring for women in relation to increased confidence, bodily control and the positive influences that sport can have on the rest of women's lives (Lenskyj 1986, Talbot 1990). Our research extends the existing work by providing rich qualitative data on how women experience sport in their lives, focusing on intrinsic factors such as their concept of self, body awareness, the culture of the body, and more extrinsic factors such as sport in relation to lifestyle, social networks and their future life plans. These qualitative experiences of sport in the lives of women will provide crucial knowledge about how women themselves experience and define their participation.

An exciting aspect to the research is the cross-national data that has been generated. There is no space in this brief outline of the research to discuss in detail the rationale behind the cross-national study. However, as colleagues with distinct cultural backgrounds and experiences we were keen to break from the ethnocentricity of much research (not only that focusing on women and sport) and awaken understanding of the situation and experience of women in different sporting cultures and to enrich theoretical debate around possible universal structural constraints in relation to cultural resistances and diversities.

To summarise, therefore, the research team decided to conduct sixty indepth qualitative interviews in each of the four participating countries, that is England, Germany, Norway and Spain. This includes ten interviews in each of the three sports selected for study – soccer, tennis and gymnastics – and with both recreational and highly competitive participants. The interviews on average have lasted between one and a half and two hours. They have been fully transcribed and have taken place over the same period of time in each country.

The research schedule was developed after many hours discussing the key issues that we identified originally by sharing our own experiences and which developed out of our main research questions. The themes that eventually structured the research schedule were identified as:

- Sportbiography
- Sport and Social Networks
- Sport in Everyday Life
- Sport and Life Plans
- Sport and Self
- Femininity and Masculinity
- Sport and the Body.

These were broad themes which we wanted to explore in as open a way as possible with the women we interviewed. The need for the structuring of our interviews in order to allow some degree of comparability across the different countries, and the problems this raises for research that we define as feminist and qualitative, will be discussed later.

As our research focus developed we applied for funding from a variety of agencies in each of the countries. Each of us secured some funding, although to different levels. The main outcome was that research students/assistants were employed in England, Germany and Norway, with Spain receiving some financial support but not securing a specific post. Immediately our research team grew, which not only widened our team and gave depth to our discussions, but raised, also, major questions for the process in terms of working collectively. This will be discussed in the final section of the chapter.

In order to reflect on the research process, Denzin and Lincoln (1994) provide a useful identification of five moments or phases of the qualitative research process. These they suggest are:

1 The researchers – our histories, who we are, how we came together and the ethics and politics of the research process.
2 Theoretical paradigms and perspectives.
3 Research strategies – the design of the research and the identification of research questions.
4 Methods and data management.
5 Art of interpretation and analysis.

Denzin and Lincoln's stages or phases are useful to encourage reflexivity and a reassessment of the research process. However, what becomes apparent is that when this neat structure is overlaid with issues raised in conducting qualitative research that we define as *feminist* and research that is *cross-national* and involves *a research team*, then the whole process becomes less ordered, and more messy, contradictory and confused. In fact, the true experiences that, I suspect, underpin the majority of research. For we are engaged not only in producing understanding and knowledge based on empirical and theoretical 'findings' but also understandings and knowledge about how the research process intersects, relates to and is a part of these 'findings'. In other words epistemological, ontological, methodological issues are all integral to theoretical and empirical questions.

The following section, therefore, focuses on Denzin and Lincoln's first three phases of the research process, considering who we are as researchers and what we have brought to the research process; the theoretical perspectives that inform our understandings; the strategies that we have adopted in order to respond to some of the practical and political challenges that we have faced during the research process. It is clear, however, that these phases overlap, at times run concurrently and most of all influence the research while it is in progress.

THE RESEARCHER

In the research it has proved important that the researchers are not only women but also women who are, or have been, keen sportswomen themselves. Our histories as women and as sportswomen are an integral part of the research and as such have informed the questions we have asked and the methods that we have adopted. It was our experiences as feminist academics working in the area of women and sport that initially drew us together. Issues around what constitutes 'feminist' research continue to be debated and remain controversial and on-going (see Holland and Blair 1995). Certainly the mid-1990s provide a wealth of discussion about epistemologies, methodologies and whether there can be any universal label attached to feminism. At the outset of the research process, although acknowledging disciplinary differences, we had agreement around our shared commitments. Our shared understandings accepted that feminist research is fundamentally linked to feminist politics with a primary aim being to contribute directly or indirectly to change and improvement in women's lives. It is research *for* women which will provide new understandings that, hopefully, will inform policy initiatives and perhaps contribute to new meanings and definitions of sport.

The research developed, therefore, out of our experiences as sportswomen and as feminist academics. Liz Stanley and Sue Wise (1993: 32), writing about feminist methodology, argue that it is important for those engaged in feminist research to have a 'feminist consciousness that is rooted in the concrete, practical and everyday experiences of being, and being treated as, *a woman*'. In our research it has proved important that we have an awareness and understanding of being, and being treated as 'a sportswoman' and some understanding of the subcultures of different sporting activities.

We are interviewing women in gymnastics, tennis and soccer who play or perform at a recreational level as leisure and those who play or perform at a highly competitive level as representatives at Regional or First Division club level. We have chosen these sports because they represent activities that have been defined traditionally and stereotypically as 'feminine' (gymnastics), 'masculine' (soccer) and gender-neutral (tennis), although we do recognise the potential cultural differences in definition and meaning attached to each of these sports. For example, soccer in Norway has a far higher and more acceptable profile for women than in Spain. However, each of these sports carry with them gendered expectations that relate to presentation of self including dress, behaviour, the spatial setting of the sport, for example, the tennis club, soccer pitch or gymnasium, and the specific characteristics of each sport that are inherent in the rules, regulations, organisation (individual or team) and language. Our understandings and awareness of these sporting contexts and cultures informs how we present ourselves at interviews, what we wear and so on, and it allows some degree of shared experience that enhances the confidence and trust of both the researcher and the researched.

However, although the researchers may share some common experiences this does not mean that the power differentials within the research process are eliminated. As Caroline Ramazanoglu (1989a: 55) argues 'Since, by and large, people do not choose to be investigated, they are logically the objects of the research chosen by the feminist for the purposes defined by the feminist'. At most these power differentials can be reduced by a heightened sensitivity and by acknowledgement within the research process that they do exist.

Who we are as researchers and our cultural backgrounds and histories have been central to the research process from the first phase. It is vital that the research is located culturally and historically: our own backgrounds and our current status and experiences are central to this process. A key issue is that we are working in four different 'mother' languages. Any cross-national or cross-cultural research has the problem of language and the use of non-equivalent concepts and meanings of key terms and definitions. As feminists we are dealing with not only patriarchal language and 'male' definitions but also cultural variations. Terms such as 'gender', 'leisure', 'housework', 'motherhood' do not easily translate across languages without variance in meaning and context. This problem of equivalence of terms and concepts became apparent at the first meeting when we attempted to define and use the term 'sport'! It was obvious that historical and contemporary cultural contexts affect recognised meanings and definitions and that sport in different cultures cannot be divorced from the political and economic context of particular societies in which gender relations are articulated, experienced and structured in specific ways. It has been important, therefore, to research into the institutional setting of sport in each of the four countries and to provide some evidence of women's status through statistics on women's employment, domestic division of labour, violence, education and so on. Furthermore, it became apparent that considerable time must be set aside for full consideration of key terms and concepts and that any interview schedule must be thought through carefully in relation to both male-defined language and culturally specific meanings. Feminist, cross-national research is time-consuming for it must allow for a full consideration of these issues. It is problematic because, as women researchers, we are not divorced from the patriarchal structuring of our own lives. Some of us have children and domestic responsibilities, we all work within a patriarchal system of paid employment and most of us have to constantly juggle the many commitments that we face. It is no coincidence that very few women have been involved in cross-national research that is very time-consuming and involves a considerable amount of travelling. As a research team we have to be aware of the structural constraints that we individually face and ensure that the research process acknowledges and deals with these issues.

THEORETICAL PARADIGMS AND PERSPECTIVES

Having come together as researchers and recognised the separate histories and cultures that we have brought to the process, we acknowledged that the research is grounded in our shared experiences as sportswomen and is underpinned by a broadly shared notion of feminist research. Our initial theoretical considerations reflected our thoughts and knowledge in the late 1980s/early 1990s in that we took as our starting point the social construction of gender and gender relations, with political action and change an inherent part of our research intentions. We wanted to learn more about women's sporting lives to help us understand more fully physicality, the pleasures and problems of being physically active and how women incorporate sport into their lives. From this we might perhaps develop new definitions and meanings of sport. These issues have implications for future policy planning and thus the intention was to gain information that ultimately will open up and improve women's sporting experiences and opportunities.

The research, therefore, started from the premise that women's personal experiences are valid and constitute a legitimate and important source of knowledge. The women who are engaged in sport are the 'knowers' in their 'everyday worlds' (Smith 1987) and are not the 'objects' of the research with us, the researchers, the 'experts' or holders of knowledge. However, at an early stage, we discussed the problems of resorting to a relativism that individualises experience and loses the social and political agenda that is at the heart of feminist research and theory (Scraton 1994). Our research aims to address questions of difference through focusing on experiences, while placing these experiences within the material context of a sports world at a specific historical moment in time. That moment within each nation state, remains dominated and largely defined by men and is within an economic context of market forces and consumerism. This context was confirmed by an initial investigation that we made into women's position in sport in each of the four countries, using existing research, statistics and survey material.

Thus, from the outset, our fundamental research question was concerned to explore how far women's everyday worlds are influenced and constrained by the material world and an institutionalised sporting context. To what extent do individuals (the women engaged in sport) have the influence and freedom to define their sporting contexts and experiences? This structure-agency debate, which continues to engage social theorists (Giddens 1991) and has informed the malestream sociology of sport (Gruneau 1983 and Hargreaves 1986), has largely been a theoretical debate with little supportive empirical work and, as Jenny Hargreaves reminds us in her recent book *Sporting Females*, has failed also to look specifically at the complexities of *male* hegemony in sport. Within these analyses gender remains secondary to a class analysis. Jenny Hargreaves has pioneered the way within sports sociology for a sports feminism that challenges through exploring and understanding male hegemony and centralises gender relations (Hargreaves 1994).

However, our research started from a recognition that rigid disciplinary boundaries have created barriers to a full exploration of the interface between the individual and the social. Sport has tended to be researched and studied within relatively rigid disciplinary boundaries, for example physiology, sociology, psychology, education. Furthermore, more recently postmodernist discourse has challenged these rigid, disciplinary boundaries and argues that foundationalist theories are 'old' voices of a past modernity. Sport, within this discourse, must be understood within the 'new' conditions of postmodernity in which the 'old' structures on which modernity was based are no longer relevant to the 'new' world of fragmentation, dedifferentiation and hyperreality (Baudrillard 1988). The feminist analyses of the 1970s and 1980s (that is the taxonomy of liberal, radical, marxist and socialist) are seen in postmodern discourse as an unachievable and inappropriate attempt to provide universal explanations for all women's experiences of exploitation and subordination. They seek to discover the cause of women's oppression be that defined as the structures of patriarchy, of capitalism or of some combination of the two such as a capitalist patriarchy. Postmodern feminism emphasises deconstruction, subjectivity, the significance of language, semiotics, diversity and difference. As a research team we acknowledge that many of the claims of postmodernism are linked to, and are compatible with, some radical claims of feminism, for example the significance of difference as highlighted throughout the 1980s by black feminists and women of colour (bell hooks 1982, 1989; Hill Collins 1990); the inadequacy of 'grand' theory (malestream of knowledge) and the rejection of dualities such as public/private, rational/emotional, mind/body.

However, as Liz Kelly, Sheila Burton and Linda Regan (1994: 30) argue:

> Postmodernist concerns are discussed at a level rather far removed from the practical questions which preoccupy researchers: how to get access; how to build a sample; what methods to use; what questions to ask and how to word them; how to make sense of the information we have collected.

However, we have not been so preoccupied with the practical and methodological concerns of 'doing' feminist research that we have failed to engage with current theoretical debate or have neglected to try to locate our research within a theoretical perspective. There is little doubt that theoretical debate did inform, and to a certain extent underpin, our research process, including the questions we ask, the methodology we explore and the methods we have adopted. We began our theoretical discussions from the stance of a socialist feminism that situated our research within the structures of a capitalist patriarchy. We thus locate our research interests around: the sexual division of labour in the home and paid employment; sexuality and questions relating to physicality and the body; sport as an institution that structures gender relations and is structured by such relations; and the significance of ideologies of gender. As the research has progressed, our own understandings remain influenced by 'new' theoretical debates within postmodernist discourse. It is an on-going engagement with the intersection of theory, research and practice, in that we did not set out with a grand theory to 'prove', rather we have addressed theoretical debates and continue to develop our theoretical understanding not only as we conduct the research and new questions emerge from the data/material but also as we, as researchers, develop through the experiences of being part of the research process.

We are constantly, therefore, exploring the interface of practice, experience and theory. The research team has a range of disciplinary backgrounds in sociology, history, social psychology and education. Therefore the research set out from a rejection of the restrictions of disciplinary enquiry and an enthusiasm to attempt to transcend the traditional distinctions and boundaries of disciplinary-based research. We want to recognise individual subjectivity, locating the possibility of responsibility and power within the individual while acknowledging the social, political and economic determinants of power and oppression in a capitalist patriarchy. We are not content solely to theorise around issues such as difference and diversity nor to be content with universal concepts such as 'women'. These theoretical debates are important and continue to be reflected in our research practice and focus as the research unfolds. However, in addition, we want to find out more empirical detail about women who participate in sport in order to contribute to the challenge to male hegemony in sport and to support the development of sport and physical activity as a liberating, pleasurable medium providing women with a potential forum for the development of bodily confidence, collectivity and support.

THE PROCESS: POLITICAL AND PRACTICAL CHALLENGES

The main methodological debates that have arisen relate to the traditional 'problems' encountered in conducting qualitative research, our attempts to work collectively in feminist practice and the implications of attempting feminist comparative research across different European countries. The following are some of the issues raised, but through necessity they are selective and do not discuss all the methodological debates that have emerged in our research.

Working Collectively

A major issue for any research team, particularly on a project that involves researchers from different countries and is extensive in terms of data gathered and time used, is how to work collectively. Feminists are concerned not to conduct work that is exploitative, which raises issues of working *within* a system that revolves around the hierarchies of power, status and responsibility. These problems have not been resolved for us. The structure that has financially supported the research in Britain is a higher education structure that, to its credit, has financially supported research that is overtly feminist and concerned with women and sport (none of these – feminist, women or sport have much status traditionally in a competitive research atmosphere where there is little money available). However, the structure of higher education in the 1990s produces, also, massive constraints on all those within the system. One example is that it is difficult to limit hierarchies and status when, in the words of Liz Kelly, Sheila Burton and Linda Regan (1994: 42) struggling with similar debates neither... 'good intentions nor feminist research practice change differential wage structures, formal status or the ways we were constructed by others'. Issues of time, confidence, experience, accountability, giving papers and academic lectures are all complex, especially within a formal structure that gives differential status to certain activities and certain positions.

Thus the outcomes of the research in terms of publication and conference presentations are afforded higher status than the research process which involves interviewing women, literature searches and so on. These issues are on-going struggles which to some extent highlight clearly the tensions at the interface of practice and theory. Problems can become individual and interpersonal yet reflect broad political, economic and social structures.

For feminists it raises a fundamental debate that has raged since the 1970s within feminism, that is the liberal notion of working *within* the system, emphasising reform and change from within, versus a more radical strand which argues that incorporation reinforces the system and that 'real' change must come from alternatives *outside* the status quo. Working within the system means that we are working within a dominant research culture that reinforces hierarchies and quantifies outcomes in terms of traditional academic criteria. The structure-agency debate about how much we are constrained by and reproduce the structures, that is a traditional male research culture within a 'new' University, and to what extent we can be agents within a process to recreate new structures that challenge the existing power relations, is a question for the research process.

As yet we have few answers to these real dilemmas that many of us face in our research. We need to reflect and act on the problems that arise in the day-to-day situation of 'doing feminist research'. Personally this involves reflecting on my situation as a professor whose status and experience have helped the research progress, who ultimately carries the accountability and responsibility, and who gains kudos from the 'outside world' for the research. I have, however, no official work time given for the research in an over-committed schedule of teaching, development and research responsibilities, yet recognise the considerable personal and academic power which is held within the traditional hierarchies and the very real potential to exploit research colleagues. These issues need to be in the public forum as they become the lived experiences of those engaged in collective, collaborative work. Most research reports on a 'nice', organised process which involves aims, methods, analysis and findings. However, this neat process rarely, if ever, exists and it is important to recognise and debate the anomalies and difficulties that are ever-present.

Our research, therefore, faces the challenge of working collectively as feminists but is supported too by the solidarity and strong networks that have developed between women committed to women and sport. Networks are an essential feature of cross-national research and our networks in the field of women and sport, in all four countries, together with existing European networks, were fundamental to both the instigation of the project and the ongoing support and dialogue developed in the research process.

Researching Sensitive Areas of Experience

There is a growing literature on researching sensitive issues that tends to
be outside the mainstream debates in sport research methodologies (see
Ellis and Flaherty 1992; Ranzetti and Lee 1993). Much feminist research
could be defined as research into sensitive issues, especially when the
focus is on women's own experiences. It is only with the development of
feminist sport research focusing on areas such as physicality and sexuality,
for example Helen Lenskyj (1986) and Pat Griffin's (1990) work on
homophobia and heterosexism in sport, that these questions have been
transferred onto the sport research agenda. (See also Gill Clarke's Chapter
3, in this collection.)

   In our research we are asking women to reveal personal and sensitive
information. Although we have spent hours debating how we should ask
questions, the structure and format of the interview, and so on, a major
difficulty arises because we are conducting comparative work that requires
translation into German, Norwegian and Spanish. The debate around how
open-ended we should have our interviews is a serious one which has been
compounded by doing comparative, cross-national research. In order to
'compare' we have been pressurised to create a structure that can be replicated in all the interviews across the four countries. Yet there is a problem
in defining themes and questions so closely that they do not allow women,
as 'subjects' rather than 'objects', to make their own experiences visible
and defined in their own terms. This delicate balance is one that remains
an issue in cross-national research (Oyen 1990).

Interviewing Women

There is much written in feminist literature on the interview as a method
of allowing women's experiences a voice (Oakley 1981; Roberts 1981).
We have attempted to address some of these issues which involve a
concern to reduce the power differential between the researcher and the
women being interviewed, allowing women some control in the process in
that they dictate the time that they have available and where they wish to
be interviewed. However, as discussed earlier the issue around power differentials remains complex and there remain many areas where power
remains unequally distributed in our research process (see Scraton and
Flintoff (1992) for further discussion).

   Within the interview situation the issue of self-disclosure has been debated. We would argue that sharing our experiences of sport or our personal lives and responding to questions asked to us provides an open agenda where women seem to gain the confidence to express an opinion or feeling. Rather than biasing the data, it builds trust in the research relationship.

However, building this research relationship is very dependent on the interviewer, on how questions are asked and on how we interact in the interview situation. No two interviews or interviewers will be the same. As feminists and, in fact, many qualitative researchers have agreed, the process is not and never can be 'objective', 'neutral' or 'hygienic' (Stanley and Wise 1993). Again this raises interesting questions for our analysis and interpretation of the material, particularly in relation to cross-national research which traditionally has been premised on notions of comparability, generalisability and equivalence (Oyen 1990).

We set out with little understanding of the issues raised in attempting to do cross-national work that is both qualitative and feminist. We are now more acutely aware of some of the issues! Constantly we have to question whether we are being led by traditional methodologies that are within a malestream tradition of research. Although we may have no 'answers' it is important to question some of the traditional assumptions. Our research is as much about experiencing and reflecting on the process as it is about providing empirical data. That does not mean that the empirical data is unimportant, for what we have as we reach the interpretative stage of the research process is a wealth of data generated by 60 in-depth interviews, each lasting approximately two hours, in each country, that is 240 qualitative interviews, that give us a privileged and unique insight into the lives and experiences of women who participate in sport.

At the stage of interpretation and analysis, it is important to recognise what the women themselves have prioritised in their responses. We have a huge amount of detailed, qualitative information and to a certain extent *we* have to enter the research by prioritising issues, identifying themes and interpreting the material. At this stage we need to question the validity of us as academics interpreting other women's worlds. We are back to the debate about 'experience as knowledge' and how far our particular standpoints will inevitably determine our interpretations. In agreement with Janet Holland and Caroline Ramazanoglu (1995: 133), when addressing the 'art of interpretation' in their research:

> Feminists have had to accept that there is no technique of analysis or methodological logic that can neutralise the social nature of interpretation. We cannot read meaning *in* interview texts, allowing them to

propose their own meanings, without also reading meanings *into* them, as we make sense of their meanings. Feminist researchers can only try to explain the grounds on which selective interpretations have been made by making explicit the process of decision making which produces the interpretation and the logic of method on which these decisions are based. This entails acknowledging complexity and contradiction which may be beyond the interpreter's experience, and recognising the possibility of silences and absences in their data.

These are important points that reflect the commitment of feminists to an acknowledgment of their own position in the research process, including the recognition that all research is based on value judgements and therefore cannot be the objective and neutral process that traditional research has laid claim to.

CONCLUSION

Inherent in our research is the acceptance that sport is a gendered world where sporting knowledge is not neutral but founded on relations of power. In the world of sport most knowledge has been presented by men, validated by them and constructed such that it is represented as neutral and applicable to all humanity. Our research argues that sporting knowledge must be ontologically based, grounded in 'the interests, competencies, experience and understandings of knowledge-producers' (Stanley and Wise 1993: 191). In other words we need to recognise that women who participate in specific sports are the 'knowers' and that their experiences are not only 'legitimate knowledge' but are a vital source for our understanding of sport. However, care must be taken not to deconstruct social categories, such that 'woman', or indeed 'sportswoman', loses political and social relevance. This theoretical starting point is implicitly tied to methodological debates about the research process and the decisions taken about the methods used for gathering data.

Cross-national research means working with colleagues from different countries, cultures and, in this case, with different academic backgrounds. We have had the privilege of visiting countries involved in the research, gained immense experience from integrating with people interested and involved in our academic areas and, in particular, with women involved in sport and those politically committed to an increased understanding and support of women and sport.

Cross-national research demands time and extensive discussion. Oyen

(1990: 17) poses an interesting question when she asks: 'Are cross-national studies simply so time- and energy-consuming that they are incompatible with the combined role of mother, wife and comparatist?' There is no doubt that there are few women involved in this area of research and that gender is central to an explanation of why this is the case. My experiences of the research process have reaffirmed that gender relations must be central to our social analysis and theorising for this research exists within a context of higher education, paid work, family responsibilities, leisure, relationships and emotions, all of which are gendered and impinge on our research experiences.

References

Baudrillard, J (1988) *Selected Writings*, Stanford: Stanford University Press.

Bredemeir, B. (1990) 'Epistemological Perspectives Among Women who Participate in Physical Activity'. *Unpublished paper*, University of California at Berkeley.

Dyer, K. (1982) *Catching Up the Men* London: Junction Books.

Denzin, N. and Lincoln, Y. (1994) *Handbook of Qualitative Research*, Thousand Oaks: Sage.

Ellis, C. & Flaherty, M. G. (1992) *Investigating Subjectivity*, London: Sage.

Ferris, E. (1978) 'The Myths Surrounding Women's Participation in Physical Activity'. *Report to the Langham Life International Conference on Women and Sport*, London.

Giddens, A. (1991) *Modernity and Self-identity*, Cambridge: Polity Press.

Gruneau, R. (1983) *Class, Sports and Social Development*, Amhurst: University of Massachusetts Press.

Griffin, P. (1990) 'Addressing Homophobia in Physical Education: Responsibilities for Teachers and Researchers' in Messner, M. and Sabo, D. (Eds) *Sport, Men and the Gender Order*, Champaign, Il: Human Kinetics, pp. 211–221.

Hall, M. A. (1988) 'The Discourse of Gender and Sport: From Femininity to Feminism; *Sociology of Sport Journal*, 5, pp. 330–340.

Hargreaves, John (1986) *Sport, Power and Culture*, Cambridge: Polity Press.

Hargreaves, Jennifer. (1994) *Sporting Females*, London: Routledge.

Hill Collins, P. (1990) *Black Feminist Thought*, London: Harper Collins.

Holland, J. and Blair, M. (Eds) (1995) *Debates and Issues in Feminist Research and Pedagogy*, Clevedon: Multilingual Matters Ltd. with Open University Press.

Holland, J. and Ramazanoglu, C. (1995) in Holland, J and Blair, M. (Eds) Debates and Issues in Feminist Research and Pedagogy, Clevedon: Multilingual Matters Ltd. with Open University Press

hooks, b. (1982) *Aint I a Woman? Black Women and Feminism*, London: Pluto Press.

hooks, b. (1989) *Yearning: Race, Gender and Cultural Politics*, London: Turnaround.

Kelly, L., Burton, S., & Regan, L. (1994) 'Researching Women's Lives or Studying Women's Oppression? Reflections on what Constitutes Feminist Research' in Maynard, M. and Purvis, J. (Eds) *Researching Women's Lives from a Feminist Perspective*, London: Taylor and Francis.

Lenskyj, H. (1986) *Out of Bounds: Women, Sport and Sexuality*, Toronto: Women's Press.

Oakley, A. (1981). 'Interviewing Women: A Contradiction in Terms' in Roberts, H. (Ed.) *Doing Feminist Research*, London: Routledge & Kegan Paul.

Oyen, E. (1990) *Comparative Research as a Sociological Strategy*, Newbury Park: Sage.

Ramazanoglu, C. (1989a) *Feminism and the Contractions of Oppression* London: Routledge.

Ramazanoglu, C. (1989b) 'Improving on Sociology: The Problems of Taking a Feminist Standpoint', *Sociology*, 23, 3, pp. 427–442.

Ranzetti, C. M. and Lee, R. M. (1993) *Researching Sensitive Topics*, London: Sage.

Roberts, H. (1981) *Doing Feminist Research*, London: Routledge & Kegan Paul.

Scraton, S (1994) 'The Changing World of Women and Leisure? Feminism, 'Postfeminism, and Leisure', *Leisure Studies*, 13, 4, pp. 249–261.

Scraton, S. and Flintoff, A. (1992) 'Feminist Research and Physical Education' in Sparkes, A. (Ed.) *Research in Physical Education and Sport: Exploring Alternative Visions*, London: Falmer Press.

Smith, D. (1987) *The Everyday World as Problematic*, Milton Keynes: Open University Press.

Stanley, L. and Wise, S. (1993) *Breaking Out Again: Feminist Ontology and Epistemology*, London: Routledge.

Talbot, M. (1991) '"It means a Lot to Me" An Investigation of Place of Sport in Women's Lives and Leisure', PhD Thesis, University of Birmingham.

13 Challenging Dominant Ideologies in the Research Process

Barbara Humberstone

This is an autobiographical account which narrates particular resistances, dilemmas and struggles in the production of knowledge. It considers tensions encountered throughout an ethnographic research project on physical and outdoor education. Through the 'telling' of this account, I intend to explore briefly some of the emergent 'issues' which have been and are part of on-going debates around research/theory within contemporary feminism. This account raises and revisits a number of aspects and dimensions which were embedded in, and are a consequence of, my commitment to ethnographic research. The chapter is concerned with my first major research project, which involved me in intensive field work for three months as a participant observer in an outdoor education centre.[1] The autobiographical account given here focuses upon two issues. Firstly, I examine my dilemmas as a feminist researcher in the process of analysing data with regard to conventional/orthodox feminist theories of that time. Secondly, I highlight my experience in challenging specific research assessment criteria which arguably have their roots in a positivistic (masculinist?) paradigm. Through this exposition of personal experience, I hope to reveal something of the struggles at the interfaces between active agent (woman as research medium) and diverse ideological frameworks.

In the research project, I was committed to the concept of reflexivity. Reflexivity is generally seen as an important aspect of ethnographic research involving in-depth reflections upon and critiques during the whole research process by the researcher (Hammersley and Atkinson 1983; Stacey 1988). It is through these written comprehensive reflexive accounts that readers of the research may make a more informed interpretation of the findings. Reflexivity is thus a form of intellectual autobiography (Stanley 1993). Since ethnographic and feminist research challenge traditional notions of objectivity in research and argue that all research is in some way subjective, then the authenticity of the research product may, in part, be ascertained by readings of autobiographical accounts of the research process. Thus my unpublished research thesis, like many other ethnographic and feminist dissertations, consisted of a high percentage of detailed autobiographical accounting of the research process, discussing my feelings and the dilemmas which I encountered before and during the collection of the data and whilst analysing it (Humberstone 1987). Throughout the research I followed the process of 'grounded theorizing' in which theory is generated during the process of the research. 'Generating theory from the data means that most hypotheses and concepts not only come from the data, but are systematically worked out in relation to the data during the course of the research' (Glaser and Strauss 1967: 6). Stanley (1990a) similarly advocates the importance to feminist theory of its derivation from the experience of the research process. She argues,

> ... feminist theory would be directly derived from 'experience' whether this is experience of a survey or interview or an ethnographic research project, or whether it is experience of reading and analyzing historical or contemporary documents. Thus its analysis would centre on an explication of the 'intellectual autobiography' ... of the feminist researcher/theoretician: it would produce *accountable* knowledge, in which the reader would have access to the details of the contextually-located reasoning processes which give rise to the 'findings', the outcomes. (Stanley 1990a: 209)

Consequently, for both critical ethnographers and feminist researchers, the visibility of the researcher's personal experience and a self-interrogation of their own values and motivations embedded in the particular research process are pivotal. Such reflexivity not only provides the reader with some access into the ways in which the researcher constructed (theoretically, methodologically, emotionally and perceptually) the research and analysed the findings, but also it can provide some insight into the ways in which webs of power work in both the culture under exploration and within the particular research process. Researchers' struggles to avoid compromising their principles and their dilemmas surrounding relationships of power within the research are now becoming more available through such written reflexive accounts of research.[2]

(RE)-CONCEPTUALISATION OF POWER IN THE DEVELOPMENT OF FEMINIST THEORIES

Feminist sociology of sport, and perhaps to a lesser extent feminist sociology of physical education (PE), have until recently, I would suggest, tended to adopt and legitimate 'traditional orthodoxies and aspirations of the women's movement' (Cooper 1994: 435) in both theoretical frameworks and conceptualisation of power.[3] Yet, more widely, many feminisms have developed which challenge some of these orthodoxies. Embedded in many of these contemporary approaches is a reconceptualisation of power (Cooper 1994; Weedon 1987).[4] The importance for me of this reconceptualisation is that it acknowledges the idea that power lies not only in structures, but also at the centre of social relations and practices. Furthermore, it allows for the conceptualisation of possibilities for radical social transformation which I, like many others, have found problematic and absent within conventional feminisms (Humberstone 1995).

Power is a contestable concept which nevertheless realises its effects through historically specific forms. These forms are mediated as ideologies embedded in language, cultures and knowledge[5] and are central to the ways in which power works both productively and relationally.[6] Cooper's (1994) work reconceptualises power and resistance in feminist theory through an engagement with the writings of Foucauldian feminists. Significantly, she argues that she is concerned not to categorise rigidly but rather to construct a framework, albeit fluid, which can apply to 'issues of agency, inequality and social change' (Cooper 1994: 449).[7] In this reconceptualisation, power is constituted as all-pervasive.[8] Moreover, she reminds us that the relationship between the physical and the social is dialectical, both aspects influencing and informing each other. Power thus operates throughout particular sites such as institutions and the body.[9] From these perspectives, power is seen to permeate the research process and is implicated in the knowledge constituted by any research.

The production of 'valid' knowledge from research takes place through its legitimisation by various dominant ideologies. Knowledge constituted by research becomes acceptable/unacceptable, valid/invalid depending upon whether it 'fits' with the values, assumptions and ideologies of those in a position to legitimate its credibility. Many feminist researchers and critical sociologists are concerned with the question: 'What constitutes valid knowledge and in whose interests does it operate?'[10] This critical awareness of the all-pervasiveness of power and the wish not to abuse the possession of power has led to a greater emphasis by many on personal narrative in the research product (see, for example, Stanley 1990b). But despite this openness through autobiographical accounting in some ethnographies and feminist research, rarely are issues to do with power, such as ideological struggles, made visible during the processes of analysis of the data or at the level of assessment of the credibility of research. Seldom are the processes surrounding sensitive issues to do with research credibility,

validation and legitimisation made available for scrutiny. At such junctures, institutional knowledge meets 'new' knowledge whose epistemology may be built on alternative paradigms from those which the former is
charged with crediting.[11]

By presenting this autobiography, I am making visible expressions of
power at particular times and junctures and exploring mediating processes
and practices. Clearly, by the very nature of this presentation, these are my
views, values and assumptions which are exposed and which are open to
scrutiny as well as those underpinning the ideologies which I critique. In
the following, for each case which I raise, it is the ideological form of
knowledge which is being contested. But in one case it is institutional and
malestream, and in the other, I make visible my own struggles within the
counter-ideology of traditional feminisms. I make no apologies for
drawing attention to the latter struggle. Feminism(s) is now credible and
powerful and has clearly influenced Western society at many levels, even
if not to the practical extent feminists would want.[12] As such feminism(s)
(and so society) can only benefit from entering into critical dialogue both
with 'outside' agencies and within its own traditions of thought (cf.
Kitzinger 1994). I shall begin with the latter.

IDEOLOGICAL STRUGGLE 1 – FEMINISM(S) AND ETHNOGRAPHY

The issue of whether or not there can be feminist ethnographies was being
debated (Strathern 1987; Stacey 1988; Abu-lughod 1990) whilst many
feminists from a variety of backgrounds, including PE, were adopting
ethnographic approaches to their research. Clearly, many of the chapters in
this book highlight ethnographic research undertaken by feminists.
Nevertheless, there seem to me, on occasions, to have been misguided
assumptions made by traditional macrotheorists that researching culture
and thence interaction through participant observation is in some way
'non-theoretical' and that such research cannot contribute to our
understanding of how inequality works or identify contexts in which
power relations or images may be challenged. The latter contexts, in
which there may be challenges to power relations, are perceived not to
exist or at best may be thought to be illusory by many adherents to traditional macroperspectives.

Ethnographers, and more recently critical ethnographers, have a history
of negotiating their position and world view within prevailing positivistic
paradigms and dominant sociological traditions. Sparkes (1992) gives an

excellent overview concerning the various paradigm debates, including that of feminist research. But neither he nor Scraton and Flintoff (1992) appear to raise as problematic issues around the relationship between ethnographic research from feminist perspectives and traditional feminist theory. However, Chapter 11 (Flintoff) and other chapters in this book do identify this as problematic. Here, I shall draw attention to this tension through exemplifying my own dilemmas when faced with the limiting effects of traditional macrofeminist theory while attempting to address ethnographic research concerned with relations and agency.

I undertook my first major ethnographic research into outdoor education for a variety of reasons, mainly as a consequence of my own experience in teaching which included teaching physical and outdoor education. There seemed to me to be a change in relations between teachers and girls and boys, and between the pupils themselves, when involved in out-of-school outdoor/adventure activities. Through 'valid' research, I wanted to explore whether I was under an illusion or whether, if there were changes, what they were and then to disseminate that knowledge. I also thought that any findings would only be taken seriously if the research was given credibility through being undertaken and subsequently evaluated for a PhD degree.

After much searching, I came across ethnographic research which seemed to be most appropriate for the purposes of my research and to fit with my values (see Humberstone 1987). I spent three months as a participant observer in an outdoor education centre collecting data, including that concerned with forms of communication through a variety of methods. Ethnography, for me, allowed for respect for the participants involved in research, giving them a voice to be heard. That is not to deny that other methodologies may have a similar capacity.

Furthermore, for Stacey (1988) ethnography is compatible with feminism, which she argues is sensitive to issues of abuse of power and to the amelioration of oppression:

> ... like a good deal of feminism, ethnography emphasizes the experiential. Its approach to knowledge is contextual and interpersonal, attentive like most women, therefore, to the concrete realm of every day reality and human agency. Moreover, because in ethnographic studies the researcher herself is the primary medium, the 'instrument' of research, this method draws on those resources of empathy, connection, and concern that many feminists consider to be women's special strengths and which they argue should be germinal in feminist research. Ethnographic method also appears to provide much greater respect for and power to one's research subjects. (Stacey 1988: 22)[13]

The importance of a reflexive account for both ethnographic and feminist research is that it makes visible the ways in which the researcher, who is central to the research, influences and is influenced by it. It highlights the ways in which the researcher weaves her way through the webs of power, whilst attempting to remain true to her principles. As she navigates her pathway through the research, different conflicts may arise and need to be negotiated. Clearly, then, such an autobiography will not try to hide 'problems' but will wish to explore and expose them. I described the stress, tensions and dilemmas encountered during the field research in my dissertation. Here I shall draw attention to the particular intellectual tensions and dilemmas which I contended with during the analytical stage of my research.

I collected vast amounts of data which I then categorised. Patterns began to emerge concerning forms of communication which identified empowering relations between teachers and pupils, and between girls and boys. Girls appeared more confident in themselves and boys seemed to respect themselves and girls. I was in something of a quandary in relation to my recognising and acknowledging structural inequalities and relations of power and yet emphasising human agency, its constraints *and* potential for change. My motives were to research teaching and learning in outdoor education to see if there were challenges to social/gender relations and if so how this shift in power relations operated. It seemed to me that, on occasions, I had identified this shift. However, feminist theoretical frameworks, which I had read prior to and during my research in the field, seemed to me to be over-determinist. They appeared to exhibit little flexibility which might allow for the possibility of change or emancipatory contexts. Like all critical feminists I see, and at times experience, the realities of oppressive structures. Yet I also believe that individuals, especially the less powerful, amongst whom I include children and young people, should be given voice and credibility. So it was something of a dilemma for me to develop my research thesis beyond the conscious awareness of the participants in the research. In addition, I was concerned, in a sense, not to impose a framework upon the data. 'What right had I to claim superior knowledge to that of the participants?' was something that I asked myself. In addition to this, feminist theory at that time seemed unable to explain or provide concepts with which to analyse my data. To me, then, feminism appeared to be fixed in structural relationships which were inadequate to get to grips with exploring the dynamic processes of communication which constituted the relations emerging from my ethnographic research.

After the field research and during the second cycle of data analysis, I began to read the works of feminist theologian Mary Daly (1973). As a consequence of this reading, my thinking was able to shift. I could identify, at a personal level, with her values and her work gave me the confidence to move from analysis at a microanalytical, interpersonal and interpretive level and to enter into dialogue with broader theoretical issues. She legitimated the possibility of empowerment and drew attention to issues surrounding oppression, affecting men as well as women. At that time, for me,

> Her work ... recognised oppressive machismo affecting both men and women. At this point, [after the intensive field research] I felt it necessary to engage in more depth with theoretical conceptualisations of power: constraints and independence [empowerment] ... This formed a critical period both in my own thinking and the development of the thesis ... My frame of reference which had located me largely within a radical naturalist orientation had blocked me from moving beyond the conscious awareness of teachers and pupils in analysis towards a structural perspective. (Humberstone 1987: 264)

I was then not only able to give voice to the girls' and boys' experiences – the nuances and subtleties of the situation and contextual variation – but also, in part, able to locate the research within wider structural frameworks which allowed for an interpretation of process and for possibility, but which did not fit neatly into conventional feminisms of that time (cf. Humberstone 1987). The resulting conceptual model which I developed to explore interaction and social change located communicative practices within wider structural factors. These structures drew upon frame factors (Evans 1982), but my model placed gender at the centre and provided for the identification of empowerment at the level of communication and interaction.[14] Arguably, in this way, it can be possible to compare ethnographic studies of teaching and learning in different contexts, framed by various factors, and so identify and contrast subtleties and nuances of contextual variability (Humberstone 1995). By making these conceptual links between studies in various areas of PE, we may develop further insight into the criteria by which disparate forms of pedagogy may help to give material substance to our feminist ideals of social change. Such research, rather than creating 'closure', may provide the opportunity to open up pathways towards equity.

IDEOLOGICAL STRUGGLE 2 – POSITIVISM; 'MALESTREAM' CREDIBILITY AND ETHNOGRAPHY

Rarely are ideological struggles at the level of assessment of credibility of research made visible. We perhaps assume that researchers, of either a positivistic orientation or an interpretative orientation, are not easily seduced by each other's world view.[15] Correctly, in my view, it is argued that the quality of research may only be judged from the criteria embodied in whichever paradigm the research purports to belong to (Sparkes 1992). Like Stanley (1990b) and Sparkes (1992), I agree that whilst quantitative data can be part of research within an interpretive paradigm, it is unnecessary for such data to be used, through the imposition of positivistic criteria, to confer 'validity' upon that research project as a whole. The problem raised here is concerned, not only with resolving misunderstandings and apparent antagonisms which may be created between antithetical academic world views, but also about addressing issues of hierarchy and power embedded within and between particular paradigms.

The positivistic paradigm is still very powerful, albeit highly contested, not only in the world of PE, sport and leisure (Harris 1983; Sparkes 1992; Hemingway 1995), but also more widely. It has held a position of considerable dominance for many years and is underpinned by taken-for-granted notions of hierarchy (Silverman 1985; Harding 1987). Its pervasion at a fundamental level may still be effective in influencing an individual or group's perceptions of what constitutes 'valid' research.[16] This I highlight in the following account.

Like all who undertake research which is to be assessed for a doctorate qualification, I had to attend a meeting at which I was called upon to defend my thesis. Immediately after this, I was asked to wait outside the room whilst the outcome was discussed and debated. After almost an hour, I was called in again. There seemed to have been some disagreement between the external examiner, who was a noteworthy professor of education having worked for some considerable time within ethnographic paradigms, and the internal examiner, a lecturer in education, early in his academic career, who had come originally from a psychological (positivistic) background. The latter had only relatively recently become interested in ethnography and seemed to assume that he knew much of what there was to know about this approach to research. The upshot of this was that the internal examiner's view held sway and I was asked to make certain brief additions to the thesis which would satisfy his positivistic leanings and perhaps his machismo.

This I could not and would not do. I was committed to working within an interpretive paradigm and could not resort to using positivistic criteria to make the thesis 'valid'. Instead, despite much of the thesis already being taken up with methodological issues and reflexive accounts of the research process, I wrote an additional chapter in which I took the internal examiner by the hand through the research process, whilst spelling out more strongly and in greater detail the various ways in which I had attempted to provide for the credibility and authenticity of the research within its ethnographic paradigm. I could indeed have compromised my principles and provided an additional paragraph to an earlier chapter which would have satisfied the internal examiner and saved me stress, time and effort. Instead, I worked at helping him to understand the criteria by which, I felt, ethnographic research might be authenticated. The aspects which were of concern to him were to do with 'triangulation' and the use of the quantitative data which I had collected.

During the participant observation, I had decided to collect quantitative data concerning all the pupils who attended for the weekly residential adventure courses in order to locate the case study pupils in terms of age, sex and social class. I asked all the pupils to fill in questionnaires at the end of their stay at the centre. I had been hesitant about this as I did not want to disrupt the pupils' experiences or distort the research. But I needed this information and other details of the pupils, and thought I would additionally use Osgood's Semantic Differentiation (Osgood 1975; Thomas 1978) to compare pupils' perceptions of themselves, each other and their teachers in the contexts of the centre and mainstream school. The results from the questionnaire I then analysed using The Statistical Package for the Social Sciences (SPSS). I excluded from the main body of the thesis the results from this quantitative data but added a brief appendix which included them. The internal examiner wanted me not only to utilise this quantitative data to validate the qualitative data, but also to use triangulation to identify 'objective' reality.[17] The final paragraph in the additional chapter, entitled 'Principled Enquiry – Epistemological Purity?', which I wrote in order to guide the internal examiner through the thesis, sets out the case against using triangulation positivistically and argues for alternative ways of assessing credibility in ethnography:

> Triangulation of participants' perspectives when used in attempts to demonstrate objective reality can, I would suggest, foreclose understanding and stultify the emergence of insight. ... The pupil questionnaire data was used primarily to locate case study pupil characteristics within the general characteristics of the pupils who attended. ... Its inclusion as a methodological tool ... touched a discordant note for me. The data generated through Osgood's Semantic Differential technique, T-tested for significance, supported my own subjective interpretation, which I had held before entering the field, and the findings which emerged from the various data sources (of difference between school and the outdoor centre). However, it was the essence of this difference

and how it was accomplished in and through classroom interaction which were my abiding concerns. The culmination for me of the research ... was through the ways in which I was able through ethnomethodological analyses to make available the complex and subtle processes in which images and relations were accomplished, in lessons, on occasions. By presenting the teacher's 'practical reasoning' as a topic of inquiry my own analyses were made accessible. Ethnographically informing this 'practical reasoning' by presenting pupils' and teachers' accounts further illuminated the ways in which messages were received and understood. This version of 'triangulation' is not incompatible with the philosophical assumptions underlying a naturalistic paradigm since the intention is enhancement of sociality and not verification. In this case, the methodological technique remains more epistemologically true to its naturalistic paradigm since it is the making available of the reflexive awareness which is attempted (not the verification of 'fact'). (Humberstone 1987: 275)

Despite being placed under tremendous pressure to utilise positivistic criteria, in the form of triangulation of the data sources and methods, to make valid the thesis, I was able to resist but under considerable stress. What is more, the internal examiner, immediately after the viva, offered to help me with the recommended additions. Needless to say, I declined this offer. To me this incident was not only an issue of paradigmatic corruption but also an expression of oppressive gender power relations. In hindsight, I think that this offer was made in good faith. Even so, the events highlight the ways in which assumptions by some men and women whose backgrounds lie in positivistic, 'malestream' paradigms may hold sway over women and men ethnographers. This case exemplifies the processes by which knowledge made available by 'woman as researcher', particularly in ethnographic research in which the researcher is the primary medium of research, can be considered insufficient to render that knowledge 'valid'. For this male examiner, and perhaps for others with similar research groundings, research can be authenticated only in positivistic terms. Further, this arguably demonstrates the ways in which some academics need to demonstrate their 'superior' knowledge and understanding of research despite evidence to the contrary.[18]

Clearly, this account shows that whilst some people may be seduced by the richness and variety that ethnographic research can afford, it may still be difficult for them to shed both their positivistic leanings and gendered assumptions and identifications. This is problematic for ethnographic research and for researchers. Such sensitive issues, like other dilemmas created and encountered during the research process, are significant and rarely brought out into the open. 'Doing' research is about creating new knowledge. Whilst much ethnographic research is concerned with the construction of cultural contexts, critical and feminist research is about social change. All forms of critical research, arguably, are overtly political acts and as such they are embedded in ideological struggles. As is evident from other contributions in this book, we need to be aware of and sensitive to the ways in which power is realised at all levels throughout research. Perhaps, in a sense, this latter incident provided the opportunity through which the issue of ethnographic research credibility could be raised more fully for the internal examiner and maybe the event had some influence on his subsequent thinking and practice.

CONCLUDING REMARKS

Through this feminist 'intellectual autobiography', I have drawn attention to the importance of reflexivity, while data are collected, during and after analyses. This chapter, I hope, comes some way to illuminating the dialectic between ideology, structure and personal struggles. Merton (1988), cited in Stanley (1993), argues that:

> Among other things the sociological autobiography is a personal exercise – a self-exemplifying exercise – in sociology of scientific knowledge. (It is) The constructed personal text of the interplay between active agent and social structure ... (Merton 1988: 19–20)

I have made visible aspects of research which are generally not made visible and issues which are not generally open to debate or wider scrutiny. Using autobiography to raise these discussions, I could be charged with self-indulgence or even paranoia. This is for the reader to judge. For a woman as ethnographer engaged in feminist-orientated research, there seems a double bind. Not only is she the main instrument of the research process and therefore, in a patriarchal society, vulnerable in many ways, but also as a feminist ethnographer she seeks a more complex conceptual framework than orthodox structural feminism can provide, a framework which can accommodate and examine social change and transformation at both microanalytical and structural levels. This, I suggest, requires feminist ethnographers and researchers of PE and sport to critically engage with postmodern and poststructural feminist notions and analyses of power.

Notes

1 Some of the findings can be found in Humberstone (1986; 1987; 1990a and 1990b). Detailed methodological discussions can be found in the accounts given in Humberstone (1987).

2 Oakley (1981) was amongst the first to raise the issue of power relations with research subjects. Flintoff in this book (Chapter 11) covers this in more detail. Farran (1990) draws attention, in her research of a water activity centre, to issues surrounding commissioned research and the problems created as a consequence of time restrictions placed upon her in producing her results.

3 Scraton (1992) and Hargreaves (1994) give excellent overviews of conventional feminist theories.

4 I draw upon the work of Davina Cooper (1994) for this discussion. She is concerned with the ways in which Foucault's framework has been 'worked' by Foucauldian feminists and she engages with their work, not with that of Foucault directly. She carefully teases out the strengths and weaknesses of these approaches, developing further ideas which enable a greater sophistication in rethinking an understanding of the ways in which power operates. Importantly, she argues for the fluidity of frameworks which can adapt to analyses of power which are infinitely more complex than previously conceptualised.

5 Other modes through which particular ideologies mediate the effects of power are force, discipline and resource. Force constitutes physical strength, which is less used publicly in Western societies but is still present in private interaction such as abuse in the home. Discipline constitutes hierarchy, surveillance, structure and discourse. Money, time, and legal rights are resources.

6 The notion of power as productive and power as relational are discussed in detail in Cooper (1994). A number of tensions and difficulties are raised. I draw on the notion that power, rather than purely repressive, is also productive. Suffice it to say for the purposes of this chapter that by using the term 'productively', I acknowledge the ways in which power at all levels shapes, creates and transforms social relations, practices and institutional processes. By using the term 'relationally' I recognise more than relationships of inequality, subordination and domination. In this latter way, we can draw attention to those exercising power and to the resistance which is almost always an integral part of power. What is important in considering social change, however, is that an emphasis only upon resistance rather than transformation implies a form of closure.

7 I perceive these developments as something akin to the developments this century in physics. Newtonian theory is still applicable to everyday life and gives a valid understanding of the movement of objects, but the development of quantum theory makes more complex and contradictory explanations (see Hawking 1988).

8 Poststructuralist approaches which tend to emphasise social construction as opposed to biological and material determinacy have been questioned by some feminists for their 'idealism' and pluralism and apparent inability to acknowledge the realities of oppression. An excellent critique of

'postfeminism' is found in Scraton (1994). However, issues which focus around the processes by which power operates and is all pervasive are not yet fully addressed.

9 Shilling (1993) points to the body as a significant site in social theory. Gilroy, in Chapter 7, explores links between physical activity and social power, highlighting women's possible empowerment through bodily control and bodily skills.

10 See Bernstein (1977); Harding (1987) and Stanley (1990b).

11 See the letter, 'Conspiracy of Silence' (name withheld) in the May 1993 issue of the British Sociological Association Newsletter-*Network* (p. 7). This letter raises issues around PhD assessment by examiners from different disciplines who apparently found sociological theory and method, at least as utilised by the student, inadequate.

12 Despite the influence which feminism has achieved in Western society, we cannot, however, ignore the resistances and challenges to these successes by those whose privileges appear threatened by it (cf. Faludi 1992).

13 When researching those in positions of power, however, it is not desirable, nor the researchers' intent, to provide them with greater power (see Anne Flintoff's Chapter 11 which considers this further). There is recognition that it is relevant to apply critical feminist perspectives to research into men's experiences, to explore how forms of masculinity are constituted in and through sport and PE (cf. Messner and Sabo 1990).

14 Evans (1982) draws upon the work of Dahllöf (1971), Lungren (1981) and Bernstein (1977) in the construction of a model which offers a conceptualisation of the ways in which teachers and pupils make sense of and act upon the learning process within 'academic' classrooms. Space, time, resource, physical and other features are seen as constraining action but also mediated by teacher and pupil.

15 See Brenda Grace's Chapter 2, in which she discusses and critiques different paradigms.

16 I emphasise this concern in relation to cross national research into outdoor adventure education (see Humberstone 1996).

17 I am not suggesting that the use of triangulation is in any way an inappropriate research methodology. Rather, I am advocating care and understanding in its use, together with greater awareness of epistemological issues.

18 Harrison and Lyon (1993) draw attention to associated ethical issues surrounding 'intellectual autobiography'. Clearly, in presenting this section of my account, I am exposing and interpreting relations with another person. I do this to reveal the ways in which power is exercised and resistance to it played out. My ethical concern here is to do with anonymity. However, I am certain that the examiner to whom I refer cannot be identified other than by those most closely involved with the viva who are least likely to read this.

References

Abu-lughod, L. (1990) 'Can There Be a Feminist Ethnography?', *Women and Performance: Journal of Feminist Theory*, 5, 1, pp. 7–27.

Bernstein, B. (1977) 'On the classification and framing of educational knowledge' in Bernstein, B. *Class, codes and control*, London: Routledge, Kegan and Paul.

Cooper, D. (1994) 'Productive, Relational and Everywhere? Conceptualising Power and Resistance within Foucauldian Feminism', *Sociology*, 28, pp. 435–454.

Dahlöf, U. (1971) *Ability Grouping, Content Validity and Curriculum Process Analysis*, New York: Teacher's College Press.

Daly, M. (1973) *Beyond God the Father, Towards a Philosophy of Women's Liberation*, Boston: Beacon Press.

Evans, J. (1982) 'Teacher Strategies and Pupil Identities in Mixed Ability Teaching. A Case Study'. Unpublished PhD thesis, University of London.

Faludi, S. (1992) *Backlash. The Undeclared War Against Women*, London: Chatto and Windus.

Farran, D. (1990) 'Seeking Susan. Producing Statistical Information on Young People's Leisure' in Stanley, L. (Ed.) *Feminist Praxis. Research, Theory and Epistemology in Feminist Sociology*, London: Routledge.

Glaser, B. and Strauss, A. (1967) *The Discovery of Grounded Theory*, Chicago IL: Aldine.

Harris, J. (1983) 'Broadening Horizons: Interpretive cultural research, hermeneutics and scholarly inquiry', *Quest*, 35, pp. 82–96.

Harrison, B. and Lyon, S. (1993) 'A note on ethical issues in the use of autobiography in sociological research', *Sociology* 27, 1 pp. 101–109.

Hammersley, M. and Atkinson, P. (1983) *Ethnography. Principles in Practice*, London: Tavistock.

Harding, S. (1987) *Feminism and Methodology*, Milton Keynes: Open University Press.

Hargreaves, J. (1994) *Sporting Females, Critical Issues in the History and Sociology of Women's Sports*, London: Routledge.

Hawking, S. (1988) *A Brief History of Time. From the Big Bang to Black Holes*, London: Bantam Press.

Hemingway, J. (1995) 'Leisure Studies and Interpretive Social Inquiry', *Leisure Studies*, 14, 1, pp. 32–47.

Humberstone, B. (1986) 'Learning for a change' in Evans, J. (Ed.) *Physical Education, Sport and Schooling: Studies in the Sociology of Physical Education*, Lewes: Falmer Press.

Humberstone, B. (1987) 'Organisational factors, teachers' approach and pupil commitment in outdoor activities: A case study of gender and schooling in outdoor education'. Unpublished PhD Thesis, University of Southampton.

Humberstone, B. (1990a) 'Gender, change and adventure education', *Gender and Education*, 2, 2, pp. 199–215.

Humberstone, B. (1990b) 'Warriors or Wimps? Creating Alternative Physical Education' in Messner, M. and Sabo, D. (Eds) *Sport, Men and the Gender Order*, Champaign, IL: Human Kinetics.

Humberstone, B. (1995) 'Bringing Outdoor Education into the Physical Education Agenda: Gender Identities and Social Change', *Quest*, 47, 2, pp. 144–157.

Humberstone, B. (1996) 'Other Voices: Many Meanings? The Case of women', *Techniques and Philosophy in Outdoor Adventure Education, Conference Proceedings, Journal of Adventure and Outdoor Leadership*, 13, 2, pp. 44–48.

Kitzinger, C. (1994) 'Take it Like a Man?', *Times Higher Educational Supplement*, June 24, p. 15.

Lungren, U. (1981) *Model Analysis of Pedagogical Processes*, Stockholm: CWK Gleerup.

Merton, R. (1988) 'Some thoughts on the concept of sociological autobiography' in White Riley, M. (Ed.) *Sociological Lives*, Newbury Park: Sage.

Messner, M. and Sabo, D. (Eds) (1990) *Sport, Men and the Gender Order: Critical Feminist Perspectives*, Champaign, IL: Human Kinetics.

Name withheld (1993) 'Conspiracy of Silence', *Network, Newsletter of the British Sociological Association*, 56, p. 7.

Oakley, A. (1981) 'Interviewing Women: A Contradiction in Terms' in Roberts, H. (Ed.) *Doing Feminist Research*, London: Routledge and Kegan Paul.

Osgood, C. (1975) *The Measurement of Meaning*, Chicago: University of Illinois Press.

Scraton, S. (1992) *Shaping up to Womanhood. Gender and Girls' Physical Education*, Buckingham: Open University Press.

Scraton, S. (1994) 'The Changing World of Women and Leisure: Feminism, Postfeminism and Leisure', *Leisure Studies*, 13, 4, pp. 249–261.

Scraton, S. and Flintoff, A. (1992) 'Feminist Research and Physical Education' in Sparkes, A. (Ed.) *Research in Physical Education and Sport. Exploring Alternative Visions*, London: Falmer Press.

Shilling, C. (1993) *The Body and Social Theory*, London: Sage.

Silverman, D. (1985) *Qualitative Methodology and Sociology*, Aldershot: Gower.

Sparkes, A. (Ed.) (1992) *Research in Physical Education: Exploring Alternative Visions*, London: Falmer Press.

Stacey, J. (1988) 'Can There Be a Feminist Ethnography?', *Woman's Studies International Forum*, 11, pp. 21–27.

Stanley, L. (1990a) 'Feminist Auto/Biography and Feminist Epistemology' in Aaron, J. and Walby, S. (Eds) *Out of the Margins: Women's Studies in the Nineties*, Lewes: Falmer Press.

Stanley, L. (Ed.) (1990b) *Feminist Praxis: Research, Theory and Epistemology in Feminist Sociology*, London: Routledge.

Stanley, L. (1993) 'On Auto/biography', *Sociology*, 27, pp. 41–52.

Strathern, M. (1987) 'An awkward relationship: The case of feminism and anthropology', *Signs*, 12, pp. 276–292.

Thomas, K. C. (1978) *Attitude Assessment*, Nottingham University: School of Education.

Weedon, C. (1987) *Feminist Practice and Poststructuralist Theory*, Oxford: Basil Blackwell.

Index